THE SCHOOL SUPER-INTENDENCY

M. William Konnert, Ed. D.
Kent State University
John J. Augenstein, Ph. D.
Marquette University

THE SCHOOL SUPER- INTENDENCY

LEADING EDUCATION INTO THE 21st CENTURY

TECHNOMIC
PUBLISHING CO., INC.

LANCASTER · BASEL

The School Superintendency

a TECHNOMIC‡publication

Published in the Western Hemisphere by
Technomic Publishing Company, Inc.
851 New Holland Avenue, Box 3535
Lancaster, Pennsylvania 17604 U.S.A.

Distributed in the Rest of the World by
Technomic Publishing AG
Missionsstrasse 44
CH-4055 Basel, Switzerland

Printed in the United States of America
10 9 8 7 6 5 4 3 2

Main entry under title:
 The School Superintendency: Leading Education into the 21st Century

A Technomic Publishing Company book
Bibliography: p.
Includes index p. 281

Library of Congress Catalog Card No. 95-60956
ISBN No. 1-56676-286-3

CONTENTS

Leadership Subsection B—Personal Philosophy and Leadership

Leadership Subsection C—Superintendent Leadership Competencies:
Personal (The Superintendent as . . .)

FOREWORD

One of the greatest challenges of the twenty-first century is to revamp, reinvent, or transform the institution of education. There is little doubt that the world of school administration is increasingly more complex as schools are confronted with such contemporary issues as multiculturalism, inclusion, authentic assessment, standards, and a myriad of new curricular programs. There are no formulas for success but rather a need for reflective and sensitive practitioners who are knowledgeable, open-minded, compassionate, and reasonable.

At the center of the educational enterprise in most communities in the United States is the superintendent, the symbolic leader of the schools. If education is to be transformed, we need reasoned and balanced analyses that focus on the role of the superintendent. Often, superintendents are viewed as villains in the plot to oppress and suppress as they manage schools in a top-down fashion. Such criticism is not without some justification, yet it seems counterproductive to criticize without suggesting constructive alternatives. This book is critical and yet constructive. *The School Superintendency: Leading Education into the 21st Century,* is written by two successful former superintendents, Bill Konnert and Jack Augenstein, who understand the complexities of contemporary educational organizations and the need for schools to transform themselves as we enter the next century. Their audience is two groups—those preparing to be superintendents and those already serving as chief executive officers of school districts; this is a book to prepare, as well as to improve, superintendents.

Too often, textbooks in school administration are merely listings of how-to-do-its, e.g., seven steps to the successful superintendency.

This is not such a text. Rather, the attempt is to sensitize administrators to some of the contemporary educational dilemmas confronting superintendents, examining those issues in broad frames from multiple vantage points—political, cultural, historical, and professional. Relevant theory is used to place the perspectives of experienced practitioners into a large context of meaning and explanation. The theory serves as a heuristic guide to analysis, and the experience grounds the theory with meaning and firsthand explanation.

This is not to say the book contains no practical suggestions for administrators; indeed, it does. But the overriding perspective is one that supplies superintendents with both conceptual capital and suggestions to enable them to effectively solve the problems of practice. The text is an interesting blend of theory and application. A major strength of the book is that two successful administrators underscore the importance of theoretical analysis without relinquishing what they do best—providing concrete examples and useful ideas. Their goal is to write a book for reflective practitioners, and they have succeeded.

I believe that, if we are to improve the practice of educational administration, then we must prepare practitioners to be reflective and systematic in their inquiry. Intuition, impulse, and the biases of dubious beliefs need to be replaced by thoughtful, open-minded administrators making reasonable and informed decisions. Administrators need to be secure enough to provide the vision and leadership that will be demanded in the future. Ironically, the leadership of the future will likely require a transformation of both the structure and functions of education. Teachers will have to play a more central leadership role, and administrators will need to learn how to facilitate that role. The challenges of the future are great; the superintendent is a critical player, and this text is a strong beginning in helping thoughtful administrators understand what they must do.

WAYNE K. HOY
The Ohio State University

INTRODUCTION

This book addresses the unique position in the school systems of the United States known as the superintendency and the individual, known as the superintendent, who occupies this position. This individual is the chief executive officer (CEO) of the school system. As such, the superintendent has no peers within the school system and is *the* leader of the system. The occupant of this position must possess a sense of vision of what the system can be and have a view of the system that is broad in its perspective and, thus, different than anyone else's. The superintendency is more than knowing *how to do;* it is knowing *how to think* and *how to feel.*

The traditionally accepted definition of the superintendent as the implementer of policy established by the board of education is far too simplistic. The reality of the situation is that a dynamic and ever-changing relationship exists between the superintendent and a host of people and agencies, including such publics as parents, community groups, students, school personnel, and state and federal agencies. The superintendent, at different times and in different situations, is a leader, coach, manager, follower, motivator, philosopher, missionary, policymaker, politician, sales person, evaluator, and distributor of scarce resources. The degree to which this individual is able to establish a value system and mission for the school system and persuade *others* to share these commitments and be motivated to work toward their attainment determines superintendency success.

The basic purposes of this book are to provide information that will help individuals prepare for, obtain, and be successful in their first superintendency and to help practicing superintendents improve their CEO skills. The size, demographics, or geographic location of the school system does little to alter the primary responsibilities of the position.

The book is divided into four parts. An overview of each part follows.

PART ONE (the milieu of the superintendent)

We feel that an overall perspective and understanding of the setting in which the superintendent functions is a prerequisite to studying and understanding the superintendency. Part One begins with a brief history of the superintendency. This is important because organizational research indicates that the history of an organization has a meaningful influence on the current state of affairs within the organization.

Following the historical perspective, the contemporary setting for the superintendency is explored from a *macro,* or *big picture,* perspective. This exploration is followed by a discussion of organizational dynamics at play within a school system. The contemporary scene concludes with a view of the school system as a political system.

Part One then moves to a discussion of the superintendent's role during the nineties and into the next millennium, because important changes are on the horizon. There is evidence that the superintendent is emerging as more of a mentor and coach than an order giver. There is a shift away from a hierarchical authoritarian organization to a more horizontal organization, where people experience more ownership, both literal and psychological, and where they can experience personal growth. Individuals are becoming more concerned with how their work relates to the rest of their lives, and this attitude represents an increased emphasis on individual concern for the quality of life, including work life.

One other important change that presently is occurring and, in all likelihood, will continue throughout the nineties and into the next millennium is a focus on women and minorities in educational administration. With respect to the superintendency, women and minority superintendents currently are few in number; however, with each passing year, their numbers continue to increase. There is every reason to believe that this trend will gain in momentum during the next decade.

This book has been written in an effort to provide useful insights for any superintendency aspirant or incumbent, regardless of gender or race. In an effort to convey this message, the authors have used inclusive or nonsexist language throughout the text.

PART TWO (the superintendent as a leader)

As the most extensive part of the book, this section discusses the superintendent as the *leader* of the school system. For the sake of clarity, it is presented in four subsections.

The Broader Leadership Perspective

In order to establish a common understanding of *leadership,* this subsection presents a brief history of leadership that is followed by a discussion of the differences between providing leadership from the superintendent's chair and from other positions within the system. The superintendent must constantly be thinking about the "big issues" and how they may be addressed without violating personal philosophical commitments. For example, the United States has entered into an information age, and the time is rapidly approaching, if not already here, when the touch of a couple of keys on a computer keyboard can *pull up* any information or facts one desires. In fact, computers can continuously and simultaneously monitor a number of information providing networks and compile a bank of relevant information in very short order. This development has tremendous implications for the mission of education since much of what is taught in the schools is factual in nature. If one can obtain facts at will by mechanical means, then what facts are still worthy of being taught in the schools?

Personal Philosophy and Leadership

This subsection addresses the important role one's personal philosophy plays in providing leadership to the school system. Before the superintendent can select an orientation and mission for the school system, a well-established personal value system must first be in place. Further, it is necessary to know how one's personal value system applies to the education of individuals from birth through early adulthood. In short, the superintendent must have a consistent, comprehensive, and workable personal philosophy; must know how this personal philosophy influences education; and must clearly communicate these beliefs to all publics. The concept of transformational leadership and the importance of system culture and values are also explored.

Superintendent Leadership Competencies: Personal

This subsection identifies desirable personal leadership competencies. These competencies are necessary, but not sufficient attributes, for general leadership success. In and of themselves, they do not guarantee leadership success; however, success will be difficult to obtain without them. The superintendent is viewed as a divergent thinker, motivator, empowerer, and communicator.

Superintendent Leadership Competencies: Professional

This final leadership subsection identifies and discusses some important professional competencies a successful superintendent must possess. These competencies are addressed specifically from the perspective of the superintendency. The superintendent, as the board's chief executive officer, is the first topic addressed. This may be the most important topic with respect to the survival of the superintendent. Second is the superintendent as strategic planner. The strategic plan of a school system is extremely important because it will serve as a guide to the superintendent as s/he functions in each of the professional competency areas. Third is the superintendent as negotiator. Probably nothing has a greater impact on the day-to-day working life of the superintendent than the negotiated contract and the process that led to the contract. The section concludes with chapters on the superintendent as business manager, lobbyist, and consulter of specialists.

A Final Leadership Comment

The study of leadership is exciting, in part because it is so elusive. Long (1988, p. 21) expresses this elusiveness well when he states,

> Analyzing leadership . . . is like studying the Abominable Snowman: you see footprints, but never the thing itself. Leadership is like elec-

tricity. You can't see it, but you certainly can't miss its effect. And yet, this elusive, intangible thing we call leadership might very well be the most essential ingredient in personal and business success.

PART THREE (preparing for, obtaining, and departing a superintendency)

This part discusses the processes of preparing for, obtaining, and departing a superintendency. The socialization process that occurs as one is preparing for the superintendency is discussed and is followed by specific suggestions relative to obtaining a superintendency. The part concludes with a discussion of post-superintendency opportunities. A superintendency does not have to be the final step in one's career.

PART FOUR (health, happiness, and the superintendency)

If one is to provide committed and enthusiastic leadership for the duration of a professional career, it is necessary to achieve an integrated lifestyle with which one is comfortable. Therefore, this last part considers what is necessary for maintaining one's health, happiness, and, yes, even sanity while serving as a superintendent. Life in the fishbowl and the unique problems encountered by single superintendents are explored. These are followed by ideas for controlling personal stress.

CONCLUDING COMMENTS

The book concludes with a potpourri of comments on the superintendency. It does more than summarize: it talks about the synergism and excitement that await a superintendent.

This book is written to blend theory and practice in a forward-looking mode. The information included has been obtained through research, interviews with hundreds of successful superintendents, and contributions from selected superintendents and other professionals with special knowledge, experiences, and/or expertise.

There is no *how-to-do-it* list that will guarantee a successful tenure as a superintendent. If something can be "done by the book," then, by definition, it is not leadership. Each individual must take the information contained in this book, with other relevant information, and integrate and apply it to one's individual likes, strengths, and beliefs in order to be a leader. There is no substitute for the arduous process of thinking.

REFERENCE

Long, G. H. (1988). Leadership and the pursuit of excellence. *Directors and Boards, 12,* 21–25.

PART ONE

The Milieu of the Superintendent

An overall perspective and understanding of the setting in which the superintendent functions is a prerequisite to studying and understanding the superintendency. Thus, this subdivision on the milieu of the superintendent sets the stage for everything that follows.

CHAPTER 1

The Historical Perspective

History is "an unending dialogue between the past and present" (Carr, 1961, p. 35), and a knowledge of history helps one understand the present. This is equally true of the superintendency. Contemporary attitudes towards and expectations of the superintendent are products of the history of the superintendency.

A detailed history of the superintendency is not available. Perhaps the reason for this is that the superintendency evolved as a product of growth in the educational arena. It was not a carefully orchestrated and planned addition to education. As such, a history of the superintendency must be pieced together from sketchy recordings dating back to the end of the eighteenth century. Wilson (1960) produced one of the few chronologies of the public school superintendency, and the National Catholic Education Association Archives is one of the few places that has material chronicling the development of the superintendency in the nonpublic arena namely, the diocesan superintendency.

THE STATE AND COUNTY SUPERINTENDENCIES

In the late eighteenth century, the states became involved in education through the tenth amendment to the Constitution, which says, "The powers not delegated to the United States by the Constitution, nor prohibited by it to the states, are reserved to the states respectively, or to the people." Since the word *education* is never mentioned in the Constitution, the states assumed responsibility for education when the citizens began expressing interest in mass education. The legislatures passed laws permitting public education and allocated small amounts of money to help local communities with their educational efforts.

When state funds began to be appropriated for education, the lawmakers wanted some accounting of the funds. They often appointed volunteer committees to oversee these limited fiscal activities. These committees, formed at the beginning of the nineteenth century, were the forerunners of state boards of education.

As more communities availed themselves of state funds for education, work loads became burdensome for the volunteer committees. These committees then proceeded to identify a paid state officer to handle the accounting activities for them. Overseeing the state educational funds was but one part, and often a small part, of the state official's total responsibilities.

As the number of communities involved in state funding continued to grow, the oversight function became a full-time job. Thus, the first state superintendencies were established. New York is credited with appointing the first state superintendent in 1812. This practice was quickly adopted by the other states.

With but a few notable exceptions, such as Horace Mann in Massachusetts and Henry Barnard in Connecticut, state superintendents seldom exerted a strong educational influence. They primarily performed data collecting and oversight functions. These same functions are readily apparent in present-day activities of state departments of education. For instance, establishing and enforcing minimum standards and equalizing educational opportunities through the distribution of state funds are still important functions of state departments of education.

As the population of this country continued to grow and expand westward, many hundreds of small local school systems sprang up. The task of visiting and inspecting these local systems became an impossibility for a single state school officer or committee. As a result, these responsibilities were gradually delegated to area committees. These area committees quickly became county committees. And, as happened at the state level, the volunteer county committees soon found the oversight activities too burdensome and proceeded to delegate them to a county official already on the payroll. As the responsibilities continued to grow, they required the attention of a full-time person. Thus, the county superintendency was born. More than a dozen states had adopted the county form of educational supervision before the Civil War. Today, the county superintendency is still very much in evidence in the educational governance structure of this country. In many states, the county office still serves as the intermediary between the local districts and the state department. In some states, the county office serves as the primary administrative unit, and the county superintendent serves in the capacity of a local superintendent.

It is interesting to note that Thomas Jefferson had great foresight in comprehending the value of a county unit in the administration of public education. In his *Bill for the More General Diffusion of Knowledge,* which he introduced in the Virginia Assembly in 1779, he proposed that the citizens of each county in the state elect three aldermen to have general charge of the schools. The aldermen were to appoint one overseer for every ten school districts in the county. The duties of this appointee were to include appointing teachers, supervising teaching, examining pupils, and carrying out instructions of the College of William and Mary (Cremin and Butts, 1953).

THE LOCAL SUPERINTENDENCY

The local superintendency was not the result of a sequential progression of the state and county superintendencies. Instead, it developed simultaneously with these positions. It evolved from local initiative and was not established by constitution or statutes as the state and county superintendencies were (Nolte, 1971).

Like its state and county counterparts, the local superintendency was preceded by a school committee that was appointed by the local councilmen, or selectmen. Often, the local minister served on the school committee because he usually was the most highly educated layman in the community. Unlike the state and county committees, these local committees were generally more reluctant to turn the supervising of the schools over to one individual. Perhaps this was because the responsibilities were generally limited to one facility, or perhaps it reflected the strong and much cherished independent spirit.

The first local superintendencies were established in the larger cities. Buffalo and Louisville are generally credited with establishing the first ones in 1837 (AASA, 1952). The practice slowly spread, and, by 1870, more than thirty large cities had their own superintendents (p. 28).

Until the 1870s, local superintendents were employed by school boards without specific statutory authority to do so. They relied on the concept that the authority to operate schools also gave them the implied authority to hire an individual to administer them. The most famous case that legitimatized the authority of a local board to hire a superintendent was the Kalamazoo case in 1874 (Nolte, 1971). Although this meant that the local superintendency now had legal status, the duties and responsibilities of the position were left largely to the discretion of the local boards of education. To a large extent, this is still true today. As evidence, Garber (1956) performed a study of state statutes and concluded that the superintendent's legal status was nebulous at best. Also, Cunningham (1962), in a study of the decision-making behavior of a large number of local school boards, found that many administrative decisions, usually considered to be the province of the superintendent, were made, instead, by boards of education.

It was not uncommon at this time for the board members to maintain control of the business operation of the school, the part of the school operation with which they felt the most comfortable, and to delegate the instructional functions to the superintendent. They also were very often involved in the personnel employment process.

It is interesting to note that the word *superintendent* has a Latin derivation. It comes from the Latin words *super*, meaning over, and *intendo*, meaning direct. This fits the description of the responsibilities of the early superintendents, which were to oversee and direct the school operations; however, the derivation does not address the leadership and change functions. Perhaps history, and even the name itself, serve to make the leadership and change functions so difficult for today's superintendents.

THE DIOCESAN SUPERINTENDENCY

Private schools educate over 5 million students, or more than 11 percent of the school-age population in the United States. The Catholic schools, with an enrollment of over 2.5 million students, represent the largest private school segment.

Historically, Catholic schools began before the founding of the country when Ursuline Sisters arrived from France in 1727 to open the first Catholic school in New Orleans (Ellis, 1969). As the country's population grew, so, too, did the number of Catholic schools. By the mid-nineteenth century, diocesan school boards (equivalent to district boards) were established, and these became important in the organization of diocesan school systems. As of 1992, there were 197 dioceses in the United States, and each has a designated head of the schools who, most often, had the title of superintendent. These superintendents provide leadership for Catholic schools in a large geographic area. For example, in Ohio, there are six diocesan superintendents covering the same geographical area as over 600 public school superintendents.

As noted above, in the nineteenth century, Catholic dioceses first established school boards, sometimes called school inspectors, to oversee the growing numbers of parochial elementary schools. These were composed primarily of pastors appointed by their bishop who were responsible for checking the teachers' qualifications, reviewing the curricular program, testing students, and inspecting the facilities. As the number of schools continued to grow and the time required of the board members increased, the board members decided that their board responsibilities were infringing upon their primary positions as pastors.

Thus, in February 1888, the Archdiocese of New York board members recommended that a "salaried inspector" be appointed, and in April, 1888, the Rev. Dr. William E. Degnan was appointed superintendent of parochial schools for the Archdiocese of New York. The next year, the Archdiocese of Philadelphia appointed a diocesan inspector of schools, and, by the turn of the century, Baltimore, Boston, Brooklyn, and Omaha dioceses had also designated superintendents. Today, each diocese has someone designated to oversee its schools.

SUPERINTENDENTS' NATIONAL ORGANIZATIONS

In 1865, a few months after Lincoln's assassination, a group of public school superintendents, who were in Harrisburg, Pennsylvania, attending the National Teachers Association meeting, met and organized the National Association of School Superintendents. Henry Barnard (Rice, 1964) reported on that meeting in the *Journal of Education*, in which he wrote,

During the session of the National Teachers Association at Harrisburg for 1865, a meeting of State and City Superintendents there present was held, of which Rev. B. G. Northrop, Agent of the Massachusetts Board of Education, was Chairman, and Rev. L. Van Bokkelen, LL.D., State Superintendent of Public Schools of Maryland, was Secretary. At this Convention it was decided to hold a meeting in February, 1866, at Washington, for the purpose of forming a National Association of School Superintendents, to be composed of those devoted to the supervision of schools in the several States and Cities of the country, and the discussion of topics appropriate to such meeting. (p. 2)

In 1870, the group became a part of the National Education Association (NEA) and was then known as the Department of Superintendents. It remained under that banner until 1937 when it became the American Association of School Administrators (AASA). Finally, in 1972 AASA separated from NEA and became a freestanding organization.

Diocesan superintendents, who were part of the Parish School Department of the Catholic Educational Association (CEA) that was formed in 1904, met informally at the 1906 CEA Convention in Cleveland to discuss the "many phases of diocesan school organization" (*Catholic Educational Association Report of Proceedings and Addresses of the Third Annual Meeting*, 1906, p. 37). They met again informally in Milwaukee in 1907 and proposed the establishment of a section for superintendents within the Parish School Department. They organized formally and held their first meeting in 1908 at the CEA Convention in Cincinnati. At that initial meeting, by-laws were adopted, noting that the group "formed a union for the purpose of preparing and discussing papers, and the exchange of ideas on subjects pertaining to the general and special work of superintending and supervising parish schools" (*The Catholic Educational Association Bulletin*, 1908, p. 369). In 1935, the organization became a separate department within the National Catholic Educational Association. In 1972, it reorganized, modified its by-laws, and changed its name to Chief Administrators of Catholic Education to accommodate the changing diocesan central office organizations. Its last modification came in 1979 when it developed three divisions, with one serving school superintendents, another diocesan directors of religious education, and the third vicars for education who had broad educational coordinating responsibilities.

IMPORTANCE OF THE HISTORICAL PERSPECTIVE

Since 1950 when the first concerted efforts to study educational administration as an academic discipline came to the forefront, much research has been performed on school systems as organizations and on superintendents as educational leaders. As a result, we know more about school systems, leadership, boards of education, and superintendents than at any time in the past. However, it is interesting to observe that many of the factors that influenced the development of the superintendency still impact upon the superintendency today.

The public school superintendent as an employee of the board of education is still the law in most states. (In a few states, the superintendent is elected to the office.) The diocesan superintendent is usually appointed by the local bishop but is often recommended by the diocesan board of education. Unlike many professionals, the superintendent cannot operate autonomously. He/she depends on the board both for the establishment of policy and the approval of many administrative recommendations.

While progress has been made in defining the responsibilities of the superintendent, there is still much left to the discretion of the board. With some boards, the distinction between policy formation and administration is blurred, at best. This is particularly true in the financial and personnel areas. Seldom do boards get deeply involved in the mechanics of the instructional program. These contemporary relationships between superintendents and boards are remnants of past practices.

The early superintendents were expected to be reporters and managers but not leaders. To a large extent, this is true today. A superintendent must possess a great deal of leadership acumen, knowledge about change processes, and patience if he/she is to function as the instructional leader of the school system. Citizens and parents tend not to view the superintendent as an educational authority whose ideas and views about education should be accepted as gospel. Instead, they develop their own beliefs relative to education in general and their local school system in specific. Furthermore, they often bring considerable pressure to bear on the local board and superintendent to have their views implemented.

In conclusion, an understanding of the historical development of the superintendency should offer some solace to beleaguered superintendents that things were not easy in the old days either. It also should lend a helpful perspective to the next chapter, which discusses the contemporary setting of the superintendency.

REFERENCES

American Association of School Administrators. (1952). *The American School Superintendency, 30th Yearbook.* Washington, D.C.: The Association.

Carr, E. H. (1961). *What Is History.* New York, NY: Vantage Books.

Catholic Educational Association Report of the Proceedings and Addresses of the Third Annual Meeting. Cleveland, Ohio, July 9, 10, 11, 12, 1906, Columbus, OH: Secretary's Office, Catholic Education Association.

The Catholic Educational Association Bulletin. (1908). Columbus, OH: Secretary's Office, Catholic Education Association, V (1).

Cremin, L. A. and Butts, F. R. (1953). *A History of American Education in American Culture.* New York, NY: Holt, Rinehart & Winston.

Cunningham, L. L. (1962). Decision-making behavior in school boards. *American School Board Journal, 144,* 13–16.

Ellis, J. T. (1969). *American Catholicism* (2nd edition revised). Chicago, IL: University of Chicago Press.

Garber, L. O. (1956). Superintendent's legal authority depends on his contract. *School Law, 57,* 63–64.

Nolte, M. C. (1971). *Law and the School Superintendent.* Cincinnati, OH: The W. H. Anderson Co.

Rice, A. H. (1964). *AASA The Centennial Story.* Washington, D.C.: American Association of School Administrators.

Vlaanderen, R. B. (1971). Statutory status of the public school superintendent. In M. C. Nolte (Ed.), *Law and the School Superintendent,* pp. 5–50, Cincinnati, OH: The W. H. Anderson Co.

Wilson, R. E. (1960). *The Modern School Superintendent.* New York, NY: Harper & Brothers.

CHAPTER 2

The Contemporary Setting

THE BIG PICTURE

Before discussing the contemporary milieu in which the superintendent functions, it is important to realize that each individual is unique with respect to the combination of personal beliefs and competencies that are brought to the position. These unique combinations are very influential in determining how each individual behaves in the superintendency setting and how others react to the superintendent; thus, no two individuals will react the same in the milieu of the superintendency. Furthermore, one's own behavior should change over time as one's personal beliefs are scrutinized and restructured via a self-assessment process, which should be ongoing, and as one's competencies are honed and new ones acquired.

The competencies needed by a superintendent have grown rather rapidly in recent years, and existing ones have increased in importance. Table 2.1 presents a sample of the types of competencies required of a superintendent to function successfully in the contemporary educational milieu. In addition to these competencies, there are also a number of task areas in which the superintendent must be knowledgeable. Table 2.2 presents some of the more important task areas. As can be seen from these two tables, competencies and task areas are not mutually exclusive. For instance, strategic planning is both a competency and a task area.

The totality of the competencies needed by a superintendent and the

Ms. Rochelle Steininger provided the basic material for the "school system as a political system" portion of the chapter. She is a doctoral student at Marquette University.

TABLE 2.1. Superintendent Competencies

Leadership	Change agent
A. Human	Computer literacy
B. Technical	Delegating
C. Conceptual	Enabling
Communicating	Empowering
Decision-Making	Organizational dynamics
A. Problem identification	Group dynamics
B. Alternative identification	Resource management
C. Alternative selection	A. Human
D. Implementation	B. Material
E. Evaluation	C. Time
Strategic planning	Public speaking
Goal setting	Law
Motivating	Stress management
Risk taking	Time management

TABLE 2.2. Superintendent Task Areas

Finance	Instruction
Budgeting	Policy development
Business management	Community relations
Personnel administration	State and federal relations
A. Pupil	Site management
B. Staff	Co-curricular activities
C. Evaluation	Strategic planning
D. Staff development	Transportation
E. Labor relations	Food management
Curriculum	

number of task areas, some of which are quite complex, in which the superintendent must have a working knowledge is staggering. It is evident that the learning and inquiring processes are never over for the superintendent. There is always something new to be learned and skills that need to be refined.

The personal beliefs of the superintendent are used to help formulate a vision for the school system and serve as guideposts in determining how the superintendent's personal competencies will be applied in fulfilling superintendency obligations. Figure 2.1 depicts the application of personal beliefs and competencies to the educational organization or school system.

In addressing the contemporary milieu in which the superintendent functions, one is directed to the set of concentric circles in the middle of Figure 2.1. Two points should be noted. First, the largest concentric circle represents the world and second, what is usually considered the educational organization is depicted only by the innermost concentric circle and the five overlapping circles within it. This graphically illustrates that the milieu of the superintendent is far greater than just the internal educational organization represented by the innermost concentric circle.

Primary responsibilities of the superintendent are to provide leadership in establishing a vision for the educational organization and then converting this vision into a set of goals and priorities for the organization. In order to do this, the superintendent must ascertain how students can be positive contributors to not only the nation, but to the world. Indeed, the technological age means that a world view must be developed. In the years ahead, products of the schools must be able to function on a global basis. The process of determining future global, as well as national, needs and resolving conflict between the two is of great importance.

Worldwide events can have an impact on the daily operation of the schools. For instance, trade deficits and, in general, the relation of the United States' economy to the world economy have an impact on the level of educational funding. Thus, world events and trends have both *macro* and *micro* significance for the educational organization and are of considerable importance to the superintendent.

The national impact is similar to the world impact, except that it is of greater magnitude and urgency. Changing national priorities, demographics, political climates, and outlooks on education have a significant influence on the superintendent's formulation of a vision

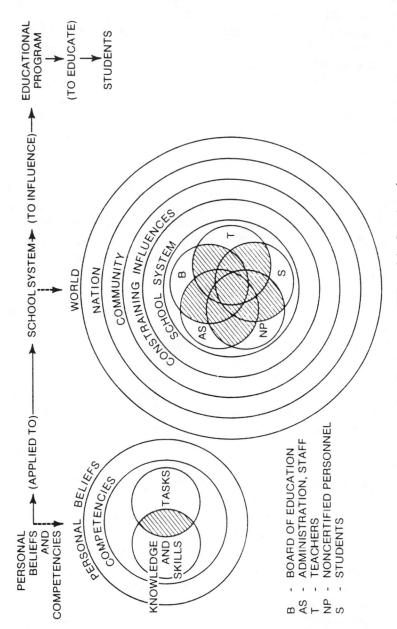

FIGURE 2.1. The Contemporary Milieu of the Superintendent.

for the school system and the degree to which the vision is able to be fulfilled.

Community mores, values, needs, and educational expectations are of utmost importance to the superintendent. As noted in Figure 2.1, the community is closer to the internal educational organization than the nation or world and, thus, it exerts the greatest immediate pressure and influence on the school organization. However, community concerns are often very parochial in nature, ranging over such matters as board member selection, coach selection, student transportation, facility utilization, etc. The superintendent must incorporate community needs and educational expectations with those of the nation and world in such a way that neither community mores or values nor the superintendent's are violated. Needless to say, this is no simple task.

The first concentric circle outside the school system represents constraining forces. These are forces brought to bear on the educational organization by people and organizational bodies outside the school organization that dictate, or attempt to dictate, how the organization will function. They serve as substitutes for leadership and include policies of the U.S. Office of Education, mandates and policies of state departments of education, federal and state legislation, judicial decisions at all levels, local referenda, and special interest groups. The school system and superintendent must operate within the confines of these parameters and, at the same time, not violate local community mores and values.

Finally, we have arrived at the innermost concentric circle, the school system. The actors within the system are represented by the five intersecting circles within the concentric circle. Theoretically, the board of education is elected by the community to set policies for and oversee the local educational program, and a superintendent is employed to operationalize and implement the policies. In reality, this is not the case. While the board does adopt policies, it is influenced in its adoptions by a number of significant others, with the superintendent being a very significant other. At times, such as in collective bargaining, the teachers and noncertified personnel can be significant others. At other times, the students fill this role.

The intersecting circles also represent overlapping efforts and responsibilities in the administration of the organization. The traditional hierarchal relationship is changing. As collaborative decision making becomes more sophisticated, as organizations have fewer layers of management, and as decision-making becomes more decentralized, the intersecting circle segments will continually increase in size.

The superintendent must bring personal beliefs and competencies to bear on the educational milieu in an effort to influence the educational program. Everything that a superintendent does should work toward the development and implementation of an effective educational program that fulfills the vision, goals, and priorities of the local educational organization.

The superintendent is the only individual who must be deeply concerned about all areas of the educational milieu. Others will have their special concerns, interests, and responsibilities, but it is the superintendent who must juggle all of the balls in such a way that the local school system accomplishes its mission of providing a quality education for its students in an effective and efficient manner.

THE SCHOOL ORGANIZATION

The School System as a Bureaucratic, Open, and Loosely Coupled Organization

Schools as bureaucracies

Institutional environments use mechanisms such as rules, regulations, and inspections to produce their organizational effects. The survival of the organization is dependent upon conformity by most of the personnel within the organization to the institutional norms and procedures (Meyer and Scott, 1983). These mechanisms combine to form what is called the bureaucracy of the organization.

School systems commonly exhibit the bureaucratic characteristics of: a high degree of role specialization, centralization of authority in a vertical hierarchical structure, control achieved through formal policies, rules and role prescriptions, and functionally specialized units (school facilities). These attempts at formality are designed to promote maximum organizational efficiency and effectiveness. Examples of these bureaucratic characteristics are

- *Division of labor:* Elementary and secondary teachers; art, music, and physical education specialists; and administrative, psychological, and counseling specialists are examples of *job* groupings designed to permit greater efficiency of oversight and function.

- *Rules and procedures:* Job descriptions, administrative procedures, teacher and student handbooks, and board of education policies are examples of formal rules and procedures created by school districts.
- *Hierarchy:* The superintendent, assistant superintendents, principals, department or grade-level chairpersons, and teachers represent a traditional chain of command within school districts.

Detailed rules and procedures are also developed to help limit disruption by the external environment. For example, school boards adopt policies and procedures that limit public access to classrooms during the school day, parent communications with school personnel, and citizen participation at board meetings.

Another approach to limiting the impact of outside influences has been the creation of staff specialists who are not directly involved in the teaching-learning process. Personnel specialists, for example, are responsible for screening applicants to ensure that they possess the desired organizational characteristics and that nondesirable characteristics are either eliminated or, at least, minimized. In larger school districts, community relations staff persons attempt to serve as buffers between the system and its external environment. However, despite attempts to close the school organization off from these environmental influences, it is impossible and unwise to do so. In the broader perspective, the external environment provides the lifeblood of the school system and is the essence for its existence.

Meyer and Scott (1983) postulate that educational bureaucracies have emerged as personnel certifying agencies. They argue that, "They use standard types of curricular topics and teachers to provide standard types of graduates, who are then allocated to places in the economic and stratification system on the basis of their educational background" (p. 72).

Frymier (1987) suggests that, in recent years, the states have assumed a greater governing role in education. The impetus for much of this change has been the national trend for greater accountability and reform in public education. The pressures for reform have "forced superintendents to exercise tighter control at the central office level" (p. 19). He concludes that, even though educators have been told to run schools like a business, they are being forced by these pressures to centralize and to do things only poor businesses do.

In conclusion, it is important to note that no formal organization can function without an operational bureaucracy in place. There must be guidelines for operations that are repetitive in nature. Consistency, stability, and formally established communication channels and ways of doing things are necessary to the efficient functioning of an organization. It is the role of the superintendent to see that the bureaucracy within his/her system is functioning properly. One must be alert to detect when the bureaucracy is too rigid and inflexible, inappropriately stifling creativity and innovation, delaying decision-making, causing decisions to be made by the wrong people, functioning in inappropriate situations, and inappropriately influencing interaction and communication with external constituent groups. A properly functioning bureaucracy can save time for all members of the organization and, thus, free them to spend more time on their primary functions and enable them to be more creative and innovative.

Schools as open systems

Daft (1983) describes an open system as one that "must interact with the environment to survive; it both consumes resources and exports resources to the environment. It cannot seal itself off. It must continually change and adapt to the environment" (p. 11).

Open systems can be very complex. Internal efficiency sometimes is just a minor issue. "The organization has to find and obtain needed resources, interpret and act on environmental changes, dispose of outputs, and control and coordinate internal activities in the face of environmental disturbances and uncertainty" (p. 11). In this context, the organization should be viewed as a set of interacting elements (people and departments who depend on one another and must work together) that acquires inputs from the external environment, transforms them, and returns outputs back to the external environment. Thus, school systems that depend on their external environments for significant support and students and that were, in fact, created by an external environment are open systems. This necessary open relationship with the environment often creates uncertainty for the school district. The local community, state legislatures, governmental agencies, pressure groups, and employee unions are examples of external publics that can provide uncertainty.

It becomes a major ongoing responsibility of the superintendent to help the school organization cope with the uncertainty created on an almost daily basis by these external influences. This requires the superintendent to provide leadership that will help the district make the adaptations necessary to keep on course. Appropriate and timely responses to influential external environments result in a dynamic school organization that is constantly reacting, changing, and adapting, in a positive manner.

However, if one is not careful, responses to external demands can lead to unplanned substantive changes in articulated organizational goals. Thompson (1967) has suggested that organizational survival itself can become the central goal superseding formal and explicitly articulated goals. In order to cope with the pressures created by a changing environment, organizations may seek to satisfy basic primary needs, especially those that help ensure organizational survival, rather than seeking maximum efficiency in goal attainment.

There is evidence today that many school systems and individual educators perceive organizational survival as a major priority. This emphasis has been brought on by such things as student/parental choice, the use of outside contractors, competency-based education, continuous progress, relaxation of certification standards, forced consolidations, etc. The approaches often used by superintendents and educational organizations to counteract these forces are reactionary in nature. After the issue(s) has surfaced, educational lobbying groups become highly critical of the legislature or other groups promoting the change.

A key question that arises is whether school organizations should be more proactive in scanning their external environment in order to attempt to influence it proactively *before* critical events occur. A study by Cameron (1986) suggested that the effectiveness of organizations was related to and improved by proactive strategies with an external focus. He stated that "top managers exercise a great deal of choice and can have major impact on organizational effectiveness and long term survival. They do this by exerting influence on, changing, or selecting the environment in which they operate . . ." (p. 107). This suggests that long-term success is enhanced by an external, proactive strategy. Superintendents should seriously examine their current leadership mode in the external arena and make appropriate adjustments if needed.

Schools as loosely coupled organizations

School systems have a penchant for planning. When this penchant is combined with the aforementioned bureaucratic and structural nature of school districts, it might be assumed that there exists a logical progression from mission statement to vision statement to goal development to development of implementation strategies to evaluation and revision of goals and strategies. If school districts were isolated from external influences, this probably would be a true assumption; however, due to the uncertainity brought on by external environmental dynamism, there often exists what Karl Wieck (1974) calls a loose coupling. In reality, action often precedes planning, and policies and practices are adapted later to reflect previous actions. This reversal is brought on by the system's need to respond to environmental contingencies, constraints, and changes. The threats and uncertainties presented by these changing environmental elements can cause school systems to react quickly in ways that are not closely related to formally articulated goals and plans. The reactions often are more closely related to survival than to legitimate organizational needs.

It would be disruptive and counterproductive for the entire school organization to respond to each external pressure. One way in which a system avoids this general disruption is to create a new division or program within the organization to deal with a particular external influence. At times, there is a very loose coupling between the new division or program and the school system's goals. Two examples of such responses would be a drivers' education program and an alcohol or drug abuse program. It is important that these societal and individual needs be addressed, but they do not fit closely with what most would view as the primary mission of a school system. Perhaps these needs could be better and more efficiently addressed by other organizations and agencies.

It is the responsibility of the superintendent to recognize when a quick response is needed to an external demand. Should the school address the demand, or should it be directed to a more appropriate organization? If the school is to address the demand, the superintendent must provide leadership to help ensure that the involvement of the system does not detract from, and hopefully supports, its primary mission.

It is worthy of note that some programs that are initiated to address a specific, legitimate need often attain lives of their own and live on after the initial need has been satisfied. These programs, in short, become organizations within an organization, and they have their own survival as a paramount concern, as opposed to the mission of the school system. For this reason, it is wise to review the program history during periodic program evaluations to see if the original need for the program formation still exists and if the program continues fulfilling the need.

Internally, loose coupling causes problems with some very vital functions. Two of the problem areas, personnel evaluation and curriculum, are ones that are central to the recent school reform movement. In personnel evaluation, there is generally a weak formal inspection of teaching and student output (Meyer and Scott, 1983). These are delegated to the local school and are infrequent. Principals and teachers have little interaction regarding teachers' work. (This is particularly true of tenured teachers.) Limited day-to-day working relations often exist among teachers at the same grade/subject levels. Student achievement is rarely used in teacher evaluations.

In the curriculum area, there are "few detailed standards of instructional content or procedure" (Wieck, 1974, p. 75). Students often are passed to the next grade with little regard for how much they have actually learned. Interdependence among instructional programs tends to be minimized.

Finally, it must be recognized that there is, indeed, a need for the school organization to be flexible and have the ability to respond to problems with dispatch when necessary. However, there also is a need to keep the school system headed in a direction leading to goal achievement. The system cannot function effectively if it is reacting at random to either external or internal pressures for change. To this end, it is important to understand that a loosely coupled organization is not synonymous with a properly functioning decentralized school system where school building–level personnel are empowered. In a loosely coupled organization, decisions and activities occur that have little relation to organizational goals, and often events have weak connections to the formal organizational structure; i.e., events have a separate identity (Wieck, 1974). Inherent in loosely coupled systems are the problems of lack of personal accountability, independence of individuals from organizational goals, and difficulty in achieving unified action; however, in a decentralized school system that is functioning properly, the individuals within the organization must know the mission and goals of the organization and be motivated to work toward their accomplishment. They must know the roles they play within the organization, and individual accountability must be the norm. Chapter 7, "Transformational Leadership," addresses the leadership role of the superintendent in reducing loose coupling within the school organization.

The School System as a Political System

Definitions of politics

One of the dictionary definitions of *politics* is "competition between competing interest groups or individuals for power and leadership" (*Webster*, 1981, p. 1,755). This definition fits the authors' view of the school system as a political system more closely than other definitions.

Tracy (1987) describes the school system as one "influenced by formal and informal power groups both within and external to the system" (p. 223) and adds that "an educational system can be assumed to have interest groups and conflicts similar to those found in cities, states, and other political entities" (p. 224). She adds as indicators of "the political nature of education," the existence of "differing goals and values represented by various interest groups," conflict as "the norm rather than the exception," and the fact that "external interest groups exert a strong influence over the policymaking process" (p. 224).

Cuban (1985) emphasizes that what is called "public relations," because of "occupational taboos," is actually politics: trying "to establish coalitions of groups and individuals who will support the mission of the schools and to minimize any damage done by critics" (p. 29). In the making of policy, "hammering out a consensus and the tugging and pushing that accompany this process are political activities" (p. 29).

Millman (1982) views politics in education, not as a negative, but simply the way things are. "Politics can be understood as the art and science of the possible. The main goal is achieved in pleasing the greatest number of people. . . . In effect, political decision making is a way of distributing the scarce resources among competing interests" (p. 26).

In a somewhat different vein, Bates (1987) discusses "cultural politics." He first defines "culture" from the perspective of the cultural studies movement as "a description of a particular way of life [of a group or society], which expresses certain meanings and values, not only in art and learning but also in institutions and ordinary behavior" (p. 25). Thus, cultural politics is a "concept . . . that emphasize[s] the ideological nature of cultural constructions" and the part they play "in the struggles between different groups" (p. 87). "Schools [school systems] can, therefore, be seen both as an ideological apparatus over which struggles for control will take place within the wide society and as sites within which struggles to maintain or challenge the existing hegemony are likely to take place" (p. 90).

Carnoy and Levin (1986) present another view as they describe the origins of conflict in the schools. They see the schools as an arena of conflict because they have the dual role of preparing workers and citizens. That the educational system

is charged with both these responsibilities creates within it the seeds of conflict and contradiction. The ensuing struggle between the advocates of two different principles for their objectives and operations tends to fashion schools that must necessarily meet the demands of both masters imperfectly. (pp. 40–41)

Politics in the history of schools

Early rural schools were the "focus of people's lives outside the home" (Tyack, 1974, p. 15).

They were the places where ministers met their flocks, politicians caucused with the faithful, families gathered for Christmas parties and hoedowns, the Grange held its baked bean suppers, . . . and neighbors gathered to hear spelling bees and declamations. (Tyack, 1974, p. 16)

From their earliest days, schools were the places for gatherings but also for struggles of control. New schools were sometimes founded as the result of neighbor feuds (Tyack, 1974).

The population explosion, particularly in the cities, between 1820 and 1860 brought enormous organization problems to the task of education. Cities had neither the trained personnel nor the physical facilities to provide education for all children. Educational leaders looked to the emerging technology in the cities to help them "discover and implement" what they thought must be one best system of education—the division of

labor in the factory, the punctuality of the railroad, the chain of command and coordination in modern businesses. . . . They sought to re-

> place confused and erratic means of control with careful allocation of powers and functions within hierarchical organizations; to establish networks of communication that would convey information and directives and would provide data for planning for the future; to substitute impersonal rules for informal. . . . In short, they tried to create a more bureaucratic system. (Tyack, 1974, p. 29)

Thus, the burgeoning pluralistic society was confronted with new challenges, and, as in earlier days, there were competing interests with solutions for those challenges.

The period from 1890 to 1940 was an era of centralization. Again, the struggle over schools as an ideological apparatus can be viewed as the central dynamic of this period, with "the members of a movement composed mostly of business and professional elites, including university people and the new school managers" (Tyack, 1974, p. 126) forming the group that came to dominate the schools during this period.

Spring (1984) provides an even closer look at the mechanisms by which this business and professional power elite came to control the school system during this same period in Cincinnati. Interestingly, Spring reports that it was the very notation of keeping politics out of school government that enabled this power elite to dominate Cincinnati's schools. Legislation was passed limiting school board size and providing for general, as opposed to district or ward, election. Thus, campaigning became a very expensive proposition. Since political parties were expressly excluded from this area, only those with considerable financial backing could afford to campaign. In Cincinnati, the business and professional interests formed the powerful Citizens' School Committee, which effectively controlled elections by controlling nominations and providing funds for campaigns. Challenges to this controlling elite arose in the 1960s, when "schooling had become one of the prime weapons in the war on poverty and a central concern not only of policy makers but also of the dispossessed, especially the people of color struggling for a greater share of power in the cities" (Tyack, 1974, p. 270).

Carnoy and Levin (1986) place these changes in emphasis within the context of the inherent conflict in the task of educating workers/citizens. Since schools tend to be "conservative institutions," they will

> tend to preserve existing social relations. . . . In historical periods when social movements are weak and business ideology is strong,

schools tend to strengthen their function of reproducing workers for capitalist workplace relations and the unequal division of labor. When social movements arise to challenge these relations, schools move in the other direction to equalize opportunity and expand human rights. (p. 41)

From an economic perspective, Viteritti (1986) interprets the gains made in the 1950s and 1960s as the result of "client politics" that allowed the political system to respond to the needs of minorities, the poor, and the noninfluentials (p. 243). But, as he notes,

Client politics works when the incentive for a small influential group to support policy outweighs the incentive for a broader political population to oppose it. In such cases, the client is the only active political constituency in the policy arena. It achieves victory by default because of the apathy of the larger community. (p. 243)

The client of the urban schools, in spite of being composed of minority groups, is not small in numbers; hence, the costs are high and even "particularly conspicuous in a period of decline (Viteritti, 1980, p. 244). Thus, Viteritti presents an economic rationale, as opposed to class differences, as the basis for recent setbacks to programs for minorities.

Danis (1984) presents a microcosmic view of the political dynamics at work over recent periods with her case study of the school board of Santa Barbara, California, from 1930 through 1979. She concludes that, before the major shifts in public attitudes could be translated into policies by the school board, school board membership had to be changed over several elections. Two periods of complete change during those years were highlighted by her study: 1931–1934 and 1973–1979. In the more recent period, three elections, in 1975, 1977, and 1979, resulted in a completely new school board and a new superintendent. Major changes in school organization and policies were effected during this period. By 1979, Danis notes, "The progressive era was over. Although the belief in individualization was never erased, in reality, the emphasis was on subject and/or functional proficiency, the ultimate goal being employment, not intellectual growth or social awareness" (1984, pp. 141–142).

More recently, Spring (1993) believes that the New American School Development Corporation established under the Bush administration is an example of the complexity of politics and conflicting interests. This is a private nonprofit corporation funded by business but working cooperatively with the federal government to provide examples of effective schools. It illustrates, according to Spring, three major political groups affecting education, namely, major government actors, special interest groups, and the knowledge industry.

The major government actors include politicians, educational politicians, boards of education, and the courts. Politicians, certainly at the state and national levels, must have educational positions or policies related to current educational problems to offer their constituencies. Educational politicians he defines as "administrators whose tenure depends on the favor of elected politicians or on voter support" (Spring, 1993, p. 5). Boards, even with diminished power, still influence such critical areas as budget and district organization. Courts have affected equality of and equity within education among education's many aspects.

The "big three" among special interest groups are foundations, teachers' unions, and the corporate sector. However, there are also educational interest groups such as the American Educational Research Association and single-interest groups that advocate such things as prayer in the schools, competency-based education, sex education, etc. (Spring, 1993).

Finally, an area not often listed under political groups is the knowledge industry. Spring delineates three principal categories: creators (funding agencies and researchers), gatekeepers (knowledge brokers and testing organizations), and distributors (publishers). Spring (1993) defines gatekeepers as "individuals and organizations that influence the distribution of research and new knowledge" (p. 18), and knowledge brokers are the researchers who often decide what shall be studied. Finally, the primary purpose of publishing companies is to make a profit in a very competitive market.

From this perspective of politics of education, superintendents must broaden their categories of political groups to extend beyond politicians, voters, and the previously limited definitions of interest groups. They should now begin to include foundations and the various groups within the knowledge industry in their observation and study.

Implications for superintendents

Since history and current literature have clearly revealed the political nature of the educational system and since "keeping politics out of education" is no longer a credible excuse for denying the participation of diverse groups and interests in the process of this system, what insights might be offered for superintendents who must be immersed in this political milieu?

Political Savvy

Danis (1984), after a close look at the processes by which the will of the majority of the voting public manifested itself by replacing incumbent school board members, suggests that "the new superintendent, after an incumbent defeat, must not only understand the new mandate but must be capable of articulating and implementing policies and programs" (p. 142).

Millman (1982) advocates the understanding and expedient application of political behavior. He proposes some political maxims that may serve educators as well as they do politicians; for example, "Do not raise to the policy level those issues that can be handled satisfactorily at a lower procedural level" (p. 27).

Superintendent/board relationships

Causes of conflict between school boards and superintendents are misperceptions of roles and changes in membership that affect the balance of power according to Hayden (1986). He has some practical advice to offer, including clear definition of roles, a strong policy manual, and avoidance of any appearance of favoritism on the part of the superintendent. He urges superintendents to maintain a positive attitude, to be honest, and, if all else fails, to recognize that there are times when it is best to "terminate the relationship" (p. 19).

An ethical framework for politics in education

Beyond the behavioral applications of political savvy is the question of the very purpose of the superintendency in the political system that is education. Bates (1987) notes that the definition of "success" will vary, depending upon the notion of culture to which one adheres. If culture means "high culture . . . one that claims to identify and celebrate the greatest achievements of the human mind" (p. 85), then

> Administration can be judged as successful or unsuccessful according to how well it can reproduce that culture among those who have in-

herited it and produce that culture among those who have not or at least persuade those who lack such an inheritance that they are devoid of talent or worth. (p. 91)

If however, one adopts the cultural studies definition of *culture* as the "whole way of life of a particular society" (Bates, 1987, p. 86), then

Educational administration can be judged successful when it helps articulate and develop the aspirations and maps of meaning that are the cultural inheritance of its members, thus, helping them to articulate and defend their interests in the wider social context. (p. 91)

Bates's view of administration, he admits

is far from the "scientific," apolitical maxims of current administrative theory . . . for it involves not simply the formulation and implementation of reliable and neutral techniques of management but rather the active embracing of a political role involving analysis, judgment, and advocacy and the adoption of an active stance toward issues of social justice and democracy. (p. 110)

In order to accomplish this in a particular school or system, Bates calls for an analysis of the actual culture, an analysis that may reveal that the culture of a given school or system is quite different from what it is believed to be.

Finally, Bates makes a strong case for an advocacy role for administrators.

Advocacy, whether administrative or not, is inevitably suffused with values and ideology. The question then becomes: what overriding values are to inform the work of the school [or system]? Clearly, in any society that calls itself democratic, principles of respect for persons, social justice, and equity are fundamental. A case can also be made that the educational process, at its best, is also closely associated with such principles. (p. 111)

Summary

As noted at the outset of this section, politics is defined as competition between competing interest groups or individuals for power and leadership in government or other groups. This competition for power and leadership has been evident in school and system history from earliest times to the present.

The superintendent, the leader of the system, according to Bates, cannot "keep politics out of education" but, rather, must provide leadership in the political arena, which is rooted in the "principles of respect for persons, social justice, and equity."

CONCLUDING COMMENT

This chapter has attempted to "paint a picture" of the contemporary milieu in which the superintendent functions. The result is a chapter that is both lengthy in number of pages and diverse in content. This length and diversity reflect the extremely complex milieu with which the contemporary superintendent must cope in his/her efforts to provide educational leadership.

REFERENCES

Bates, R. J. (1987). Corporate culture, schooling and educational administration. *Educational Administration Quarterly, 23*(4), 79–115.

Cameron, K. (1986). A study of organizational effectiveness and its predictors. *Management Science, 32*(1), 87–112.

Carnoy, M. and Levin, H. M. (1986). Educational reform and class conflict. *Journal of Education, 168*(1), 35–46.

Cleveland, H. (1972). *The Future Executive.* New York, NY: Harper & Row.

Cuban, L. (1985). Conflict and leadership in the superintendency. *Phi Delta Kappan, 67,* 28–30.

Daft, R. L. (1988). *Organizational Theory and Design.* New York, NY: West Publishing Co.

Danis, R. (1984). Policy changes in local schools: The dissatisfaction theory of democracy. *Urban Education, 19,* 125–144.

Frymier, J. (1987). Bureaucracy and the neutering of teachers. *Phi Delta Kappan,* (Sept.), 9–16.

Hayden, J. G. (1986). Crisis at the helm: Superintendents and school boards in conflict. *The School Administrator, 43*(10), 17–19.

Meyer, J. W., and Scott, R. W. (1983). *Organizational Environments.* Beverly Hills, CA: Sage Publications.

Millman, S. D. (1982). Don't get mad, get even! *Community and Junior College Journal, 52*(7), 26–28.

Simon, H. A. (1957). *Models of Man, Social and Rational.* New York, NY: The MacMillan Company.

Spring, J. (1993). *Conflict of Interests—The Politics of American Education* (second edition). New York, NY: Longman Publishing Group.

Spring, J. (1984). The structure of power in an urban school system: A study of Cincinnati school politics. *Curriculum Inquiry, 14,* 401–424.

Thompson, J. D. (1967). *Organizations in Action.* New York, NY: McGraw-Hill.

Tracy, S. J. (1987). The positive politics of education. *Clearing House, 60,* 223–225.

Tyack, D. B. (1974). *The One Best System: A History of American Urban Education.* Cambridge, MA: Harvard University Press.

Viteritti, J. P. (1986). The urban school district: Toward an open system approach to leadership and governance. *Urban Education, 21,* 228–253.

Webster's Third New International Dictionary. (1981). Springfield, MA: Merriam Webster, Inc.

Wieck, K. E. (1974). Educational organizations as loosely coupled systems. *Administrative Science Quarterly, 21*(1), 1–18.

CHAPTER 3

The Future Scenario

Visualize, for a moment, the environment for which the schools will be preparing students to function in the twenty-first century. Science and technology will have reached a level of sophistication that is difficult to comprehend today. Cybernetic intelligence will be well along the path to implementation. Computers will be running many machines by responding to the verbal commands of the operators, and interactive electronic media will allow people to visualize events around the world and verbally interact with them. Medical capabilities beyond one's wildest dreams will be commonplace. Genetic engineering and bionic limbs will be in use. Many diseases will have been eradicated, and life expectancies will be longer. A revolution in the speed of electronic and transportation systems will have occurred.

Food supplies will be grown more extensively using hydroponic techniques. Sea farming will be commonplace. Scientific breakthroughs in fertilizers and harvesting techniques will enable even greater yields per acre.

The technological information society will have made quantum leaps. Businesses will be totally automated with electronic mail and filing systems, and paper letters and paper storage will be virtually unknown. Perhaps all homes will be equipped to handle electronic mail. The only paper mail one might receive would be the junk mail that is so prevalent currently.

Dr. Holly Genzen provided the material from her original research for "The Woman Superintendent" section.

Mr. Robert Gudgel provided material for the "technology" section. He is a private consultant in organizational development.

Dr. David Kircher provided material used throughout the chapter. He is an assistant superintendent.

The future also has population changes in store. In 1992, the U.S. Census Bureau found it necessary to revise its twenty-first century projections developed in 1988. In 1988, it had predicted that the U.S. population would reach 268 million by 2000 and 300 million by 2050; however, because of the increase in new immigrants (legal and illegal) and newborn infants, it now predicts that the population will reach 275 million by 2000 and 383 million by 2050. Among its other revisions for 2050 are the following:

1. The number of individuals eighty-five years old and older will increase from 3.3 million to 17.7 million.
2. Persons 100 years old or older will increase from 45,000 to more than 1 million.
3. The Afro-American population will increase from 32 million to 62 million.
4. The Asian-American population will go from 8 million to 41 million.
5. Hispanic-Americans will increase from 24 million to 81 million.

It also notes that the median age for Americans will rise from thirty-three to thirty-nine by 2035, and the white population will reach 208 million in 2029 and then stop increasing (Pear, 1992).

Futurists such as John Naisbitt feel strongly that human resources are the key to future productivity. He feels that the human element is far more important than structural and/or organizational considerations (Naisbitt, 1985). In other words, as we progress into the technological and information ages, human relations will become ever more important in determining success or failure in business. Thus, the teaching of respect for and tolerance of individual and cultural diversity will assume a position of increased stature and importance in the educational process.

As education moves into the twenty-first century, some significant changes will occur in the superintendency. The face of the superintendency will literally change as the number of women and minorities occupying the position increases dramatically. There will be significant paradigm shifts in the educational process, curriculum content, organizational structure, and role definition. These paradigm shifts will require a new understanding of and commitment to visionary leadership on the part of the superintendent. Each of these areas will be addressed in the following subsections.

THE WOMAN SUPERINTENDENT

Introduction

Currently, there is a striking lack of women in the superintendency. K–12 education is, overall, a female-dominated profession, but the people who fill the leadership role of superintendent are predominately men. Current statistics from the American Association of School Administrators (1993b) indicate that women hold only 6.7 percent of the superintendencies in the United States.

There has been much speculation as to why this is the case and as to whether there will be a trend toward increased representation by women in the superintendency. The authors strongly believe that the number of women holding superintendencies will increase dramatically during the nineties and beyond.

The issues surrounding women as superintendents that will be addressed here are a demographic description of the average woman who currently holds the superintendency, the barriers to women achieving the superintendency, personality characteristics of women who hold superintendencies, the leadership style of these women, aspects of the superintendency that serve as either job satisfiers or dissatisfiers, and the dilemma of retaining women once they achieve the superintendency.

Demographic Description

The 1992 *Study of the American School Superintendency* by the American Association of School Administrators (1993a) offers a description of the "typical" woman superintendent. The average woman superintendent is younger than the average male superintendent although she was older when she was appointed to her first administrative position. She is more often a Democrat than is her male counterpart. She comes from a more urban background than the average male superintendent. She has spent more time in the classroom before entering administration, and her first administrative position is more commonly the staff position of coordinator of special programs, rather than the line position of principal, which is the most common first administrative position for men.

Interestingly, the woman superintendent is more likely to look to the research when addressing educational issues than is the male superintendent.

Barriers

There are both internal and external barriers to women achieving the superintendency. Internal barriers may include conflicts related to family and career, internalization of socialized sex roles and gender characteristics, and the absence of role models. External barriers to women achieving the superintendency are their exclusion from the "good old boys' club" and continuing sex discrimination both in practice and in attitude (Edson, 1988; Pigford, and Tonnsen, 1993). Once a woman obtains a superintendency, these barriers may remain as obstacles to achieving success and satisfaction in the superintendency and may serve as the final stimulus toward leaving the superintendency.

Job Satisfaction/Dissatisfaction

As active superintendents, women face many of the same satisfactions and frustrations as their male counterparts. Recent research (Genzen, 1993) indicates that both men and women superintendents express high satisfaction with community/superintendent relationships, student/superintendent relationships, and staff/superintendent relationships.

In the same study, both genders expressed a similar frustration with the way education is funded and with enactments of the state board of education. Women superintendents indicated a greater dissatisfaction with their compensation, which may be a result of women's serving in smaller school systems (American Association of School Administrators, 1993b).

Motivators

What sort of women aspire to the superintendency? Those who have become superintendents are high achievers with dominant personalities (Genzen, 1993). They show little dependence on others and have strong determination and persistence. It is possible that these qualities are necessary for success in achieving and retaining this male-dominated position.

Leadership Style

The debate continues as to whether men and women have different styles of leadership. There are those who contend that effective leadership is unrelated to gender, while others believe that, because of sex role socialization, men and women lead in different ways.

Some literature suggests that women may lead in a style quite different from men. Because of past socialization, women may put a higher value on enabling and empowering. This style of leadership is described as horizontal or "web-like," rather than as top-down and controlling (Aburdene and Naisbitt, 1992; Cantor and Bernay, 1992; Helgesen, 1990). As Burns (1978) states in his classic work, *Leadership,*

> The male bias is reflected in the false conception of leadership as mere command or control. As leadership comes properly to be seen as a process of leaders engaging and mobilizing the human needs and aspirations of followers, women will be more readily recognized as leaders and men will change their own leadership styles. (p. 50)

Research has indicated that women assume the characteristics of transformational leaders (Genzen, 1993), that in their relational style of leadership, they bring both themselves and their followers to new levels, that they do not "treat pawns like pawns, nor princes like princes, but all persons like *persons*" (Burns, 1978, p. 462).

Retention

Women face both internal and external barriers in achieving the superintendency. A critical problem to address is that of retaining the women who do become school superintendents. In a recent publication on women who exit the superintendency (Tallerico, Burstyn, and Poole, 1993), the authors found that reasons for leaving included the attraction of new job opportunities, child-rearing concerns, and the strong negative effect of politics. Women superintendents who left the job were disenchanted with the politics of school board "dysfunction," of union influences, of noneducational foci, and of moral clashes. A telling quotation from this qualitative study was, "I began to realize that the superintendency is not a position in education but a position of politics" (p. 7).

In a recent study of the career paths of women school district administrators in Wisconsin (Lundin, 1993), a woman superintendent stated that "women have less tolerance for politics than men" (p. 83). Another woman superintendent in the same study advised that "women must develop a tolerance for the politics of the position" (p. 87).

All the women interviewed in Lundin's (1993) study expressed the desire to provide a positive educational experience for children. Their belief that they would make an impact on others allowed them to put up with politics, time demands, and family issues.

Future

It is likely that this scenario of male dominance in the superintendency may change. We may be living through the end of the era where the "good old boys' " network prevails, where analogies from sports and from the military as guides for the running of organizations may fade, where the effective manager role of the superintendent no longer dominates the role of educational leader. The 1992 *Study of the American School Superintendency* (American Association of School Administrators, 1993a) clearly shows that women superintendents see instructional program leadership as more essential than do men superintendents.

One cannot foretell the future, but the increasing numbers of women enrolled in programs of educational administration in our universities seem to suggest that the pool of future school administrators will be predominately female.

THE MINORITY SUPERINTENDENT

In 1993, there were nearly 14,000 superintendents in the United States. In this same year, the American Association of School Administrators (1993b), in their report, *Women and Racial Minority Representation in School Administration*, noted that racial minority and women superintendents increased only slightly from 2.2 percent in 1981–82 to 3.5 percent in 1992–93. The report stated that

> Each racial minority group . . . is most highly represented in areas where persons of the same race are living in greater numbers. Blacks are more highly represented in the South Atlantic and East South Central states. For Asians and Pacific Islanders, the highest representation in the superintendency is in the Pacific. Hispanic and American Indian

superintendents are more highly represented in the Mountain States. (p. 5)

Most of the literature on minority superintendents is devoted to blacks who are the largest group within this category. Although the history of black superintendents begins around 1965, there were some earlier.

The National Alliance of Black School Educators (NABSE)

identified four Blacks as forerunners of current Black superintendents . . . Lillard Ashley of Boley Oklahoma (1956); Lorenzo R. Smith of Hopkins Park, Illinois (1956); E. W. Warrior of Taft, Oklahoma (1958); and Arthur Shropshire of Kinloch, Missouri (1963). (AASA, 1983, p. 28)

Blacks were first selected in all-black southern school systems. For example, blacks led the all-black system of Taft, Oklahoma from 1930–1958 (AASA, 1983, p. 28).

Systems in which they are often found are those with financial problems where minorities represent a large percentage of the students and community and where the system is no longer attractive to aspiring superintendents (Moody, 1985). As Nancy Amez (1986) wrote, "Even a cursory observation can lead one to the conclusion that when big city systems went bankrupt and when they became overwhelmingly black, black men and women were recruited" (p. 398). When they did assume the position, the challenges and expectations were at times unreal. They were expected to perform at a level beyond that of others, to provide immediate or miraculous solutions to social, financial, and racial problems that had developed over years. Their tenure in the position was often short because of such expectations.

Their sparsity in the ranks is the result of several factors. The usual ways of securing a superintendency include encouragement of administrators and professors, networking (tapping into the old boys' network), consultant nomination, notification by placement personnel, and mentoring or sponsorship. Historically, blacks received little encouragement by their professors. High-level administrators in local systems seldom took them under their wing and mentored them, and they frequently lacked the right connections to consultants and organizations who worked in the superintendent placement arena.

As noted in the previous section regarding women and male dominance, it is equally as likely that the number of racial minorities, including blacks, will increase as the nineties conclude and the twenty-first century begins. This will occur because professors (minority and white) will identify, encourage, and sponsor minorities with the potential and desire for a superintendency. Blacks and other minorities will locate and/or be introduced to networking. Consultants will develop lists and portfolios of potential minority candidates and nominate them when openings occur. In fact, the NABSE already includes a "superintendents' commission" that assists black superintendents in networking and other important services.

PARADIGM SHIFTS

Joel Barker (1989), in his video *Discovering the Future: The Business of Paradigms*, defines a paradigm as a set of rules or regulations that 1) define boundaries and 2) tell one how to be successful within those boundaries. He indicates that a paradigm shift occurs when there is a change to a new set of rules and different boundaries. Individuals can be blinded by their investments and successes in the current or old paradigms to the extent that they ignore data that don't fit the old mold. This paradigm paralysis, or the lack of ability to comprehend shifts that are occurring, can spell big trouble for superintendents.

Education currently is being conducted very much like it has been for the past 100 years; i.e., a group of students are assigned to a teacher on a regular basis for instruction at a facility called a school. To be sure, pedagogy has advanced to the point where different learning styles and abilities can be identified and accommodated, but the basic delivery process remains the same.

A number of educational fads have come and gone and continue to do so. Thus, it is very easy to understand why one may not be in a hurry to get on the paradigm shift bandwagon. However, the authors believe there is ample evidence to support the concept that education will undergo dramatic paradigm shifts during the remainder of the nineties and into the next millennium. An overview of the key shift areas that the authors believe must receive serious introspection and analysis follow.

Educational Process and Content

Superintendents must be involved in the rethinking of what the word *education* means. Does education take place only in the classroom? Or, with modern technologies, can students learn as well at home via computer or television? Toffler (1980) said that the notion that learning takes place only in the classroom is dated. What will the new literacy mean? Will workers still need to know how to read? Or will they merely need to know how to interpret information given to them by talking machines and computers?

It will no longer be possible to teach students facts alone, because facts are increasing at an exponential rate. Problem solving will be a key need for students. In their rapidly changing world, they will have to adapt and learn through a variety of modes. They will be on their own to learn new concepts. They will also need to be able to synthesize and analyze what is taking place around them in order to function effectively in a rapidly changing world and job market.

Adaptability and flexibility will be keys to success for students. It will not be uncommon for students to change jobs a number of times during their working lifetimes and careers. Therefore, they will have to be able to learn new skills at a rapid pace.

What are some of the paradigm shifts that could emanate from these changes looming on the horizon? The almost total individualization of instruction seems to be a paradigm shift that already has gathered a head of steam. Ultimately, this could mean such things as doing away with the Carnegie unit at the high school level, development of more comprehensive and reliable individual authentic assessment techniques, and progressing through topics at one's own pace. These shifts, in turn, could mean that the time-honored K–12 grade divisions will become blurred, if not nonexistent. The distinction between K–12 and higher education could also become blurred.

As much of society and schooling become individualized, perhaps a primary function of the school will be to educate students in such things as human relations skills, functioning successfully in group problem-solving situations, understanding and accepting individual diversity, and accepting of responsibility for one's own actions. In other words, perhaps the school will bear a primary responsibility for teaching individuals to live and work together in harmony.

Student/Parental Choice

Among the many areas in the superintendent's future with which s/he must be knowledgeable is the multifaceted topic of school choice. Although it is not new, its impact and possibilities continue to grow.

During the early years of this country, parents chose whether, where, and when to formally educate their children. When the states began to establish compulsory attendance laws, parents' ability to make educational decisions for their children was curtailed. [Tyack (1974) notes that compulsory attendance for minority children was not included in these laws.] For a number of years, the states continued to enact more restrictive attendance legislation. This trend came to a head in 1922 when Oregon enacted a law that, in essence, said to parents that their children could only be considered "in attendance" when they were attending a public school. The constitutionality of this legislation was challenged in *Pierce v. Society of Sisters,* and, in 1925, the U.S. Supreme Court set aside the law and allowed only limited interference by the state regarding parent control of their children's education when it wrote:

> In this day and under our civilization, the child of man is his parent's child and not the state's. . . . It is not seriously debatable that the parental right to guide one's child intellectually and religiously is a most substantial part of the liberty and freedom of the parent. (Alexander and Alexander, 1992, p. 201)

The student/parental choice plans replace the age-old process whereby school boards divide their districts into geographic attendance areas and require a student to attend the designated school facility within the attendance area in which his/her parent or guardian resides. Conran (1990) notes that choice concepts are built upon certain assumptions, namely:

1. There is no best school for everyone.
2. Diversity is necessary in schools.
3. Students perform better in schools they've chosen.
4. There is more teacher commitment and satisfaction in schools they've selected.
5. There is more parental satisfaction and support for schools they've chosen.
6. There is a creation of shared values and expectation in choice schools.

Choice plans are being increasingly authorized by individual states as the school reform and accountability movements gather steam. In a like manner, more students/parents are taking advantage of the choice options available to them.

Choice plans have been supported, and at times promoted, by business, industry, and parent groups. These plans come in many forms and with varying options. Pienkos (1993), citing testimony given before the Tennessee House Committee on Education, provides a synopsized descriptive list of choice plans:

- magnet schools—option of attending a facility that promotes a particular educational theme
- intradistrict choice—option of selecting the facility to attend from within the district in which a student resides
- controlled choice—separation of system into zones from which students/parents choose within their zone
- schools within schools—distinctive schools created within the same facility from which students/parents choose
- interdistrict choice—option of attending schools in other districts
- choice of curriculum within a school—option of selecting alternative curricula, teaching methods, etc.
- post-secondary options—provisions for college/university course enrollment by high school juniors/seniors
- choice for at-risk and dropouts—special target schools for those types of students
- charter schools—public schools established by teachers and others under charters issued by state and local educational agencies and other authorities
- vouchers—redeemable state vouchers that can be used for attendance at approved public or private schools within a state
- privately funded vouchers—business funding of a voucher plan that will pay a percent of the tuition when opting to attend a private sectarian or nonsectarian school
- tuition tax credits and tuition tax deductions—reduction of parental/guardian income taxes for specific educational expenses
- home schooling—parental education of their children at home subject to state and local oversight

All of the plans listed are subject to applicable federal mandates, such as desegregation statutes and court decisions, health and safety standards, etc.; state rules and regulations on such things as teacher certification and student testing; and local school district policies that

address things such as facility capacities and desegregation requirements.

Choice plans have been around since 1980, and new types are continually emerging. There are both proponents and opponents to the
various plans. However, regardless of one's position on choice, the
concept is not about to disappear from the education scene.

Organizational Restructuring and Role Definition

Naisbitt (1985) and Toffler (1980) suggest that organizations must
become less hierarchical and more responsive and innovative, meaning that there should be fewer levels of administration in school organizations. Many of the largest corporations in the world have
already reorganized along these lines. Peters and Waterman (1982)
found that the monstrous Toyota Motor Corporation operated with
only five layers of management. The 800 million member Catholic
Church also has five layers of management. Dana Corporation, which
is a multi-billion dollar corporation, has less than 100 people at its
corporate headquarters.

If schools are to follow these examples, hierarchical decision-
making will have to be reduced in favor of greater decision-making at
the building level. Collaborative networks will replace bureaucratic
networks in significant decision-making processes. Superintendents
will be spending more time in individual schools, stimulating those
directly involved with the educational process.

As collaborative teams become the heart of the management process, organizational barriers will have to be removed so that all people
can have direct access to each other on a daily basis. Free-flowing networks will develop, with people interacting with each other in the
problem-finding and problem-solving processes. Organizational restructuring will mean a redefining of many traditional roles within the
system. Superintendents are going to have to empower the people
closest to the problem to make the decisions and then help and encourage them in the implementation process.

As discussed in Chapter 2, school districts are loosely coupled
systems where activities often have little relation to each other. The
challenge is how to decentralize, reduce hierarchy, and yet foster increased collaborative efforts and teams. Visionary or transformational
leadership creates a means to empower people through common focus
on a vision for the school district and instilling a sense of pride and

mission (Bass, 1990). A vision with goals of empowerment and collaboration can help create a climate in which people will work to accomplish such role redefinition while restructuring takes place.

As a part of the organizational restructuring and role redefinition process, the quality of work life must be closely examined. There are indications that all personnel within the school system are going to be placing greater emphasis on personal fulfillment and growth needs. The superintendent will assume a major responsibility for addressing the needs of these more fully actualized individuals. These needs include the physical and psychological environments and the acknowledgement of staff as professionals.

Attention will need to be given to making the physical working environment more stimulating, comfortable, and personal. Improving this aspect of work life will take some effort and money, but it should be reasonably easy to accomplish.

Addressing and improving the psychological work environment is a much more complex undertaking. In this area, the personal and professional needs of employees are not distinct entities. Items that enhance one's professional life also contribute to the well-being in one's personal life and vice versa. In addressing the psychological well-being of employees, it will be necessary to address personal needs such as providing child-care facilities, flexible work schedules, permanent part-time and job-sharing positions, and individualized fringe benefit packages. On a professional basis, greater involvement in curriculum development, pedagogical techniques, scheduling, teaching assignments, evaluation, and professional growth opportunities will need to be explored.

In summary, the best work will be performed in school systems that exhibit a sincere interest in addressing the personal and professional needs of their employees.

A major responsibility of superintendents will be to provide the leadership so that the school structure can be adapted to effectively and efficiently support these new modes of operation and thinking. In doing this, superintendents will have to be good listeners. They will be constantly fine-tuning the organization as a result of formal and informal input from a variety of sources.

It is anticipated that superintendents will be given much greater latitude in restructuring a school organization than is now the case. For instance, in all likelihood, there will be less emphasis on professional certification and standardized curricular requirements and more on the quality of student output. There will be many fewer external constraints. Thus, the degree to which the school organization is successfully reorganized will depend almost entirely on the leadership effectiveness of the superintendent.

Finally, there is evidence that the public schools will no longer have a client monopoly based on the residence of the parent(s) or legal guardian. Individual school buildings will be in competition with other like facilities within the school district, with other school districts, with home schooling, and with private educational enterprises. The superintendent will be leading an organization that operates in a client choice environment.

Effective Use of Technology

The computer is the instrument that has ushered in the information age and has been responsible for many job changes. Computerization and robotics have made many jobs obsolete while also creating new jobs. However, the individuals whose jobs have become obsolete often do not have the skills to qualify for the new ones that have been created. Schools must address this problem by helping students understand that their learning will be lifelong if they are to remain employable.

In an age of exploding electronics technology, systems must consider how they will use such current and future technology. Such things as fax equipment, cellular telephones, and pocket computers will need to be incorporated into the curriculum. Students must be prepared to function in an electronics world.

Teachers and other school personnel need access to and knowledge of computers also. There are many functions that school employees still do manually that could be done more efficiently by computers. It is important for superintendents to develop an overall computerization plan for the system, provide the necessary hardware and software to implement the plan, and motivate and encourage employees to become active and enthusiastic participants in the plan.

Another technological advancement of the future is interactive television. This technology allows students to view television anywhere in the world and to verbally interact with the individuals at the source. For instance, world experts could be beamed into any classroom, students could enter into a dialogue with them, and small groups of students would then be able to take courses not normally offered. Possibilities for tutoring and adult education perhaps are even more far-reaching. In fact, the uses of this technology in the educational process are limited only by the imagination.

Virtual reality currently is being developed primarily for entertainment; however, it can be potentially used as an excellent educational tool. Consider a history class where students could "see" and "be present" for a reenactment of historical events. This vehicle has tremendous potential to improve student interest and understanding.

In summary, technology has the potential to change the way schools do business. Historically, students have always had to come to a central location at a specific time to be educated because this is where the educational materials and professionals were located. For the first time ever, the vehicle is present in the form of technology to break this paradigm. The potential now exists for a student to receive education from any location at any time of the day or night. Only the visionary superintendent will be able to harness and maximize the use of technology.

Concluding Comments

The paradigm shifts will mean that there will no longer be education as usual. This is very threatening, for when there is a paradigm shift, everyone goes back to zero (Barker, 1989). Past training and successes mean little. Thus, the superintendent will need to develop and implement a professional staff development program that is of unthinkable proportions by today's standards.

The superintendent will need to be very knowledgeable about the options available for both curricular content and delivery. The days when textbook selection was the big curriculum event of the year are gone. Many curriculum decisions now will be very costly and will have the potential to start a school system down a road of no return. In all likelihood, these decisions will require a significant investment of time and money for staff development and the purchase of both hardware and software.

School systems will no longer be able to "go it alone." It will be necessary to collaborate and/or negotiate with a myriad of external organizations (both educational and noneducational) in both the public and private sectors.

VISIONARY LEADERSHIP

Malphurs (1992) states that "it [vision] is a mental word. Vision is a seeing work. A good vision probes the imagination in such a way that it conjures up visual representations in the mind. Vision begins with a dream that is developed by a few leaders and is shared with others" (p. 7). Barker (1990) states that "vision is the result of dreams in action." Great leaders have a vision. Great leaders in our society such as Abraham Lincoln, Susan B. Anthony, John Kennedy, Sojourner Truth, Martin Luther King, and Elizabeth Blackwell each had a vision or dream to which s/he was totally committed. Likewise, those who are to lead education into the twenty-first century must have a vision to which they are enthusiastically committed.

Superintendents are often bogged down in the day-to-day realities of running a school system. Problems abound that need immediate attention. Such things as staff and parental concerns, financial problems, union demands, and legal problems combine to occupy vast amounts of a superintendent's time; however, if superintendents are to provide the leadership needed for the future, they must find time to transcend these immediate demands and become visionary leaders. Others need to be trained and empowered to handle many of the daily concerns. They must develop in themselves, first and then with others, a sense of mission regarding where their systems should be going and an understanding of what is important within their school systems.

One does not become a visionary leader by chance. It takes practice and effort to force one's own thinking processes, as well as those of others, to transcend conventional wisdom and thinking. It takes courage to think the unthinkable. In other words, one must make a start at being a visionary by entertaining creative and innovative thoughts and developing a personal vision for where one would like to see the system at a specific point in the future.

The second stage in becoming a visionary leader is to share the vision with the board, staff, students, and community and to seek their input and ownership of it. This will follow the development of the system's mission statement, which says this is who we are and what we are about. The vision statement must then be converted to goals that are understandable and will assist the system in making its vision a reality.

The third stage is the motivational stage. The superintendent must motivate school personnel and community to accept and work toward the achievement of these goals. When this type of commitment takes hold within a school system and community, it permeates all thinking processes.

SUMMARY

The degree to which a superintendent is able to work with his/her leadership team in formulating an educational vision for the twenty-first century, the degree to which the leadership team is able to sell the vision to the school and community, and the degree to which specific goals and plans for reaching these goals can be established and implemented will determine the operational effectiveness of the school district. Superintendents specifically and the educational community generally can't afford to be like Rip Van Winkle and wake up some day to a different world in which the nation's school systems no longer play an integral part in the education of our country's youth.

REFERENCES

Aburdene, P. and Naisbitt, J. (1992). *Megatrends for Women.* New York, NY: Villard Books.

Alexander, K. and Alexander, M. D. (1992). *American Public School Law.* St. Paul, MN: West Publishing Company.

American Association of School Administrators. (1993a). *The Study of the American School Superintendency.* Alexandria, VA: AASA.

American Association of School Administrators. (1993b). *Women and Racial Minority Representation in School Administration.* Alexandria, VA: AASA.

American Association of School Administrators. (1983). *Perspectives on Racial and Minority Women School Administrators.* Alexandria, VA: AASA.

Amez, N. L. (1986). Black public policy. *Journal of Black Studies, 16*(4), 397–408.

Barker, J. (1990). *The Power of Vision.* Burnsville, MN: Chart House International.

Barker, J. (1989). *Discovering the Future: The Business of Paradigms.* Burnsville, MN: Chart House International.

Bass, B. (1990). From transactional to transformational leadership: Learning to share the vision. *Organizational Dynamics, 18*(3):19–31.

Burns, J. (1978). *Leadership.* New York, NY: Harper & Row.

Cantor, D. and Bernary, T. (1992). *Women in Power: The Secrets of Leadership.* New York, NY: Houghton Mifflin Company.

Cetron, M. (1985). *Schools of the Future.* New York, NY: McGraw-Hill.

Conran, P. (1990). *Public Schools of Choice.* Alexandria, VA: Association for Supervision and Curriculum Development.

Craver, C. (1983). The future of the American labor movement. *The Futurist* (Oct.), 70.

Deutsch, R. (1985). Tomorrow's work force. *The Futurist* (Dec.), 8.

Edson, S. (1988). *Pushing the Limits: The Female Administrative Aspirant.* Albany, NY: State University of New York Press.

Genzen, H. (1993). A study of the leadership style, motivation, and job satisfaction of women public school superintendents in Ohio. Unpublished doctoral dissertation, Kent State University.

Helgesen, S. (1990). *The Female Advantage: Women's Ways of Leadership.* New York, NY: Doubleday.

Kirst, M. (1984). *Who Controls Our Schools.* New York, NY: Freeman & Company.

Kotler, P. (1986). Prosumer. *The Futurist* (Sept.), 24.

Lundin, S. (1993). A multiple-case analysis of the career paths of women school district administrators in the state of Wisconsin. Unpublished dissertation, Marquette University.

Malphurs, A. (1992). *Developing Vision for Ministry in the 21st Century.* Grand Rapids, MI: Baker House.

Moody, C. D. (1985). The black superintendent. *National Scene* (Magazine Supplement) (Aug. 9–14), 22.

Naisbitt, J. (1985). *Re-inventing the Corporation.* New York, NY: Warner Books.

Naisbitt, J. (1982). *Megatrends.* New York, NY: Warner Books.

Pear, R. (1992). New look at the U.S. in 2050: Bigger, older and less white. *The New York Times* (Dec. 4), A–10.

Peters, T. (1987). *Thriving on Chaos.* California: Random House Audio-Books.

Peters, T. and Waterman, R. (1982). *In Search of Excellence.* New York, NY: Warner Books.

Pienkos, M. E. (1993). Perceptions among parents, teachers, administrators, and lawmakers on the Milwaukee parental choice program involving private, non-sectarian schools. Doctoral dissertation, University of Southern California.

Pigford, A. and Tonnesen, S. (1993). *Women in School Leadership.* Lancaster, PA: Technomic Publishing Co., Inc.

Raymond, H. (1986). Management in the third wave. *The Futurist* (Sept.), 15.

Sinetar, M. (1987). The actualized worker. *The Futurist* (March), 21.

Tallerico, M., Burstyn, J. and Poole, W. (1993). *Gender and Politics at Work:*

Why Women Exit the Superintendency. Fairfax, VA: National Policy Board for Educational Administration.

Toffler, A. (1980). *The Third Wave.* New York, NY: Bantam Books.

Toffler, A. (1974). *Learning for Tomorrow: The Role of the Future in Education.* New York, NY: Random House.

Tyack, D. (1974). *The One Best System.* Cambridge, MA: Harvard University Press.

Venn, G. (1970). *Man, Education, and Manpower.* Washington, D.C.: The American Association of School Administrators.

PART TWO

The Superintendent as Leader

The leadership part is the most extensive part in this book. This is as it should be, for leadership is the essence of the superintendency. The four subsections of this part are as follows:

A. The broader leadership perspective

B. Personal philosophy and leadership

C. Superintendent leadership competencies: personal

D. Superintendent leadership competencies: professional

LEADERSHIP SUBSECTION A

The Broader Leadership Perspective

CHAPTER 4

Historical Leadership Perspectives

It is necessary to have a historical perspective of leadership in order that the more specific leadership material presented in the three subsequent subsections can be viewed from an appropriate perspective. One must have some insights and answers to such questions as: What does the word *leadership* mean? How does one know it when one sees it? How does one know when one is providing it? This chapter addresses these critical questions.

RECOGNIZING AND DEFINING LEADERSHIP

When Franklin D. Roosevelt died, Walter Lippman's syndicated column "Roosevelt Has Gone," April 14, 1945, stated that

> For the final test of a leader is that he leaves behind him in other men the conviction and the will to carry on. . . . The genius of a good leader is to leave behind a situation which common sense, without the grace of genius, can deal with successfully. (p. 4)

Lippman's definition of a leader was one who had an impact on others by giving them the conviction to continue. This conviction was not created through genius, but through common sense. Just as Lippman sought to define FDR's leadership, the definition and concept of leadership have intrigued mankind for centuries.

The Greeks, Romans, Egyptians, and Chinese have recorded observations regarding the act of leadership. Despite the varying cultures,

---

Dr. Kathleen Neal provided the basic material for this chapter. Dr. Neal is the superintendent of an urban school system.

the following attributes of a leader emerged: justice, wisdom, counsel, authority, valor, and judgment. During the Renaissance, in Machiavelli's study of leadership entitled *The Prince*, he noted that "there is nothing more difficult to take in hand, more perilous to conduct, or more uncertain in its success, than to take the lead in the introduction of a new order of things" (W. K. Marriatt, translator, 1948, p. 43).

James MacGregor Burns (1978) stated that "leadership is one of the most observed and least understood phenomena on earth" (p. 2). In his book, *Leadership*, Burns noted that, although previous centuries had been the seed bed of a richly illustrative compilation of literature on leadership, the modern age has produced a fragmented approach to the study and meaning of leadership as a concept. As an example, there are over 350 definitions of leadership in the literature (Cunningham, 1985). Burns posits that there is no school of leadership, are no standards of assessing leaders, and is no modern philosophical basis from which one can adequately assess the empiricism and theory of leadership. Consequently, modern man is left floundering in indecision on the qualities separating leaders from rulers, power wielders, and despots (Burns, 1978).

Warren Bennis, noted organizational theorist, developed a theory of managerial strengths and tactics. In a bold step to put these theories to the test, he accepted the presidency of the University of Cincinnati during the early 1970s. This was the acid test for his leadership theories and for himself as a leader—a test made more challenging by the turbulance on campuses during the late 1960s and early 1970s. Upon leaving the presidency, he wrote a book entitled *The Unconscious Conspiracy: Why Leaders Can't Lead* (1976). In this book, Bennis reflects on his experiences as president of the University of Cincinnati. At one point, he recalls that Clark Kerr, while president of the University of California at Berkeley during the heyday of student unrest, succinctly summed up the three most important jobs of a president of a university: to provide sex for students, football for alumni, and parking places for faculty. Bennis noted that, at Cincinnati, sex is taken for granted, football was still a priority, and parking was considerably worse. He then laments that the times call for leadership but that leaders are not leading. Instead, they are consulting, pleading, temporizing, martyrizing, trotting, putting out fires, and either avoiding the heat or taking the heat but spending too much energy doing both.

Essentially, Burns and Bennis echo similar themes. Burns says that man cannot distinguish between leaders and power mongers, while Bennis says that leaders themselves cannot distinguish between the concepts of leading and managing. Thus, the definition and recognition of leadership remains nebulous at best.

HISTORICAL REVIEW OF LEADERSHIP THEORIES

Great Man Theory

When Arthur Schlessinger, Jr. asked John F. Kennedy how he became a hero, Kennedy's response was, "It was involuntary. They sank my boat" (Bartlett, 1968). To paraphrase Shakespeare's great comic figure, Malvolio, in *Twelfth Night*, some are born to greatness, some achieve it, and some have greatness thrust upon them. Kennedy may have had greatness thrust upon him the moment his PT boat sank.

The great man theory of leadership embraces the notion that history is shaped by great men who have the capacity to lead the masses (Jennings, 1960). In 1841, Carlyle's *Essay on Man* reinforced the concept of a leader as a person endowed with unique qualities that capture the masses. Carlyle's hero would contribute no matter where found, because history is shaped by great men who are destined for leadership.

Would Chrysler corporation be what it is today if it were not for Lee Iococca? Would the billion-dollar Disney Enterprises be just that, if it were not for the leadership and vision of Walt Disney? Without Moses, the Jews would not have left Egypt; without Churchill, England would have submitted. As England embraced Churchill in 1940, their collective political memory forgot that he had been in exile since 1934. Without Lenin, would there have been the Russian Revolution? If Lenin had been hanged and not exiled and if the boxcar in which he traveled had not made it to the Russian border, the Bolshevik cause might have dissipated. Would American public education be what it is today if it were not for the likes of Thomas Jefferson, Horace Mann, and John Dewey?

The great man theory of leadership supports the idea that a superior leader emerges to lead a society no matter how intelligent, energized, and moral the society may be. A society cannot be led by the masses; therefore, a leader must always emerge.

Early leadership researchers reasoned that, if the great man theory was valid, then it should be possible to study these great men in an effort to discover the traits that made them great. Thus, in the 1920s and 1930s, researchers attempted to isolate the superior qualities of great men and, in the process, explain leadership in terms of personality and character traits (Bass, 1981). Many such personality and character trait lists were developed; however, no list was ever developed that guaranteed that, if an individual possessed the listed characteristics, he/she would be an effective leader. As a result, the trait approach to leadership fell into disfavor for a number of years. Currently, it is experiencing somewhat of a resurgence, in that students of leadership are hypothesizing that, perhaps, there are certain traits that are necessary but not sufficient conditions for leadership. In other words, the possession of certain traits would not guarantee that one would be a leader, but it would be very difficult to be a leader if one did not possess these traits. As an example, it might be hypothesized that it would take a reasonably intelligent individual to be a leader of other intelligent individuals, such as in a school system. However, not all intelligent individuals will be effective educational leaders.

Environmental Theory

The environmental theory of leadership emanated from the great man theory. It posits that leaders emerge not necessarily because of their own inherent greatness, but because time, circumstance, and place surround them. The German philosopher, Hegel, noted that the leader fulfilled the needs of his own time; what the great man did was automatically right to do because he fulfilled what was needed. No man, however great, could change the course of history. The great man rose within the historical condition because the time, place, and circumstance were right.

Students of the United States Civil War could argue for the environmental theory of leadership by examining the person of Ulysses S. Grant. In 1848, Grant was a hero in the Mexican War, but by the 1850s, Grant had to resign his commission in the army rather than face being court-martialed for drunkenness. He returned to his farm near St. Louis, only to find he could not farm the unyielding land, so he turned to selling real estate and failed at that. Near desperation, he beseeched his father for help. He was given a clerkship in a leather store in Galena, Illinois, and proceeded to fail again. It became evident that soldiering was his forte; consequently, the outbreak of the Civil War was a fortuitous occurrence for him. He enlisted as a volunteer in the 21st regiment from Illinois, and by 1864, the once drunken failure had risen to Lt. General of the Army.

A half a century later and on another continent, one could ponder if Mahatma Gandhi could have been the perpetual thorn in the side of British India, preaching nonviolence and civil disobedience if it had not been for the poverty, the religious and political factions, the discontent in India, and the decline of the British Raj. Could Martin Luther King have had the impact on the nation if it had not been for the emerging civil rights movement in the South? Returning attention to Vladimir Lenin, could he have returned to Russia in 1917 and begun a revolution if the time and circumstances were not there? Have the effective school and accountability movements had an impact on the type of individuals obtaining superintendencies?

The environmental theory of leadership embraced the ideas that the situation and the group were the significant factors in determining the type of leader who would emerge. Leadership was seen as residing not in the person, but in the occasion confronting the leader.

Psychoanalytical Theory

Psychoanalytical leadership theory was based on the Freudian notion of the leader as the superego made real. Bass (1981) stated that the leader was seen as the father figure, a source of love or fear, and as an outgrowth of the followers' needs. As an example, Payne (1973) explored the adult Adolf Hitler from the perspective of childhood deprivations, the culture within Germany in the early years of the twentieth century, the political milieu of the time, and Hitler's relationships with authority figures. All of the above were combined in the horror that was post–World War I Germany, a Germany that willingly accepted Hitler's philosophy.

M. F. DeVries (1977) studied the charismatic leader who, depending on his ability to control his own paranoia, serves the welfare of the group. The group, especially the dependent group, is devoted and unquestioning and succumbs to the charismatic leader in times of crisis. The charismatic leader is one who exudes confidence, dominance, and a sense of purpose and can articulate the needs and goals of the group and translate those goals into action. Charisma literally means endowed with divine grace. Qualities of the charismatic leader include fatherliness, a high energy level, the capacity to inspire loyalty, and optimism (Bass, 1981).

Were the days when a coach or band director went directly from coaching or directing duties into administration a reflection of the psychoanalytic theory of leadership in action? Many of these individuals tended to administer in a benevolent autocratic style. This style was usually accepted, and they were looked upon with favor. In essence, they were looked up to by the school staff and community.

Interaction and Expectation Theory

Interaction and expectation theory implies that something is happening between two or more members of a group. As action/interaction occurs, group members participate in the action. In addition, this leadership concept embraces the notion of sentiment wherein a mutual liking takes place between group members. The clarification of group norms occurs when these positive bonds occur within the group.

Bass (1960) proposed that the quality of leadership is dependent upon the level of interaction in a given situation. Whether or not two individuals interact depends upon the size of the group, the geographical and social proximity within the group, the opportunity for contact, the level of intimacy and familiarity within the group, and the mutual attraction and self-esteem of the group. Leadership under this theory could be likened to the lever on a pinball machine that propels the steel ball along its course. Leadership is the act of initiating or structuring interaction.

R. J. House's (1971) path-goal theory is a prime example of the interaction and expectation theory of leadership. His theory is based on the concept that leaders clarify goals for their subordinates, as well as the paths available to the subordinates to reach these goals. Leaders motivate the subordinates to perform, and, in turn, the subordinates derive satisfaction from a job well done. The leader provides appropriate rewards for the positive performance of his/her subordinates.

Ohio State Leadership Studies

In 1957, the Ohio State Leadership Studies staff, with the development of a paradigm for the study of leadership (Bass, 1960), ushered in a series of research studies and theories that viewed leaders' interactions with their groups and organizations in terms of some combination of task/relationship leadership style.

The instrument developed by the project staff was the Leader Behavior Description Questionnaire (LBDQ) and was designed to describe how leaders carried out their activities. Leadership was defined as the behavior of an individual when directing the activities of a group. Leader behavior was described in terms of two entities: initiating structure and consideration. Initiating structure defined the relationship between the leader and work group in terms of communication, procedures, and organizational patterns. Consideration referred to the affective relationship between the leader and members of the work group. The leader had a mixture of both initiating structure and consideration as part of his/her management style (Hersey and Blanchard, 1988).

Fiedler's Leader Match Concept

Fiedler's theory is composed of two essential factors: the leadership style of the person in charge and the degree to which the leader can control or influence the situation. Leadership style is determined by the Least Preferred Co-Worker (LPC) instrument. The scores, which identify a dominant leadership style, obtained via this instrument lie on a continuum with a very high task orientation (low LPC) at one end and a very high relationship or people orientation (high LPC) at the other end. The leadership style identified by this instrument is viewed as an extension of one's own personality; thus, it is not possible to alter one's leadership style.

The three components that determine the degree of control or influence a leader has in a given situation are leader-member relations, task structure, and position power. Leader-member relations is self-explanatory. Task structure refers to the degree of specificity with which a task is to be performed. Position power refers to the degree to which the position of the leader gives him/her the authority to reward and punish subordinates. These three factors combine to determine whether situational control is low, moderate, or high.

Task-oriented leaders perform best in either a low-control or a high-control situation; relationship-oriented leaders perform best in a moderate-control situation. Therefore, if one's leadership style, as determined by the LPC instrument, is known, the situational control level at which this individual will function best as a leader can be determined. If there is not a good match between one's leadership style and the situational control level, then one must attempt to alter the situational control to a level that is compatible with one's leadership style. This is referred to as situational engineering (Fiedler and Chemers, 1984).

Hersey and Blanchard

In Hersey and Blanchard's (1988) theory, one's leadership style is determined via the Leadership Effectiveness and Adaptability Description (LEAD) instrument. Like Fiedler's theory, leadership style is a combination of task orientation and relationship orientation; however, unlike Fiedler's, leadership style is not confined to a continuum. Instead, leadership style can fall anywhere on a two-dimensional grid that places task orientation on one axis and relationship orientation on the other. Also, unlike Fiedler, Hersey and Blanchard believe that it is possible to alter one's leadership style because they view it in terms of behavior, which they believe can be controlled, instead of an extension of one's personality, which cannot. They do believe, however, that one has a dominant preferred leadership style.

Situational analysis is determined by ascertaining the readiness level of an individual(s) in relation to a specific situation. Readiness level is determined by assessing the ability and willingness of an individual(s) to perform a task. The readiness level of an individual or group can range from very low to very high. A very low readiness level calls for a task-oriented leadership style, while a very high readiness level calls for a relationship-oriented style. The leader must start with a leadership style that is appropriate for the individual's or group's readiness level as he/she strives to raise it. It should be stressed that Hersey and Blanchard's definition of readiness is situation specific; thus everyone's readiness level changes with the situation.

CONCLUDING COMMENTS

As theories of leadership have evolved during the twentieth century, the emphasis has swung from the study of the leader as an individual to an emphasis on the transactional leader who assesses, alters, and reacts to specific situations. At the present time, a new theory of leadership referred to as transformational leadership is emerging. It represents more of a holistic approach to leadership and holds great promise for the superintendency. In fact, the transformational leadership concept is viewed as important enough that an entire chapter is devoted to it in the next leadership subsection.

As one looks at the history of leadership, one discovers an overlapping of the various theories. Each theory adapts and builds upon another, and it is only by looking at the history of leadership that one is able to obtain an appreciation of its complexity and elusiveness. Influencing the actions and motivations of others is a very complex process that is far from being mastered. Herein lies the excitement in the study of leadership theory in general and the application of leadership theory via a superintendency specifically.

REFERENCES

Argyris, C. (1976). *Increasing Leadership Effectiveness*. New York, NY: Wiley.

Bartlett, J. (1968). *Bartlett's Familiar Quotations*. Boston, MA: Little, Brown & Company.

Bass, B. M. (1981). *Stodgill's Handbook of Leadership*. New York, NY: The Free Press.

Bass, B. M. (1960). *Leadership, Psychology and Organizational Behavior*. New York, NY: Harper & Brothers.

Bennis, W. (1976). *The Unconscious Conspiracy: Why Leaders Can't Lead*. New York, NY: AMACOM.

Burns, J. M. (1978). *Leadership*. New York, NY: Harper & Row.

Cunningham, L. (1985). Leaders and leadership: 1985 and beyond. *Phi Delta Kappan, 67*, 17–20.

DeVries, M. F. (1977). Crisis leadership and the paranoid potential: An organizational perspective. *Bulletin of the Menniger Clinic, 41*, 349–365.

Fiedler, R. E. and Chemers, M. M. (1984). *Improving Leadership Effectiveness: The LEADER MATCH Concept*. New York, NY: Wiley.

Hersey, P. and Blanchard, K. (1988). *Management of Organizational Behavior: Utilizing Human Resources*. Englewood Cliffs, NJ: Prentice-Hall.

House, R. J. (1971). A path goal theory of leader effectiveness. *Administrative Science Quarterly, 16*, 321–338.

Jennings, E. A. (1960). *An Anatomy of Leadership: Princes, Heroes, and Supermen*. New York, NY: Harper.

Likert, R. (1967). *The Human Organization*. New York, NY: McGraw-Hill.

Lippman, W. (1945). Roosevelt has gone. *The Cleveland Plain Dealer* (April), 4.

Machiavelli, N. (translated by W. K. Marriatt) (1948). *The Prince.* New York, NY: E. P. Dutton and Co., Inc.

McGregor, D. (1960, 1966). *The Human Side of Enterprise.* New York, NY: McGraw-Hill.

Payne, R. (1973). *The Life and Death of Adolf Hitler.* New York, NY: Praeger Publishers.

Reddin, W. J. (1970). *Managerial Effectiveness.* New York, NY: McGraw-Hill.

CHAPTER 5

The Uniqueness of the Superintendency

Viewing the chief executive officer's position from other positions within the organization is a difficult task. In most instances, individuals occupying other positions in the organization have never experienced the responsibilities and pressures of being a CEO. Therefore, others' perceptions of the CEO's position are formed by drawing conclusions from fragmented bits of information that have been gained in random fashion over a period of time. The net result is that the CEO position, as perceived by the outside observer, is usually dramatically different than the actual experience. A case in point is the manner in which school-level and central office administrators in a school system view the superintendency.

This chapter discusses the uniqueness of the superintendency, as compared to other administrative positions within the school system. The principalship of a large high school comes closest to the superintendency because a principal in this situation is in charge of a self-contained operation of considerable complexity. However, as will be shown, even this position falls short of capturing the complete essence of the superintendency.

A dozen areas in which the superintendency is unique are presented in this chapter. While the sections are not entirely mutually exclusive, they do represent individual areas of uniqueness. The areas are not presented in any order of importance.

SCOPE

The most obvious uniqueness of the superintendency is the overall

Mr. Daniel McCombs provided the basic material for this chapter. He has served as a superintendent, business manager, personnel director, and high school principal.

scope of the position. The necessity to look at the "big picture" is paramount. The superintendent has to be concerned not only with the activities at the various building levels, but also with the overall fiscal and political implications of these activities.

Boards of education and the community rightly hold the superintendent accountable for the efficient and effective operation of the system. In doing this, it is their expectation that the superintendent should know *everything* that is going on in the system. By contrast, the school principals and other administrators are held responsible only for those activities occurring within their domains. As another example, the principals and other administrators are primarily interested in garnering as many resources as possible to support their own operations. The superintendent, however, must always keep an eye on the big picture when making decisions relative to the allocation of scarce resources among these individuals. These decisions must be made in the best interests of the entire school system.

PLANNING

A prime function of the superintendency is to provide planning and direction for the school system. More than any other employee, the superintendent must constantly be concerned with systemwide missions and goals and must be constantly working to motivate the other employees to accept and be committed to them. The superintendent is always concerned that the system is pulling together in a synergistic effort, rather than operating as individual entities with missions and goals that may not support, and may even detract from, systemwide concerns. It is the superintendent's responsibility to be sure that every subdivision and every individual understands how their activities contribute to the big picture.

RESIDENCY

The residence of the superintendent can become a significant issue with boards of education, as well as with the community. Many boards of education have a requirement that their superintendent live within the district as a condition of employment. This is in contrast to other administrators who usually are not required to reside within the district.

If one has aspirations to pursue a career as a superintendent, one should decide at the onset the stance that will be taken to a residency requirement. Because of longevity, one may be facing this decision several times during one's career. In making this decision, a superintendent must weigh both the financial and emotional consequences. Financially, most boards will pay moving expenses, but they will not assume any of the costs associated with purchasing a new residence or selling an old one. Also, depending on the socioeconomic level of the district, residences of the caliber in which a superintendent will be expected to reside may be out of the economic range of the new superintendent. Emotionally, one must ascertain how the rest of the family will react to changing geographic locations and school systems.

LONGEVITY

As alluded to in the preceding section, the average tenure of superintendents is reasonably short. By contrast, principals and other central office administrators enjoy a much higher degree of security and longevity. Declining enrollments or a shortage of finances that cause positions to be eliminated are exceptions to this generality. However, rarely are individuals in these positions as subjected to the whims of the board of education or the collective wrath of the community as the superintendent. When things go wrong in a system, it is usually the superintendent who pays the price.

FOCUS

School principals and central office personnel are usually more narrow in their focus than the superintendent. Often, they need only to be concerned with the welfare of their specific schools or programs. Actions taken by these individuals on behalf of their schools or programs sometimes are taken at the expense of other schools or programs. The superintendent must continually make economic and programmatic decisions based on the general welfare of the entire system. The potential reactions from negatively affected school-level and programmatic personnel can place a great deal of pressure and stress on the superintendent.

COMMUNICATIONS

Central office personnel often spend the greater part of their day communicating within the organization. Principals have a greater responsibility to communicate with constituencies external to the organization, but, with the exception of the high school principal, the greatest part of their day is usually spent on communications internal to the system and their respective facilities. The principal of a comprehensive high school comes closest to experiencing the complexity of internal and external communication demanded of the superintendent; however, any communication problem at any level will eventually find its way to the superintendent's office; therefore, the superintendent must be concerned with the communication efforts of the individual administrators in addition to fostering and enhancing a systemwide image.

The superintendent must be extremely precise in his/her communications. Sloppy, incomplete, and/or misleading information furnished by the superintendent is taken more seriously and evokes a greater reaction than that coming from other sectors of the system, and such information can cause a great amount of chaos and damage to the organization.

FISCAL EXPERTISE

In this age of expanding accountability and shrinking financial resources, most superintendents must become financial wizards in order to keep their districts financially solvent. School funding in most states is a very complex process, and woe to the superintendent who doesn't understand it. The business manager is the only other administrator in the system who has expertise in this area on a level of that required of the superintendent.

Many individuals enter the superintendency well-versed in educational matters but lacking in fiscal and business management skills. Exposure to business management concerns before entering the superintendency is a great asset. The experience gained from working daily with transportation problems, leaky roofs, unexpected utility increases, federal asbestos legislation, civil service laws, and obsolete physical plants will serve one well in the superintendency.

LEVY CAMPAIGNS

In many states, boards of education have to go before the citizenry to obtain approval to levy taxes for current operating and/or capital outlay purposes. In these situations, it is the superintendent who is responsible for providing the leadership to determine such things as the type of levy, amount of money to be raised, and type of campaign to be run. Other administrators within the system probably will get involved in campaigning for the passage of the levy or bond issue; however, the overall coordination of the campaign and, in the final analysis, its success or failure will rest with the superintendent.

LABOR RELATIONS

The superintendent and other administrators differ significantly in their roles in the area of labor relations. The other administrators, or their representatives, often serve on the negotiating team, and the principals are responsible for the day-to-day implementation of the negotiated contract. However, it is the superintendent who must help the board decide the system's priorities at the bargaining table. The superintendent must provide leadership on the following concerns: On which items can concessions be made and on which will the board hold fast? What issues are worth taking a strike over? What is the total cost of the proposed package?

Constant and complete communication with the board of education while negotiations are in progress is an extremely important responsibility that is solely the superintendent's. Others can help, but the superintendent must be in charge.

Determining the total cost to the school district of a proposed package is another important responsibility of the superintendent. One must be alert for hidden costs in a contract, such as professional leave, personal leave, class size changes, change in number or length of working days, and potential arbitration and fact-finding costs. In some states, the superintendent must sign a legal document stating that monies will be available to adequately fund the negotiated contract.

LOBBYING

Superintendents must be on top of pending and recently enacted state and federal legislation because it is important that they commit time and resources to influence pending educational legislation. This can mean working through and with professional groups such as the state association for school superintendents, the state school board association, the state department of education, etc., or it can mean making trips to the state capital when the legislature is in session to make personal contact with one's legislators and to testify at committee hearings. It also means getting to know one's legislators on a personal basis and keeping them informed about school-related matters. On occasion, a superintendent will go to Washington to testify at a hearing. While testifying is important and should be taken seriously, the greatest portion of a superintendent's lobbying efforts, however, will usually be spent at the state level.

Thoroughly understanding recently enacted legislation is extremely important. What does the legislation really mean for the schools? Often, innuendo and rash generalizations immediately follow the passage of significant school-related legislation. The superintendent must sort out the wheat from the chaff.

At times, state legislators pass educational mandates without supplying the necessary financial resources to implement them. The superintendent must be on top of this action immediately and inform the board of education and community of the potential impact of the legislation upon the school budget.

It is clear that no other administrative person in the system has the continuing lobbying responsibility and interest like the superintendent.

DECISION-MAKING

The school principals and the superintendent engage in a variety of decision-making exercises daily; however, the overall well-being of the school system is the superintendent's. For example, while the high school principal is anxious to make decisions that will enhance the morale within his/her building, the superintendent is concerned with the morale in each of the schools, plus the mental outlook of the board members and community. Decision-making in this milieu is extremely difficult.

TIME ALLOCATION

All administrators within the system are extremely busy and have a great need to manage their time wisely. The superintendent is, however, the only one who has almost complete control over personal time allocation. The superintendent can determine which issues are worthy of personal attention and those that will be delegated. The superintendent should be able to do a better job of planning personal time allocation than the school-level administrators, because the superintendency is more isolated from the minute-to-minute operation of the school day than the principalship.

The superintendent also influences the way the other administrators within the system spend their time. This is done by direct request and by constantly communicating with them on what is important in the system. An important way in which the superintendent communicates to others what is important is the manner in which personal time is allocated and the manner in which the immediate assistants are encouraged to allocate their time. Allocation of time by the top echelon of administrators is not lost on the others.

The superintendent has a responsibility to allocate a greater portion of personal time to thinking than the other administrators. The superintendent is paid to be creative and innovative in idea generation and problem resolution. This will not happen if the superintendent's calendar is crammed nonstop with meetings that are interrupted only to handle the latest perceived crisis in the district.

CONCLUDING COMMENTS

Twelve areas have been put forth, which, when taken together, make the superintendency a very unique position within the school system. The breadth and complexity of the responsibilities that go with the superintendency, along with the fact that the superintendent has the ultimate responsibility for the performance of all aspects of the system, make the superintendency an awesome and, at times, an overwhelming position. Some individuals thrive in this milieu. Others become hesitant and timid at the thought of making decisions that have a significant impact on many lives, both students and staff, and that will constantly be communicated broadly and receive continuing and close scrutiny. The fact that one often has to stand alone can be frightening; there are no other superintendents in the school system.

One can prepare thoroughly and conscientiously for the superintendency, but it is difficult to predict how one will function in the top chair until one occupies it. Many terrific assistant coaches never quite make it as the head coach. Any experience one can gain prior to obtaining a superintendency in assuming decision-making responsibilities that are public and have an impact on individuals with diverse interests will be beneficial.

On the positive side, some individuals thrive in this milieu. The challenge, excitement, responsibility, and opportunity to positively affect the lives of many individuals keep the adrenaline flowing and put a bounce in one's step. The job becomes more important than the individual, and the mission assumes a status that is greater and more important than personal job security.

Personal Philosophy and Leadership

CHAPTER 6

A Philosophical Discussion

A very influential member of your school board has just called and given you a strong recommendation relative to the employment of a personal friend for a teaching position. How are you going to handle this recommendation, which, as presented, is tantamount to a directive? Your personal philosophy as it is applied to the administrative process will be used as a guideline in weighing the pros and cons of the various alternatives you will consider en route to making a decision on this matter.

The preceding paragraph depicts a specific dilemma for the superintendent. A more general example could involve making decisions on how to implement the effective schools research. For instance, in the name of increasing school effectiveness, elaborate goal-setting and measurement techniques have been and are being developed along with a host of technical tools to help individuals operate more effectively within the organization. Today, more than at any time in history, more is known about how organizations (specifically school organizations) and individuals react. However, an often overlooked fact is that individuals and organizations can use this knowledge to help achieve any goals, good or bad. Thus, organizational effectiveness is determined by deciding which goals are worthy of achieving, regardless of the leadership techniques used. But how can *good* educational goals be distinguished from *bad* ones? One's personal philosophy is critical in deciding which goals will be established to achieve an effective school program.

Superintendents, like other administrators, face value conflicts daily, and because they are not just technicians, they must mediate

This chapter was adopted from an article written by William Konnert and Orin Graff entitled, "The Sine Qua Non of Organizational Effectiveness" that appeared in the Fall 1976 edition of *The Educational Administration Quarterly*.

and resolve such conflicts. Marshall (1992) studied the values that provided direction to a small group of administrators in resolving ethical dilemmas. Minority and white males and females were included in her study. She identified the following guiding principles upon which these administrators relied:

1. "guidance from God or from their moral principles inculcated by church and family" (p. 376)
2. "family background and personal values" (p. 377)
3. "justice, equity . . . fairness . . . openness, honesty, and evenhandedness" (p. 378)

Marshall (1992) also spoke to the role modeling of these administrators and the lessons learned by others, particularly their subordinates. She wrote

> When administrators vacillate and compromise, the moral lesson is "Lay low and go with the flow." When administrators take a stand for a cause or live up to an ethical principle and are punished (demoted or left hanging to take the heat alone) the moral lesson is "You'll be hurt by standing up for principles." (p. 383)

Superintendents are very visible role models and, thus, must be cognizant of their resolution of ethical dilemmas.

Finally, as Marshall notes, "Transformative leaders . . . bring to the surface our recognition that values are part of organizations and that leadership is value laden" (p. 382). Therefore, the influence of one's personal philosophy or set of values in the decision-making process is inescapable. Thus, a discussion of one's personal philosophy is not a useless academic exercise; rather, it represents an attempt to address the most important factor in the decision-making process. In fact, consistent decision-making is dependent upon adherence by leaders to a personal philosophy or set of values that keeps them honest in their behavior. What follows is a discussion of the components of a personal philosophy and the role one's personal philosophy plays in educational philosophy and professional decision-making.

THE SINE QUA NON
OF ORGANIZATIONAL EFFECTIVENESS

Every individual's personal preferences, habits, and values, in one way or another, come into play with every decision made. Preferences and habits, often unconsciously held, are for the most part environmentally acquired and, in part, custom based on experience.

Values are of a different order because they are an individual's more conscious recreations of habits and preferences, deliberately used to direct personal experience and/or to achieve personal goals. Thus, values are the stuff of which a personal philosophy is made. Yet there is a further step in the achievement of a personal philosophy: the various values held by an individual must be compatible, else an analysis of overt action is apt to reveal an amazing jumble of inconsistencies. The achievement of compatibility among values is a responsibility that only the individual can assume. Obviously, complete compatibility can never be completely achieved because intelligent action requires, as an important aspect of life, the evaluation and regeneration of one's values as new, productive experiences, both personal and vicarious, are lived.

An individual's values are not separated from one's acquired preferences and habits but, rather, are the results of choices resulting from appraisal of personal behaviors. A personal philosophy is achieved by continuously seeking compatibility among the values to which one becomes committed.

One other important aspect of a personal philosophy needs to be noted. Compatibility among values is hardly possible without arranging them in an orderly fashion from general to specific, major to minor, and concern for others to concern for self. Thus, one's philosophy is lifted from the status of a hodgepodge of specific values to an organized and understandable unity of values. A central core of values provides a person with a personal evaluative base for both present and projected action. Without such a core of values in operation, a person cannot be judged to have a philosophy.

Perhaps the most important element in the core of a personal philosophy should be the all-pervading desire to place human welfare above all other concerns. Essentially, this tenet means that whatever decisions are made and implemented, projected outcomes must be in the interests of those most likely to be affected, including, of course, the individual or individuals immediately involved.

An overriding concern for the welfare of others should then be the chief factor in integrating an individual's values into a consistent, comprehensive, and workable whole, thus achieving a personal philosophy. The concern for the welfare of others constitutes a basic and integrating factor in any personal philosophy. The neglect for the welfare of others in the creation of a philosophy is an exercise in futility for a superintendent.

It is legitimate to speak of an organizational philosophy; however, the primacy of the interaction of individual personal philosophies in establishing an organizational philosophy is self-evident. The philosophy of an organization is a constellation of consistent values, the components of which are derived from the values of those who are responsible for the management, control, and direction-setting functions within the organization. Thus, it is impossible to promote into action values that are not held and commonly supported by individuals within the organization. Further, these values constitute a strong motivating force for productivity if commonly held by a majority of the work force within the organization.

A philosophical base is the sine qua non to organizational effectiveness and sound decision-making. The real basis for decisions and, ultimately, organizational effectiveness goes far beyond the use of leadership techniques. It is only through a well-conceptualized philosophical base that worthy goals can be established and appropriate leadership techniques selected to facilitate their achievement.

DEVELOPMENT OF THE SINE QUA NON

Organizational leaders have the difficult task of avoiding the "how-to-do-it" syndrome. A checklist is easy to follow compared to the hard philosophical thought process. If practical advice and common sense are the guides to practice, then all aspects of theory are ignored as nonfunctional. Under such conditions, the value base of administrative leadership is ignored; either the persons involved falsely assume that whatever is done will generally affect others positively, or they confuse immediate self-satisfaction with the common welfare.

The formulation of a personal philosophy is a tough and time-consuming task for a mature person who, for the first time, decides to sort out personal values and reorder life activities accordingly. No one really enjoys viewing in retrospect a hodgepodge of inconsistent behavior or dealing with the problems of discarding firmly established attitudes and modes of behavior. One may know what one ought to do, but there is still a strong urge to continue past modes of behavior. Such attitudes and feelings can be controlled only if one pushes, and continues pushing, oneself into acting as one knows one ought. It is only through this kind of thinking and testing in everyday life situations that a person achieves a personal philosophy that is consistent, comprehensive, and workable.

By its very nature, a personal philosophy is a dynamic, directing, and controlling human behavior and, as such, has the capacity for growth and change. A philosophy in action should find the possessor relatively, but never entirely, satisfied with the results. There is always a definite feel that the results could be improved. This constant personal demand for higher congruity between ideals and practice is the kind of challenge needed to give lifelong attention to the improvement of one's personal philosophy—to maintain and enhance its dynamic state.

It is even more difficult for a group of persons to develop and maintain a philosophy for their organization than for each to develop and maintain a personal philosophy. However, establishing an adequate philosophic value base for an organization with a membership lacking in adequate personal philosophies is futile.

APPLICATION OF PERSONAL PHILOSOPHY TO DECISION-MAKING

To illustrate the application of one's personal philosophy to decision-making, the thinking process involved in reaching a decision to the situation put forth in the opening paragraph of this chapter will be explored.

In addressing the situation, let us assume that your personal philosophy places an extremely high priority on the welfare of others. When applied to your school system, this stance means that you have a paramount concern for the education of the students. If this is the case, then your decision regarding this particular sample situation seems rather clear-cut. You hire the best qualified teacher for the position, without regard to personal friendships. However, upon closer inspection, this decision may not be so cut-and-dried. For instance, suppose you strongly believe that a much greater emphasis on professional inservice within your system is the best way to enhance the quality of education within your system. To this end, you have been working with the board in an attempt to convince the members to add one week to the contract of each teacher. This additional week will be used exclusively for professional enhancement activities without students present. This move will mean the addition of another fifty thousand in salaries to an already tight budget. In addition, you will need another ten thousand dollars to conduct a quality program during this additional week. Presently, the community sees no need to spend more money on inservice activities. In short, if the board is to adopt and fund your plan, it will mean that each member will be making a high personal-risk decision. If your plan is to have any chance of receiving board approval, you must have the support of the influential member who just made the call to you.

In analyzing the above scenario, you might decide that, in the big picture, the students in your entire system will be better served by the inservice program. This logic could be particularly valid if the difference between the board member's friend and the other individual you would prefer to employ is not great. Thus, it might be best to employ the board member's friend in order to enhance the probability of board acceptance of the inservice program. You tend to be leaning in this direction. However, it also occurs to you that, if you hire the board member's friend, you might be setting a precedent for board member involvement in employment that could have long-term disastrous effects on the system. If this is the case, the negative precedent set by the employment of this teacher outweighs even the proposed inservice program. So, now you are beginning to think that the best plan of action would be not to employ the board member's friend. The decision is not easy. However, you are not wavering on you intention of making the decision in light of what you believe is in the best interests of the students in your system. The pros and cons of the various alternatives must be weighted against this dominant guideline. After you have made the decision, you will decide how to deal with the board member and the members of your staff.

For now, let's approach the scenario from a different perspective. Suppose you know a superintendent who is very self-serving. This individual values career advancement above all else. You suspect that this individual would find this decision, which is driving you up the wall, relatively easy to make. He would strike a deal with the board member for a strong recommendation at some future date or for something else of a similarly self-serving nature, in return for the employment of the board member's friend. For just a moment, you are a bit envious of your cohort; however, you quickly realize that this way of thinking is not you. A quick mental recap of what you expect to accomplish in the superintendency puts you in a better frame of mind and makes you both excited and confident about wrestling with the problem in light of your own values.

In summary, this discussion was intended to illustrate that your value base guides you in making the tough decisions. It doesn't make the decisions for you. For as we have seen, differing sets of circumstances can lead to differing decisions. Rather, it provides the benchmark against which various alternatives are weighed. At times, you will even make the same decision as someone operating from a substantially different value base. As this is the case, one can mask one's real values for a while, if one is so inclined. However, sooner or later, the real you and your real value system will emerge for all to see.

CONCLUDING COMMENTS

The thesis of this discussion is that the effectiveness of an organization depends on the values of the individuals involved; thus, the personal philosophies from which the individuals operate are the sine qua non for organizational effectiveness. More than any other factor, they determine the organizational philosophy and goals that will be established and to which people within the organization will be committed. They also condition the leadership techniques to be applied in reaching those goals.

In addition to demonstrating a need for the importance of a good philosophical base, this discussion has further proposed a belief that such a base should be grounded in an overriding concern for the welfare of others in achieving unity among the complex variables at play within society and within the school organization.

Judgments and decisions that are based on a well-thought-out philosophical base applied to relevant data is the only route to achieving trust and confidence among the membership of an organization and is essential for the contemporary leader seeking to cope effectively with a myriad of complex situations. Without it, a leader will find it extremely difficult to place a proper perspective on the many situations confronted daily.

This discussion has important implications for personnel selection. Often, an individual's philosophical base is not given serious consideration in the selection process. Such a process is inadequate if the aim is to select those who will be of the greatest benefit to the organization. The nature and consistency of the values of a selectee must rank high among selection criteria; in fact, they must be given top priority.

In conclusion, the philosophical base and corresponding values of individuals concerned with organizational leadership will be key ingredients to organizational effectiveness. The skill with which a leader can apply one's technical knowledge and leadership techniques to the organization and not violate one's own philosophical base will, in the long run, determine the degree of personal and organizational effectiveness achieved. A sound and internally consistent philosophy is the sine qua non upon which leadership is based and, consequently, the ethical base for organizational effectiveness.

REFERENCE

Marshall, C. (1992). School administrators' values: A focus on atypicals. *Educational Administration Quarterly, 28*(3), 368–386.

CHAPTER 7

Transformational Leadership

In order for a superintendent to bring about positive change within a school system, a mission statement with accompanying goals and objectives must be developed that is consistent with one's personal philosophy. Secondly, the development of a system culture and value system that support these goals and objectives and to which those associated with the system are committed must be created. In order to provide effective leadership in bringing all of this to fruition, the superintendent must go beyond transactional leadership to become a transformational leader.

This chapter describes transformational leadership and delineates the differences between a transactional leader and a transformational leader. It describes a different form of leadership thinking for the superintendent.

WHAT IS TRANSFORMATIONAL LEADERSHIP?

James MacGregor Burns (1978) suggested that only a portion of leadership is due to an exchange or transaction between the leader and followers. In transactional leadership, the leaders and followers approach each other with the expectation that an exchange will occur. Sergiovanni (1990) labels this bartering, which he explains as,

Mr. Richard Clapp provided the basic material for the "Transformational Leadership and Organizational Culture" section. He is a superintendent.

Drs. Holly Genzen and Keith Miller provided the material for the "What is Transformational Leadership?" portion of the chapter. Page 85 is taken directly from Dr. Genzen's research that is cited in the reference section. Dr. Miller is a business manager in a large public school district.

"Leader and led strike a bargain within which the leader gives to led something they want in exchange for something the leader wants" (p. 30). In going beyond this approach, the transformational leader "looks for potential motives in followers, seeks to satisfy higher needs, and engages the full person of the follower. The result of transformational leadership is a relationship of mutual stimulation and elevation" (Burns, 1978, p. 4). The transformational leader engages the follower in such a way that both are raised to "higher levels of motivation and morality" (Burns, 1978, p. 20).

Sergiovanni (1990), in discussing leadership types, distinguished between the Clockworks I leader who "believe[s] . . . that the purpose of leadership is to gain control and regulate the master wheel and the master pin of their clockworks organization" (p. 44) and the Clockworks II leader who "must rely on cultural cement to provide the necessary connections for coordination and control. The ingredients for cultural cement are the norms, values, beliefs, and purposes of people" (p. 46).

Bass (1985) described the transactional leader as one who recognizes what subordinates want to derive from their work and provides appropriate rewards for expected performance, i.e., responds to subordinates' immediate self-interests. His research yielded the following two factors associated with transactional leadership:

1. *Contingent reward:* The leader is seen as frequently telling subordinates what must be done to achieve a desired reward for their efforts.
2. *Management-by-exception:* The leader avoids giving directions if old ways are working; leader intervenes only if standards are not being met.

Tichy and Devanna (1990) list seven major characteristics of transformational leaders that distinguish them from transactional leaders. They

1. Clearly identify themselves as change agents. They are not hit-and-run artists. Rather, they stay with the organization throughout the entire transformational process.
2. Are courageous individuals who are risk takers and are willing to take a stand
3. Are powerful, yet sensitive to the needs of others and believe in people

4. Can articulate a set of core values and exhibit behavior that is consistent with their core values
5. Are life-long learners
6. Have an ability to deal with complexity, ambiguity, and uncertainty (Characteristics 5 and 6 are related because the more knowledge an individual has, the more he/she can appreciate the uncertainty and complexity of situations.)
7. Are visionaries in that they can visualize an organization's potential. They are also able to meaningfully articulate their visions to others.

Transformational leadership is described as both political (Quantz, Rogers, and Dantley, 1991) and moral (Burns, 1978). Needs of followers are recognized, and the leader engages followers in activities to lift both leader and followers to new levels. Such leadership acknowledges the necessity of alleviating one group's domination over another through hierarchies and bureaucracy (Ferguson, 1984; Quantz, Rogers, and Dantley, 1991). Transformational leaders do not seek power for personal gain but, rather, work toward what Bellah et al. (1985) describe in *Habits of the Heart* as a "public virtue" (p. 270), what Burns (1978) describes as "the higher levels of moral development" (p. 46).

Transformational leaders are able to excite the apathetic (Burns, 1978) to "inspire people to grab and follow their vision" (Cantor and Bernay, 1992, p. 188). Leader and follower work together toward a common vision that "will create change, transform institutions, and thus improve the quality of life" (Astin and Leland, 1991, p. 8). Transformational leaders convince followers that current realities "can indeed be changed for the better" (Foster, 1989, p. 41). In this way, a leader can turn power into a force for positive change (Feinstein, 1992).

Criticism of transformational leadership is also found. The current research and writing on transformational leadership is promising in this time of social and educational confusion. There is a real danger, however, as Foster (1989) warns, that the concept of transforming leadership will be assumed by management to serve its own purposes. For example, rather than being a vehicle for social change, it may be used only as a way of leading companies to greater profit.

There is also criticism that leaders will choose the appropriate vision, rather than listening to the people (Angus, 1989). "The leaders—in spite of their important, fundamental, and indispensable role—do not own the people and have no right to steer the people blindly towards their salvation" (Freire, 1990, p. 167). As Smyth (1989, p. 190) warns, "Those who lay claim to be the visionary thinkers in schools must be prepared to analyze their own intentions, lest they become manipulative."

James M. Kouzes and Barry Z. Posner, in their 1987 book *The Leadership Challenge*, cite ten commitments of leadership resulting from interviews with 1,200 managers. More than 70 percent of the behavior and strategies described in case study and interview analyses can be accounted for by these commitments. The commitments are the following:

1. Search for challenging opportunities to change, grow, innovate, and improve.

2. Experiment, take risks, and learn from the accompanying mistakes.

3. Envision an uplifting and ennobling future.

4. Enlist others in a common vision by appealing to their values, interests, hopes, and dreams.

5. Foster collaboration by promoting cooperative goals and building trust.

6. Strengthen others by sharing information and power and increasing their discretion and visibility.

7. Set an example for others by behaving in ways that are consistent with your stated values.

8. Plan small wins that promote consistent progress and build commitment.

9. Recognize individual contributions to the success of every project.

10. Celebrate team accomplishments regularly.

As a result of their interviews, Kouzes and Posner also developed an instrument called the Leadership Practices Inventory (LPI) to measure the degree to which an individual exhibits each of the ten commitments. The instrument has high degrees of reliability and validity and is being used extensively in research involving school administrators.

Kouzes and Posner (1990) also asked over 7,500 managers nationwide, from a variety of organizations, to describe what qualities they looked for or admired in their leaders. The qualities of honesty, competency, and the abilities to be forward-looking and inspiring appeared constantly. The most important quality of a leader, as perceived by a follower, was honesty or trustworthiness. Leaders must do what they say they will do. Follow-through and consistency are important. Trust is viewed as a two-way street, where the leader must first give trust in order to get trust.

Kouzes and Posner have been contemporary leaders in interpreting, researching, and operationalizing transformational leadership. Their work is very relevant to the superintendency.

In summary, when decision-making is becoming more decentralized and greater empowerment is being given to school-level personnel, transformational leadership becomes increasingly important. Transformational leaders become effective change agents by helping to create an organizational vision and by helping others to understand, accept, and work toward the accomplishment of this vision. The superintendent obviously must be the transformational leader among transformational leaders.

TRANSFORMATIONAL LEADERSHIP AND THE ORGANIZATIONAL CULTURE

Before a transformational leader can change an organization's culture, one must first understand what an organizational culture is and by what means it can be changed. This section discusses the concept of organizational culture and is followed by a section identifying ways in which an organizational culture can be changed.

What Is an Organizational Culture?

Schein (1987) defines *culture* as

> a pattern of basic assumptions—invented, discovered, or developed by a given group as it learns to cope with its problems of external adaptation and internal integration—that has worked well enough to be considered valid and, therefore, to be taught to new members as the correct way to perceive, think, and feel in relation to those problems. (p. 9)

In short, an organization's culture determines how things are done around here.

Johnston (1987) indicates that "at the very foundation of a culture are its values—basic beliefs that control the choices we make" (p. 80). Every organization has these values. If they are true organizational values, they are believed and subscribed to by most members of the organization. They are the bedrock of the organization, and they indicate what the organization stands for and determine how it conducts its affairs. They are institutionalized and guide and control the behavior of the individuals within the organization. Sergiovanni (1990) names this a "covenant," which is ". . . a binding and solemn agreement . . . to honor certain values, goals, and beliefs; to make certain commitments to each other; and to do or keep from doing specific things" (p. 20).

Outstanding organizations have a core set of values that are extremely important and must be observed. Organizational members display a dedication to these values that has been referred to as rigid, nonnegotiable, inflexible, and fanatical. They are willing to confront anyone within the organization who might be so brazen as to disregard them. Enforcement is placed above personal popularity (DuFour and Eaker, 1987). The unwillingness by organizational members to accept excuses for a lack of adherence to core values makes it clear that they are important and should be incorporated into daily practices (Johnston, 1987). In further support of a core set of values, Peters and Waterman (1982) state

> . . . suppose that we were asked for one all-purpose bit of advice for management, one truth that we we were able to distill from the excellent companies research. We might be tempted to reply, "Figure out your value system. Decide what your company stands for." (p. 279)

Thus, it is essential that schools develop a core set of values that are shared by teachers, administrators, board members, parents, and citizens (Deal, 1985). It is the shared values that keep the various subgroups within the school organization headed in the same general direction that will make empowerment work. For, as decision-making is decentralized, it is imperative that the decision makers adhere to a common set of values. Otherwise, a series of subgroups with different goals, heading in different directions, and, at times, working at odds with each other will be the result.

A number of examples can be put forth where an organization's values have a profound impact on its operations. For instance, in a school organization, values will determine such things as whether academics or athletics are given higher priority, whether women and minorities can obtain formal leadership positions, the importance of achievement test scores, the emphasis placed on a warm and caring environment, and the things to which employees are willing to devote extra time and effort.

Thus, transformational leadership causes important changes to take place in the school culture. New values and expectations are created; people are unified and work towards a new shared vision. Bass and Avolio (1993) believe that "in a highly innovative and satisfying organizational culture we are likely to see transformational leaders. . . . Leaders who build such cultures . . . typically exhibit a sense of vision and purpose. They foster a culture of creative change and growth rather than one which maintains the status quo" (p. 113).

Shaping Organizational Values

Organizational leaders must give high priority to the shaping and dissemination of appropriate organizational values. If these values are to survive, they must be nourished and celebrated (Deal and Kennedy, 1982). Deal (1985) identifies six ways in which organizational values may be shaped.

Document the school's history

A school system's history should be explored and documented. Important events and people should be chronicled for all to read. Shared values evolve from experience and have historical analogies. "Values detached from history rarely have meaning" (Deal, 1985, p. 616).

Anoint and celebrate heroes and heroines

These need to be individuals who embody and represent the school system's core values. They need to be recognized not only for themselves, but also for the important value(s) they represent. Thus, the recognition can be situation specific.

Recognition can be accomplished via storytelling of the type that abounds at reunions. Ways need to be devised to share these tales of the past with each new generation of students.

Recognition also can be done through materialistic symbols. The New York Yankees have celebrated their immortals with statues in center field. There is a statue of Stan Musial outside of Busch Stadium in St. Louis. Some schools have established "Walls of Fame" where they honor their distinguished graduates. Every high school has a trophy case, and most have an entire hallway devoted to athletic feats of the past.

Johnston (1978, p. 84) believes that the impact of heroes on the school is profound in that it

1. Shows that success is attainable and human
2. Provides role models for other group members
3. Creates a school image for the outside world
4. Sets standards of performance
5. Motivates people to perform

Rituals

Rituals determine much of the day-to-day behavior in any organization. The school's rituals should be reviewed periodically to be sure they are reinforcing the appropriate values. They should also be reviewed for the messages they are conveying to others. For instance, do the morning announcements over the public address system always start with the scores and heroes and heroines of the most recent sporting event? What percent of board meeting time is devoted to curriculum and/or student types of things? Is there seldom a unanimous vote by the board of education? Do negative comments consistently come out of board meetings? Are inter-office memos originating in the superintendent's office usually very directive in nature?

Ceremonies

If a symbolic event is to be effective, it must be more than a mandatory exercise; it must be viewed as a sacred occasion. Thus, graduation exercises should be conducted with pomp and fanfare. National Honor Society induction and academic awards ceremonies should also be treated similarly. Ceremonies should say that something important is being celebrated here. As with rituals, ceremonies reinforce the core organizational values.

Storytelling

Included among the purposes of storytelling are reinforcing values and transmitting culture. Historically, many cultures have perpetuated through the art of storytelling. Some are concerned that this is becoming a lost art. However, there usually is a cadre of individuals in an organization who are very knowledgeable of the organization's past and interested in sharing it with others. These individuals should be encouraged and others developed because, as Sergiovanni (1990) notes, it is important to "return to the past for inspiration, insight, and guidance" (p. 148).

Cultural network

The cultural network is the informal communication system that tells how things really are within the school system. This network is a true indication of the real core values of a school system. It disseminates only the information it considers important. Therefore, this network must be recognized and nourished with tender loving care. Its transmissions cannot be left purely to chance because they influence the formal organization.

To shape the organization, "cultural leadership" is needed. This leadership

> comes from defining, strengthening, and articulating enduring values, beliefs, and cultural strands that give the [organization] its identity over time. This is the "high priest" function of being a leader. The behaviors associated with cultural leadership include articulating . . . purposes and mission; socializing new members . . . telling stories and maintaining or reinforcing myths, traditions, and beliefs; explaining the way things operate around here; developing and displaying a system of symbols over time; and rewarding those who reflect the culture. (Sergiovanni, 1990, pp. 87–88)

One final means by which organizational culture can be shaped is with the employment of personnel. Because an organizational culture is nothing more than the collective values of its members, it is of utmost importance that new hires share a commitment to the system's core values. This value commitment could be more important to the system than a 4.0 grade point average in one's teaching area. Thus, the organization's mission and core values must be considered in the recruitment and selection of employees.

CONCLUDING COMMENTS

Transformational leadership *is* the superintendency. It's having a vision of what the school system can be and motivating all associated with the system to have pride in the system and to achieve more than they thought possible for the good of the system. It is stimulating and releases the creative energies of all for the benefit of the system.

Transformational leadership is exciting in that, while some descriptions can be given of what it is and some general guidelines can be put forth on how to become one, there is no prescription that can be put forth to produce a transformational leader. Leadership is an art as much as a science. It is a school system revitalizing "itself through the combined efforts of its people" (Ruane, 1984).

REFERENCES

Angus, L. (1989). New leadership and the possibility of educational reform. In J. Smyth (Ed.), *Critical Perspectives on Educational Leadership*, pp. 63–92.

Astin, H. S. and Leland, C. (1991). *Women of Influence, Women of Vision: A Cross-Generational Study of Leaders and Social Change.* San Francisco, CA: Jossey-Bass.

Avolio, B. J. and Bass, B. M. (1986). *Transformational Leadership, Charisma, and Beyond.* Technical Report No. 85–90. Binghamton, NY: State University of New York, School of Management.

Bass, B. M. (1985). *Leadership and Performance Beyond Expectations.* New York, NY: The Free Press.

Bass, B. J. and Avolio, B. J. (1993). Transformational leadership and organizational culture. *Public Administration Quarterly* (Spring), 112–121.

Bellah, R., Madsen, K., Sullivan, W., Swedler, A. and Tipton, S. (1985). *Habits of the Heart.* New York, NY: Harper & Row.

Bennis, W. G. (1984). The four competencies of leadership. *Training and Development Journal* (Aug.), 14–19.

Bennis, W. and Nanus, B. (1985). *Leaders: The Strategies for Taking Charge.* New York, NY: Harper & Row.

Birney, R. C. and Teevan, R. C. (1962). *Measuring Human Motivation.* Princeton, NJ: D. Van Nostrand Co. Inc.

Burns, J. M. (1978). *Leadership.* New York, NY: Harper & Row.

Cantor, D. W. and Bernay, T. (1992). *Women in Power: The Secrets of Leadership.* New York, NY: Houghton Mifflin Company.

Deal, T. E. (1985). The symbolism of effective schools. *The Elementary School Journal, 85*(5), 601–620.

Deal, T. E. and Kennedy, A. (1982). *Corporate Cultures: The Rites and Rituals of Corporate Life.* Reading, MA: Addison-Wesley.

DuFour, R. and Eaker, R. (1987). The principal as leader: Two major responsibilities. *NASSP Journal* (Sept.), 80–89.

Feinstein, D. (1992). Foreward. In D. Cantor and T. Bernay, *Women in Power,* pp. xiv–xvii, New York, NY: Houghton Mifflin Company.

Ferguson, K. (1984). *The Feminist Case against Bureaucracy.* Philadelphia, PA: Temple University Press.

Foster, W. (1989). Toward a critical practice of leadership. In J. Smyth (Ed.), *Critical Perspectives on Educational Leadership,* pp. 39–62, New York, NY: The Falmer Press.

Freire, P. (1990). *Pedagody of the Oppressed.* New York, NY: Continuum.

Johnston, J. H. (1987). Values, culture and the effective school. *NASSP Journal, 71,* 79–88.

Kirby, P. and Paradise, L. (1992). Extraordinary leaders in education: Understanding transformational leadership. *Journal of Educational Research, 85*(5), 303–311.

Kouzes, J. and Posner, B. (1990). The credibility factor: What followers expect from their leaders. *Management Review* (Jan.), 29–33.

Kouzes, J. and Posner, B. (1987). *The Leadership Challenge.* San Francisco, CA: Jossey-Bass.

Peters, T. J. and Waterman, R. H. (1982). *In Search of Excellence.* New York, NY: Harper & Row.

Quantz, R., Rogers, J., and Dantley, M. (1991). Rethinking transformational leadership: Toward democratic reform of schools. *Journal of Education, 173*(3), 96–118.

Rosener, J. (1990). Ways women lead. *Harvard Business Review, 68*(6), 119–125.

Ruane, P. (1984). Moving through and beyond transition: Barriers and bridges to a better quality of organizational life. Unpublished doctoral dissertation, Harvard University, Cambridge, MA.

Schein, E. H. (1987). *Organizational Culture and Leadership.* San Francisco, CA: Jossey-Bass.

Sergiovanni, T. J. (1990). *Value-Added Leadership—How to Get Extraordinary Performance in Schools.* New York, NY: Harcourt Brace Jovanovich.

Smyth, J. (1989). Preface. In J. Smyth (Ed.), *Critical Perspectives on Educational Leadership*, pp. 1–8, 179–204, New York, NY: The Falmer Press.

Tichy, N. M. and Devanna, M. A. (1990). *The Transformational Leader.* New York, NY: Wiley.

Tichy, N. M. and Ulrich, D. O. (1984). The leadership challenge—A call for the transformational leader. *Sloan Management Review, 26*(1), 59–68.

Wortman, M. S. (1982). Strategic management and changing leader-follower roles. *Journal of Applied Behavorial Science, 18,* 371–383.

*Superintendent Leadership Competencies:
Personal (The Superintendent as . . .)*

CHAPTER 8

The Superintendent as Divergent Thinker

INTRODUCTION

In the preceding chapter on transformational leadership, the transformational leader was depicted as one who is less willing to be satisfied with partial answers or to accept the status quo. Conversely, this individual is more likely to seek new ways to do things and to take greater risks. The transformational leader is a visionary and an intellectual stimulator. S/he is a leader who provides ideas that result in the rethinking of old ways. S/he enables followers to look at problems from many angles and encourages them to seek creative solutions.

In order to be a transformational leader, one must be a divergent thinker. The Webster's dictionary (1976) definition of divergent is "mov[ing] or extend[ing] in different directions from a common point" (p. 214). In the educational arena, this means challenging commonly held assumptions; i.e., all children must spend twelve years in a formal and organized school setting, schools are the primary dispensers of knowledge to youth, etc.

From the time one is very young, emphasis is placed on being right. Young children are encouraged to stay within the lines when coloring and not draw pink elephants. The entire grading system in grades K–12 and, indeed, on through graduate school is predicated on being right. Preparation programs in educational administration stress logical thought processes in problem solving and decision-making. Thus, almost all of one's formal educational experiences stress being *right* and the derivation of correct answers through logical thought processes. In other words, *convergent* thinking is emphasized.

When one enters the teaching profession, one is expected to teach a prescribed curriculum and to have a thorough knowledge of one's content area. When one obtains an administrative position, one is expected to apply rational thought processes to the resolution of problems, go through prescribed budget formulation exercises, promote the commonly accepted educational assumptions, and, by all means, not suggest wild ideas with any degree of seriousness. The result is that the convergent thinking to which one has been exposed during the formal schooling process is reinforced in the job setting. Now, suddenly, and with no real preparation as a superintendent, one is not only expected to be a *divergent* thinker, but also to encourage others to be divergent thinkers.

THE NEED FOR DIVERGENT THINKING

Divergent thinking is essential to the first two phases of the decision-making process, which are problem definition and idea production, whereas convergent thinking comes into play during the last three phases of the decision-making process, namely, idea evaluation, implementation, and evaluation.

Problem definition, or problem finding, is probably the most neglected phase of decision-making. There is a great tendency to assume that one knows the problem and to embark immediately on finding a resolution through the convergent-thinking process; however, a solution to the wrong problem does no one any good and has wasted a lot of time in the process. In the book *If You Don't Know Where You're Going, You'll Probably End up Somewhere Else,* Campbell (1974) aptly describes the confusion that exists when a problem has not been adequately defined. This confusion can exist in the big picture, such as in strategic planning, as well as in the day-to-day problems faced by superintendents, such as a troublesome board member.

Many of the issues one identifies as difficulties are merely only symptoms of the real problems. For instance, by applying the theories presented in the next chapter on motivation to the collective bargaining process, one should entertain the idea that salaries and fringe benefits are, at times at least, symptoms of teacher discontent in other areas. By bargaining innovatively and attempting to satisfy some esteem needs of teachers, the salary and fringe benefit issues may prove less troublesome to resolve.

In a noneducational example of problem identification, the management of a high-rise hotel was receiving a number of complaints from its guests about having to wait too long for the elevators. Some alternatives that come readily to mind for resolving this perceived problem are to put in another elevator, reprogram the existing elevators, revise the room assignment policies, offer reduced rates for the upper floors, etc. The resolution was very simple and included none of the above: pictures were hung in the elevator waiting areas. In reality, the guests were not having to wait long at all. The problem was that, while waiting for the elevator, there was nothing to do but stare at the blank walls, and time passed very slowly in this setting. The old adage that "a watched pot never boils" was very appropriate to this problem. The original ideas listed for resolution were all mechanical or logistical in nature. It was not until someone had the idea that maybe the problem was psychological in origin that the real problem emerged and, along with it, a simple and effective resolution.

The remainder of the chapter discusses some thought processes that must be developed and utilized if one is to become a divergent thinker. Or, applied to the superintendency, if one wishes to be a visionary leader, a leader who wants to identify and deal with *real* problems, and a leader who wants to identify innovative and exciting resolutions to problems, then one must develop divergent-thinking capabilities.

DEVELOPING DIVERGENT THINKING

Contrary to the thinking of many, creativity or the ability to innovate is not an inherited trait reserved for a fortunate few. While it is true that some individuals are more inclined to search for novel approaches than others, all have the potential to be creative. Interestingly, most individuals, when asked to identify something they have done within the last six months that has been innovative, will reply that they cannot recall doing anything innovative and that, in general, they just are not the innovative types. However, with some prodding, almost all will be able to identify something they have done that has been innovative. Researchers have generally concluded that a belief in one's ability to be creative is the single most important factor to being creative. To make maximum use of the ideas that follow for developing creative ideas, one must first develop the personal confidence that one does have creative potential.

Novel or innovative ideas do not spring from a vacuum. Rather, they come from the novel combination of knowledge and/or experiences stored in one's mind. Creative people know a lot about a lot of things. von Oech (1986) calls this the "explorer" stage. In this stage, one breaks out of routines and looks for new information. He suggests such things as looking in outside fields, looking for lots of ideas (nothing is worthless), and not jumping at the first solution. Campbell (1977) calls this the "experience" stage, where one picks up the background to the problem. His book addresses this knowledge-gathering phase. In summary, the components of an innovative idea are not necessarily innovative and novel in and of themselves. What is innovative and novel is the way in which they have been adapted and combined to provide an original solution to a problem.

The idea generation phase is referred to by von Oech as the "artist" stage. This is the off-the-wall stage where one should get a little crazy. Break the rules, do something different, fool around. The greatest danger the artist faces is becoming a prisoner to familiarity. Don't evaluate ideas immediately. Look at a job backwards. (How can one be a less effective superintendent?) Comedy is important; it brings to light the unexpected. Look at the same things as everyone else, but come up with new ideas. Campbell (1977) refers to idea generation as the "creativity" phase where individuals develop the ability to give up traditional viewpoints and to veer off the beaten path to explore new and novel things.

Kanter (1986) stresses contact with other individuals who do not share the same values or assumptions. Creativity often flows from uncomfortable situations where basic beliefs are challenged. The most productive research scientists have the most contact with people outside their field because creativity often emerges at the boundaries of disciplines. Outsiders can see the picture a little differently, look at a different angle, and not know enough not to ask the *dumb* question. Kanter calls this "innovation by invasion."

The relationship between comedy and creativity merits special mention. Kanter (1986) indicates that creativity is playfulness and irreverence, and goes on to say, "Every creative act is a form of play—playing with ideas, twisting the kaleidoscope of reality. Every new invention is a little bit irreverent: it challenges orthodoxy and trods on tradition" (p. 12). Indeed, there is a close connection between *ha-ha* and *a-ha*. Some things are so important that they must be taken lightly and laughed at.

The best way to have good ideas is to have a lot of ideas. One way to do this is through brainstorming. The objective of brainstorming is, in a three- or four-minute period of time, to generate as many ideas as possible. (Shoot for forty ideas.) Four rules for successful brainstorming are

1. Criticism of any kind is a no-no.
2. Freewheeling is welcomed (the wilder the idea, the better).
3. Quantity is wanted. A fast pace should be maintained.
4. Combinations and improvements are sought.

Roger van Oech (1983) has identified ten mental blocks that cripple creative potential. These ten blocks are as follows:

1. The right answer
2. That's not logical.
3. Follow the rules
4. Be practical.
5. Avoid ambiguity.
6. To err is wrong.
7. Play is frivolous.
8. That's not my idea.
9. Don't be foolish.
10. I'm not creative.

The next section identifies ways in which these divergent-thinking ideas can be applied to the superintendency.

APPLICATION OF DIVERSE THINKING TO THE SUPERINTENDENCY

It has been said that professionals today know more and more about less and less. In education, this is reflected by the English teacher who reads only English publications and associates with other English teachers (perhaps only tenth-grade English teachers). Multiply this example by the number of subject areas, grade levels, and administrative positions, and one gets a picture of massive professional isolation.

To combat professional isolationism, educators should be encouraged to do such things as attend seminars in other fields, subscribe to journals in unrelated fields and journals that espouse viewpoints contrary to one's own, and associate with individuals who question the effectiveness of contemporary educational organizations.

Within the school setting, promote cross-disciplinary activities, such as a physics teacher serving on an English textbook adoption or curriculum revision committee or vice versa. Have a teacher, or teachers, present something of interest in their academic area to the entire staff. This activity can also be done with the administrative staff.

Break routines. Do things differently on occasion for the sole purpose of doing them differently. Use a different format for a meeting and hold it at a different time. If one really wants to get far out, have the custodian, a sixth grader, or a parent run the schools for a day.

Educators, particularly administrators, tend to be serious and dedicated individuals. This demeanor is difficult to fault; however, taken to the extreme, it can have a stifling effect on the school climate and put a damper on creativity. It is important that playful activities be supported within the school system. Otherwise, one cannot expect individuals to be playful when it is important to be playful, i.e., when an innovative approach is needed to a knotty problem such as falling student achievement scores. Halloween parties, gag gift birthday parties, humorous awards, etc., help set the stage for playing over serious business.

To illustrate how difficult it is to poke fun at professional problems, particularly those in which one has a personal stake, divide a group of educators into groups of four or five. Have each group brainstorm for four minutes to identify as many ways as possible to keep bugs off the windshields of cars, and then have them post their ideas. Two things will be noticed. First, during the brainstorming session, there was much laughing and smiles abounded. Second, some rather far-out solutions were identified. These far-out ideas are important because it is ideas like these that lead to other ideas, which lead to innovative resolutions. Next, have these same groups brainstorm ideas on an important educational problem, e.g., how would formal K–12 education be affected if the passing of a competency test was all that was needed to obtain a high school diploma? Again, have the ideas posted. Three things will be noticed this time. First, there was much less humor during the brainstorming because this is serious business now. Second, there were some deviations from the brainstorming ground rule of no criticism of ideas. Third, not as many far-out ideas have been generated. It is almost heresy to think, let alone say among colleagues, that the primary function of the schools in the future may be to provide diagnostic and prescriptive services. In fact, it is a good bet that some very obvious possibilities such as schools ceasing to exist and teachers becoming private entrepreneurs commanding pay commensurate to the achievements of their students were not even mentioned.

Lest one think that this is an idle academic exercise in frivolity, a case can be made that the primary reason legislatures across the nation have demanded competency testing for students, teachers, and administrators is that the education profession ignored, for over a decade, a serious and growing public concern for an increased accountability of K–12 educational programs. Instead of identifying effective and innovative ways to be accountable, educators spent their time explaining why they couldn't and/or shouldn't be held accountable. After futile attempts to get the education profession to address this issue, the public felt compelled to address it through their elected representatives.

Campbell (1977) has identified the following seven characteristics of creative managers:

- willingness to absorb risks taken by subordinates – Leaders who encourage creativity expect that errors will be made. They are able to accept short-term failures in the hope of achieving long-term success.
- comfort with half-developed ideas – These leaders don't require every detail to be in place before accepting an idea. This requires instinct and judgment on the part of the leaders. Every "half-baked" idea cannot be pursued.
- willingness to "stretch" company policy – These leaders don't normally disregard rules and policies, but they have a *feel* for when the rules need to be stretched.
- ability to make quick decisions – These leaders have developed the ability to recognize when a partially developed idea is worth betting on, without waiting for further studies of committee reports.
- ability to be good listeners – These leaders seem to have the ability to draw out the best from their subordinates and then add to it.
- lack of dwelling on mistakes – These leaders are more future-oriented than past-oriented. They learn from past mistakes but don't wallow in them.

- enjoyment of their job—These leaders like what they are doing. They do not feel trapped. They add energy to their environments.

Being creative is risky. Professionals must feel valued and secure before they become risk takers.

Finally, there comes a time when one must become practical and assess the value of an idea and the feasibility of its being successfully implemented. It is obvious that, after a decision has been made and time, effort, and money have been spent in its implementation, any drastic changes should not be taken lightly. However, the common mistake is for educational decision-makers to become too serious, too logical, and too committed to an idea or resolution too fast.

The best way for a superintendent to get innovation started in his/her district is to lead the way. Positive and helpful innovations emanating from the superintendent's office will not go unnoticed. They need not be grandiose in scale. It is the climate setting that is important.

In conclusion, the superintendent is paid to be a divergent thinker, as well as a convergent thinker; therefore, it is necessary to build divergent thinking time and activities into one's daily calendar. Each Friday, one should do a self-analysis of the divergent-thinking time engaged in during the past week.

REFERENCES

Campbell, D. P. (1977). *Take the Road to Creativity and Get off Your Dead End.* Greensboro, NC: Center for Creative Leadership.

Campbell, D. P. (1974). *If You Don't Know Where You're Going, You'll Probably End up Somewhere Else.* Greensboro, NC: Center for Creative Leadership.

Kanter, R. M. (1986). Creating the creative environment. *Management Review* (Feb.), 11–12.

von Oech, R. (1986). *A Kick in the Seat of the Pants.* New York, NY: Harper & Row.

von Oech, R. (1983). *A Whack on the Side of the Head.* New York, NY: Warner Books.

Webster's Pocket Book Dictionary. (1976). New York, NY: Simon & Schuster, Inc.

CHAPTER 9

The Superintendent as Motivator

INTRODUCTION

During the last twenty years, the subject of motivation has provided writers and practitioners with fertile ground for research and inquiry. The result has been the emergence of a number of motivation perspectives and models, with many of these relating specifically to the child and the classroom. There is a growing body of research on motivation as it applies to educational administration in general and superintendents in particular.

This chapter defines motivation and then presents a discussion of motivational factors that may influence the leadership effectiveness of a superintendent. It concludes with the results of some recent research on superintendent motivation.

WHAT IS MOTIVATION?

Motivation is difficult to define. The word has no fixed meaning in contemporary psychology and is used in a variety of ways. For example, Hoy and Miskel (1987) define motivation as the "complex forces, drives, needs, tension states, or other mechanisms that start and maintain voluntary activity toward the achievement of personal goals" (p. 176). Another definition notes that motivation is a matter of choices a person makes regarding what one wants to experience or avoid and the amount of effort to be expended in that regard.

Ms. Mary Jane Landry and Mr. Kevin Rozman provided the basic material for this chapter. Ms. Landry has been a board member and board president, and Mr. Rozman has been a superintendent intern.

Most definitions seem to contain the following three elements:

1. Activating forces are assumed to exist within individuals.
2. Individual behavior is directed toward something.
3. The surrounding environment must reinforce the intensity and direction of individual drives or forces (Hoy and Miskel, 1987).

Theories on motivation, which are as varied as the definitions, attempt to answer frequently asked "why?" questions about human behavior. Why do people work overtime? Why do some people work harder than others? Why doesn't a salary increase improve production? Why doesn't a pupil attend class?

Motivation theory utilizes two basic approaches, content and process, to formulate answers to the "why?" questions. The content approach specifies only those things that motivate behavior, and content theories attempt to identify what things energize or initiate behavior. Theories in this group list specific needs, motives, expectancies, incentives, goals, and reinforcers.

Process theories investigate how behavior is started, sustained, and stopped. These theories attempt not only to define the major variables that are necessary to explain choice, effort, and the persistence of certain behavior, but also how the variables interact to influence outcomes (Miskel, 1982).

While research on motivation produces a number of definitions, theories, and perspectives, one concept emerges very clearly: the importance of motivation in the workplace is not a new issue. In fact, the principles of motivation have been primary concerns in business administration management ever since the realization that employee motivation has a bearing on productivity (Pastor and Erlandson, 1982). The classic Hawthorne Studies, conducted from 1927 to 1932, yielded a number of conclusions that remain important today.

In recent years, an increased interest in motivation has emerged within the educational community. A possible reason for this heightened interest might be found in the report, *A Nation at Risk*. The report focused on the problems facing American public education and stressed the serious lack of motivation for both students and teachers.

Some of the recommendations of the report center around the need to increase teachers' salaries. However, the National Commission on Excellence in Education (1983) also refers to the need to "make teaching a more rewarding and respected profession" (p. 30), implying that there is more to motivation than just money. One of the conclusions of the Hawthorne Studies notes that economic incentives are not the only significant motivators (Hoy and Miskel, 1987).

For whatever reason, motivation in the educational setting has become an area of increased interest among researchers and educators. Superintendents need to be aware of the motivational research and recognize its significance not only within the school organization, but also in the community at large.

SUPERINTENDENTS AND MOTIVATION

According to Hoy and Miskel (1987), school superintendents need to be aware of the importance of motivation within the educational organization and the teaching profession. A solid understanding of motivation is essential for explaining causes of behavior in schools or divisions, predicting effects of executive decisions, and directing behavior to achieve system goals.

Superintendents need to know how to motivate. If the superintendent is to be a strong leader, s/he must be able to motivate other administrators, teachers, parents, students, and the community. Effective leaders don't do the jobs themselves; rather, they motivate others to accomplish the goals of the organization. Patricia Duttweiler (1986) states, "Education excellence requires a leader who has the ability to gain the commitment of others to organizational goals" (p. 371).

If a superintendent is to motivate others, s/he must have a personal commitment to the importance of motivation. This individual must understand that the superintendent's enthusiasm for the goals of the system sets the tone for the system climate. The findings of a Texas school district study revealed that the superintendent was able to commit his values and behavior toward followers in such a way that all were raised to higher motivational levels (Marks, 1990).

Another leadership factor that influences motivation is the ability of the chief administrator to involve people, both board and staff, in goal setting and decision-making. Much of the research in this area involves teacher motivation and suggests that part of the solution to the problem of motivating teachers lies in involving staff in making decisions that have a direct impact on their work.

Superintendents need to be aware of the importance of sharing decision-making at all levels — not just in the classroom. State, system, school, and student levels must also be taken into consideration when delegating authority and decisions.

According to Duttweiler (1986), including employees in making decisions in their system will result in an increased sense of ownership in the results of those decisions. Job satisfaction will increase, and employees will be motivated to support decisions they have helped make. The superintendent will find that s/he has less work, fewer staff problems, and a smoother operating system.

A study by Buck (1990) focused on the leadership behaviors of forty-nine exemplary superintendents and identified the seven most frequently described behaviors:

1. Conceptualizes a specific future
2. Employs formal communication
3. Understands the organizational and community ethos
4. Provides up-to-date and accurate information for new learning
5. Advocates quality education
6. Develops and improves skills
7. Involves others in goal setting and decision-making

The conclusion of this study was that educational leaders must be able to continue to demonstrate these behaviors in order to function in a changing society and to move a school system into the twenty-first century.

In addition, the superintendent should be knowledgeable about incentives meaningful to system employees. Incentives build interest and satisfy needs. Research indicates that, if the needs that motivate an individual to work are satisfied by the organization's incentives, job satisfaction is high. If an individual's needs are greater than the rewards received for work, a discrepancy exists that leads to dissatisfaction (Hoy and Miskel, 1987). Thus, it would seem logical that superintendents who can match incentives with employee needs will be better able to motivate staff.

The superintendent has an important relationship with the school board. A study that investigated the relationship of the board members' common perception of the ideal superintendent leadership behavior to their present superintendent's work motivation found that school board members prefer a high level of supportive leader behavior by their superintendents and identified the motivation factor "potential for personal challenge and development" as a most critical variable for superintendents (Benzinger, 1988).

Not only do the system's internal groups require motivation, but external groups do as well. Community business leaders need motivation to become involved with education and understand the importance of the future work force. Parents need to be motivated to become involved with their children's education. Nonparents, particularly senior citizens, need to be motivated to utilize educational services and understand the changes and functions of today's educational process. Taxpayers and church members for church-related schools need to be motivated to support the educational investment. Legislators need to be motivated to provide continued legal and statutory support for the overall educational enterprise. In essence, every element of the community needs to be motivated to provide the best possible education for each and every child. Finally, the superintendent needs to set high expectations for self, staff, and students. Orr (1991) performed a study that investigated the job performance of superintendents by examining the relationships among motivational forces, role concepts and perceptions, and the personality traits and attributes that impact their behavior within an organizational setting (Orr, 1991). The results indicated that the superintendent must be confident in the capabilities of his/her staff to meet high expectations and organizational goals.

THE APPLICATION OF MOTIVATION THEORY: AN EXAMPLE

In the preceding section, the importance of the superintendent serving as a motivational leader was discussed. In addition, motivational tips drawn from the literature were presented. This section provides an example of the practical application of two motivational theories to the superintendency setting.

The superintendent must continually assess the personal needs of the system's administrators and teachers. In this assessment process, the work of Maslow and Herzberg (Hersey and Blanchard, 1982) can be used as a basis of operation. In Maslow, the lower order needs of security and affiliation must be satisfied before any real work can begin on raising employee productivity. This can be accomplished by the superintendent through the provision of appropriate renumeration, stability in employment, serving as a buffer with special interest groups, and practicing team management. Once these lower order (or deficit) needs are fulfilled, the needs of individuals will move to the esteem and self-actualization (growth) levels. At these levels, professionalism assumes a paramount role, and the potential for increasing employee productivity is present.

Herzberg built upon Maslow's theory. He refers to the lower order needs as hygiene factors and indicates that these factors, comprising working conditions, interpersonal relations, money, status, and security, must be satisfied before it is possible to consider raising productivity levels. The satisfaction of these factors keeps productivity from decreasing but does not increase it. In order to increase productivity, the staff must be moved to the level where their needs fall within what Herzberg refers to as the "motivators" category, which is equivalent to the esteem and self-actualization levels of Maslow. Motivators consist of such things as recognition for accomplishment, challenging work, increased responsibility, and personal growth and development. The ways in which a superintendent can address these needs are limited only by one's imagination and ability to effectively match motivators to the needs of employees.

MOTIVATIONAL PATTERNS OF PUBLIC SCHOOL SUPERINTENDENTS

One hundred fifty-six public school superintendents participated in a research study to identify superintendent motivational patterns (Jackson, 1992) by completing Form E of the Personality Research Form (Jackson, 1989). All but five subjects in this study are male. A summary of the results follows:

1. Decisions were not made on "the spur of the moment." There was a tendency to seek and study alternatives, rather than to act impulsively.
2. They were not prone to try new and different experiences. They tended to hold stable and consistent opinions and values and were likely to consider the consequences of any program change, rather than move forward impulsively.

3. Considerable effort was put forth to maximize personal safety. Taking unnecessary risks in dealing with people was avoided.

4. There was a dislike for clutter, confusion, and lack of organization.

5. There was a dislike for ambiguity.

6. They aspired to accomplish difficult tasks and were willing to put forth effort to attain excellence. They most likely served as good models for the "work ethic" and in striving for excellence.

7. They were not nearly as likely to do as many things "just for fun" as the general population. There was a tendency to be somewhat more serious than the general population.

8. There was a tendency not to break away from restraints, confinements, or restrictions of any kind.

9. There was a tendency to stick to the practical "nuts and bolts" issues. They appeared to prefer not to dwell on abstract and conceptual issues.

10. They did not utilize input from their five senses to the same degree as the general population.

11. They were definitely "take charge" people who were motivated to assume leadership and make things happen.

12. They enjoyed being with friends and people in general, made efforts to win friendships and maintain associations with people, and desired to be held in high esteem by their acquaintances.

13. There was a tendency not to be easily annoyed and not to hurt others when they got in the way. They probably accepted criticism more readily than others and were not quick to take umbrage.

14. There was a definite concern for creating a favorable impression by "putting their best foot forward."

By analyzing these motivational patterns, it is possible to construct superintendent leadership profiles in the areas of decision-making, change, and personal characteristics.

As decision-makers, the superintendents were conservative individuals who played things "close to the vest." This was evidenced by the following motivational patterns:

1. Cautious

2. Seekers and analyzers of alternatives
3. Data based
4. Stuck to "nuts and bolts" issues

The conservative nature of the superintendents in their decision-making carried over to the change agent category. This was demonstrated by motivational patterns that portray them as

1. Not likely to try new and different experiences
2. Seeking to maximize personal safety
3. Avoiders of risk taking
4. Disliking clutter, confusion, and lack of organization
5. Disliking ambiguity
6. Having a tendency not to break away from restraints, confinements, or restrictions

These superintendents were people persons. This is not surprising, because it is probably what attracted them to the educational profession in the first place. Motivational patterns supporting this profile were

1. A desire to create a favorable impression
2. A need to help others
3. A need to be held in high esteem by their peers
4. An experience of enjoyment in being with friends in particular and people in general

These individuals were also portrayed as hard workers who were more serious than the general population. The fact that they tended not to be cognizant of the information received through their five senses supports this. This could mean, on a professional level, that they are overlooking valuable decision-making information, and, on a personal level, it could mean that they just simply are not taking time to "smell the roses."

In a study conducted one year later by Genzen (1993), only the women superintendents in the same population as used by Jackson (1992) were studied. Data were collected via the Personality Research Form (Jackson, 1989) and the Leadership Practices Inventory (Kouzes and Posner, 1993). Fourteen women out of a possible twenty-eight participated in the study. In presenting the results of the study, comparisons with the Jackson study are interesting because the subjects in the Jackson study were 97 percent male. When making comparisons, the participants in the Jackson study will be referred to as the general superintendent population.

The women participants scored significantly higher on the *achieve* scale than both the standardization sample and general superintendent population. Perhaps this indicates the great drive that was needed to these few individuals to break through the "glass ceiling." In addition, the women superintendents also scored higher than the standardization sample and the general superintendent population on the *endurance* scale. They are tenacious individuals who do not quit in the face of adversity.

Both women superintendents and the general superintendent population scored significantly lower than the standardization sample on the *play* scale. This indicates that both groups of superintendents were achieving, goal-driven individuals.

The *succorance* and *autonomy* scales measure an orientation toward direction from other people. The women superintendents scored significantly lower on both scales. The low score on the *succorance* scale is particularly interesting as it contradicts the woman stereotype as dependent upon others. The women appeared to be unusually self-reliant and apparently do not readily ask for advice or assurance from others.

The *autonomous* scale provided another interesting finding, in that the women superintendents scored lower than the standardization sample but higher than the general superintendent population. This finding is contrary to much of the contemporary literature that suggests women value their ties to other people more than men do.

The women superintendents scored higher on the *exhibition* scale than the general superintendent population, and both groups scored significantly higher on the *desirability* scale than the standardization sample. This indicates that all of the superintendents want to win the attention of others, look good, and "put their best foot forward."

The *aggression* and *defendence* scales are measures of the degree and quality of interpersonal orientation. The women superintendents scored significantly lower than the standardization sample on these scales. These results are congruent with the literature, which suggests that women encourage a spirit of collaboration, rather than competition.

Both the women superintendents and the general superintendent population scored significantly lower than the standardization population on the *change* scale. This suggests that both groups are uneasy with change and more comfortable with established routine. However, the women superintendents scored lower than the general population of superintendents on the *cognitive structure* scale, which indicates that, even though they are uncomfortable with change, they can handle ambiguity and uncertainty better than the general population of superintendents.

On the *dominance* scale, the women superintendents scored higher than both the standardization sample and the general superintendent population. This suggests that they are domineering, persuasive, forceful, and attempt to control their environment. This certainly contradicts the stereotype that depicts women as yielding and deferential.

In the leadership area, the Leadership Practices Inventory developed by Kouzes and Posner (1993) was administered. This instrument has combined the ten commitments of leadership described in the "Transformational Leadership" chapter into the five leadership practices of challenging the process, inspiring a shared vision, enabling others to act, modeling the way, and encouraging the heart. The women superintendents scored significantly higher than both the "male manager" and "female manager" norming groups. This across-the-board significance is particularly noteworthy for, as has been noted in previous chapters, transformational leadership is the way school districts must be led in a future environment that is decentralized, empowered, and rapidly changing.

In summary, the superintendent decision-making and change agent leadership profiles put forth in this section tend to portray the superintendents as having a paramount concern with the day-to-day issues that must be addressed in order to keep the ship afloat and on an even keel. This may be all that can be expected of superintendents at this point in time. However, with the changes that are on the immediate horizon for education, they must make a concerted effort to alter their leadership profiles to more of a transformational approach.

Some insightful information has been presented on women superintendents. Comparisons with a general population of superintendents (97 percent male) yielded some interesting differences, and several findings clearly were not congruent with prevailing women stereotypes and literature.

As superintendents learn more about transformational leadership strategies and see the need to adopt them, they probably will become more effective and, as a result, feel a greater sense of satisfaction with their position. It is very difficult to retain a sense of helping others when one is operating in a day-to-day survival mode.

CONCLUDING COMMENTS

Motivating others to work toward the accomplishment of organizational goals is the essence of leadership. It is interesting that motivational theories are rather straightforward and easy to apply but are often ignored by leaders. Hopefully, this chapter has made a case for the importance of motivation in the superintendency and given some insights into on-the-job applications of motivational theory and contemporary superintendent motivational profiles.

REFERENCES

Benzinger, T. L. (1988). The relationship of school board members' common perception of ideal superintendent leadership behavior to their present superintendent's work motivation. Doctoral dissertation, University of Wisconsin–Madison, 1987, *Dissertation Abstracts International, A 49/03,* 386.

Buck, J. T. (March, 1990). Transformational leadership behaviors of exemplary Texas superintendents. Doctoral dissertation, University of Texas at Austin, 1989, *Dissertation Abstracts International, A 50/09,* 2716.

Duttweiler, P. C. (1986). Educational excellence and motivating teachers. *The Clearing House, 59,* 371–374.

Genzen, H. (1993). A study of the leadership style, motivation, and job satisfaction of women public school superintendents in Ohio. Unpublished doctoral dissertation, Kent State University.

Hersey, P. and Blanchard, K. (1982). *Management of Organizational Behavior.* Englewood Cliffs, NJ: Prentice-Hall, Inc.

Hoy, W. K. and Miskel, C. G. (1987). *Educational Administration: Theory Research and Practice.* New York, NY: Random House.

Jackson, D. (1989). *Personality Research Form Manual.* Port Huron, MI: Sigma Assessment Systems.

Jackson, R. F. (1992). An investigation: The relation of motivation to job satisfaction in Ohio public school superintendents. Doctoral dissertation, Kent State University, 1992, *Dissertation Abstracts International, 53,* 1343A.

Jensen, B. A. (1994). Job satisfaction of public school superintendents in the United States. Doctoral dissertation, University of South Dakota, 1993, *Dissertation Abstracts International, 54/08,* 2826.

Kouzes, J. and Posner, B. (1993). *Leadership Practices Inventory—Self.* San Diego, CA: Pfeiffer.

Kouzes, J. and Posner, B. (1987). *The Leadership Challenge.* San Francisco, CA: Jossey-Bass.

Marks, N. D. (1990). The influence of leader values and behavior on follower values and behavior. Doctoral dissertation, Texas A & M University, 1989, *Dissertation Abstracts International, 50/12,* 3825.

Miskel, C. G. (1982). Motivation in educational organizations. *Educational Administration Quarterly, 18*(3), 65–88.

National Commission on Excellence in Education. (1983). *A Nation at Risk: The Imperative for Educational Reform.* Washington, D.C.: National Commission on Excellence in Education.

Orr, D. R. (1991). An expectancy theory investigation of school superintendent job performance. Doctoral dissertation, University of Texas at Austin, 1990, *Dissertation Abstracts International, 52/02,* 45.

Pastor, M. C. and Erlandson, D. A. (1982). A study of higher order need strength and job satisfaction in secondary school teachers. *The Journal of Educational Administration, 18*(2), 172–183.

CHAPTER 10

The Superintendent as Empowerer

Empowerment is the vehicle through which transformational leadership is achieved. It is the key by which a superintendent is able to create and maintain a strong and consistent desire for excellence within his/her system. Thus, the role of the superintendent in empowering others is the focus of this chapter.

The chapter is divided into three sections. The first section provides a definition of empowerment and explores the relationship between empowerment and leadership—the what of the superintendent and empowerment. The second section examines the groups to be empowered—the who of the superintendent and empowerment. The final section focuses on empowerment skills and practices—the how of the superintendent and empowerment.

EMPOWERMENT DEFINITION AND LEADERSHIP
(the *what* of empowerment)

Definition

The word *empower* means *to give power*. Power can be understood as a coercive force or the imposition of ideas or authority. In this context, it becomes synonymous with control and dominance. This is a legitimate understanding of power, but it is not the meaning of empowerment.

Dr. Calareso contributed to this chapter and is an assistant professor at College of St. Rose in Albany, New York. He also has served as the superintendent of schools in the Diocese of Green Bay, WI.

Empowerment is *power sharing*. As such, it encourages people "to be involved in decision making . . . engenders increased commitment . . . self-respect . . . and satisfaction . . ." (Stimson and Appelbaum, 1988, p. 314). Empowerment is leadership that provides autonomy, responsibility, and freedom. It creates the environment for commitment, dedication, and the realistic accomplishment of mutually understood and accepted goals. It allows for a common vision, shared values, and mutual respect.

In the educational arena, empowerment is "a deliberate effort to provide . . . the room, right, responsibility, and resources to make sensible decisions and informed professional judgments" (Sergiovanni, 1989a, p. 5). Lest this be confused with a directionless free-for-all, empowerment in education includes acceptance of "responsibility to achieve," along with "responsibility to decide" (p. 6). Goals, objectives, and standards do exist. With empowered leadership, however, the commitment and direction are commonly developed and shared with mutual accountability.

Furthermore, the understanding of empowerment must always balance rights and duty (Bloom, 1987). With every right given to an educational leader (principal, teacher, board member, parent, etc.), there exists a clear and corresponding duty. The decisions made and actions taken must reflect what is right and good for the students and their educational experience.

Power sharing by superintendents is "power investment" (Sergiovanni, 1989b, p. 220). Leadership by empowerment brings more power back to the superintendent; however, this increased power is not a domination of people and resources. Rather, it is measured by growth, success, and accomplishments of the educational system. Increased power is reflected by efficiency, efficacy, and creativity. "Empowered individuals feel alive . . . and become part of a community with a common purpose" (Lagana, 1989). Perhaps most importantly, students learn, achieve, and develop to their full potential.

Leadership

Leadership is a process that brings about the accomplishment of goals. The methodologies of leadership are influence, authority, and/or power.

Leadership is critical to excellence. What is most important, however, is the style or philosophy of leadership that permeates the superintendent's actions.

Burns' (1978) definition of leadership as an act that induces "followers to act for certain goals that represent the values . . . of both leaders and followers" (p. 19) provides a basis for understanding of the superintendent as leader. Transformative leadership unites the superintendent with the principals, board, and others through a common goal and level of commitment that "raises one another to higher levels of motivation and morality" (p. 20). It is this understanding of leadership that is called empowerment, and the most efficacious leadership style for the superintendent is leadership by empowerment.

EMPOWERED GROUPS (the *who* of empowerment)

It is necessary to understand the scope of the superintendent's empowering relationships. Although time and attention devoted to one empowered group may be disproportionate to that devoted to others, the effectiveness of the school system depends on the empowerment of all the partners in the educational endeavor. An image that helps represent this shared responsibility and relationship is the wheel. The superintendent is the hub with the "spokes" of empowerment connected to each group involved in the system. Carrying the analogy one step further, an efficient vehicle depends on the proper functioning of every wheel. The superintendent leads through empowerment that drives the system to reach its goals. The superintendent provides the power to empower.

Board of Education

The district's board ideally provides the vision and leadership for the system. Through its development of policies and guidelines, the adoption of a budget, and its public expression of the quality of education, the board influences the limits and perception of the endeavor. An effective board is an empowered board.

The superintendent assists in setting the board's agenda, recommends policy and leadership actions, and facilitates the implementation and evaluation of policy (Ziegler, Kehoe, and Reilsman, 1985). The superintendent empowers the board to enable effective vision and leadership to develop and flourish.

Central Office Personnel

While numbers, titles, and position descriptions may vary, central office personnel constitute the superintendent's leadership team. They often represent the superintendent to the schools and community. They play a critical role in the support, resourcing, and implementation of the system's goals and programs. To the degree that these personnel are empowered to achieve the goals of the system, the superintendent and educational community are well served.

School Principals and Staff

The efficiency of empowerment is very dependent on the superintendent's direct relationship with school principals and indirectly with teachers, aides, and staff. Although a system should strive for common goals and values, the place of education is the school. It is the school that has the greatest potential to be effective and excellent.

Excellent schools are led by excellent principals. Excellent principals are leaders by empowerment, and it is the superintendent who empowers the principals.

The school principal then must empower his/her staff because these individuals articulate the vision and mission into a dynamic curriculum.

Teachers' Union

While many participate in the negotiation of collective bargaining agreements, it is through this relationship with the teachers' union that the superintendent directly *leads* the teachers. The superintendent has the opportunity to empower the teachers and their representatives through open and equitable negotiations and dialogue.

Parents and Community

Empowerment of parents and the community at large is more than public relations; it is a call to participation. Parents are the primary educators of their children. The community is the primary supporter of the system and the ultimate beneficiary of its efficacy. While schools have received recent criticism from the public (Carnegie

Report, Gallup Poll, etc.), there is also a renewed recognition of the necessary partnership between the community and the school.

Superintendents play a significant role in empowering school leaders to actively initiate parent/community programs and efforts. Superintendents must also empower the community to realize its critical role in the educational system. Parents/community are an equally important wheel as the educational system moves toward the accomplishment of its goals. The superintendent is the agent of empowerment, and, through empowering leadership, the partnership is created, strengthened, and nurtured.

EMPOWERMENT SKILLS AND PRACTICES
(the *how* of empowerment)

In his book, *Thriving on Chaos*, Peters (1987) frequently makes reference to the following axiom—there are no limits to the ability to contribute on the part of a properly selected, well-trained, appropriately supported, and, above all, committed person. Empowered school personnel (principals, teachers, board members, central office staff, parents, citizens) have unlimited potential to positively affect the quality of education. The effective superintendent must devote the time and energy necessary to develop the skills and practices of empowerment. Each is integral to the transforming style of leadership that leads to commitment and dedication of the educational partners. A discussion of required skills and practices follows.

Recruitment and Selection

The previous axiom makes reference to proper selection. It should not be presumed that empowerment is of itself a guarantee of excellence. The people with whom the superintendent interacts must be competent, professional, open, and creative: they must be people who are energized by freedom, responsibility, and participation and must be people who believe in leadership by empowerment.

The superintendent has significant responsibility for his/her staff, school principals, and teachers. Attention must be taken to build a team of capable educators. This may require some difficult personnel decisions and changes. The superintendent has far less input regarding board members and the community; however, it is important to carefully seek out and involve those individuals with the greatest ability to contribute to the team effort.

Vision and Goals

The articulation of a vision and goals may be the cornerstone of empowerment for the superintendent and the entire educational community. A vision is a statement of belief. It is a core statement of philosophy and values. Goals are specific objectives necessary to embody the vision. They are tangible actions that, if enacted, will lead to a real feeling of accomplishment and fulfillment.

The need for vision and goals must be understood in terms of the empowering superintendent and the empowered educational partners. The effective superintendent must "develop and live an enabling and empowering vision" (Peters, 1987, p. 283). Clarity of educational vision and frequent articulation of goals create the atmosphere for growth and development.

However, the vision and goals must be owned by everyone. Therefore, while the superintendent must articulate his/her values and philosophy, there must be room for adaptation and change. There must also be a process of interaction leading to a mutually acceptable and shared vision and goals. At this point, everyone becomes empowered to proclaim the vision boldly and loudly.

Finally, this vision and these goals can then become the criteria for evaluation and the substance of celebration. The reality of the vision in the lives of students and the educational community and the successful accomplishment of the educational goals will be both the sign and the experience of an empowered educational system.

Communication

The ability to communicate one's vision and goals is only a single dimension of the communications area. It is certainly necessary for the effective superintendent to be able to speak clearly, convincingly, and constantly on behalf of the educational mission. Communications has, however, two other dimensions in addition to output.

Empowerment also requires the ability to listen (input). The superintendent must not only be able to listen, but also able to create both the atmosphere and opportunities for listening to take place. Empowered people believe in and experience openness and attentiveness from their peers and leaders. Their ideas and feelings must not only be heard but acted upon. The superintendent must be available to the educational community in situations that encourage the exchange of ideas and emotions.

The third dimension of communications is networking or facilitation. As depicted earlier, the superintendent is the hub of the wheel. S/he must connect the various dimensions of the educational system to ensure a cohesive and cooperative effort.

Some would assert that there is a serious problem in the loosely coupled structure of school systems. While local schools make responsible decisions (a goal of empowerment), they often lack the connection with other dimensions of the system necessary to make the decisions effective. The necessary facilitation or networking is the responsibility of the superintendent. S/he is the link between the schools, the board, the community, etc.

Training and Resources

Empowered people need the ongoing opportunity to learn, to develop their skills, and to grow. More importantly, an effect of empowerment will be the desire for training. It will be a manifestation of the commitment of the system and a response to the freedom and responsibility. Training opportunities must be frequent, high quality, and pertinent to the vision and goals.

The need for resources speaks to the availability of materials and personnel (human resources) necessary to successfully achieve the goals. It also refers to compensation and rewards that motivate, affirm, and recognize commitment and excellence.

Delegation

Implicit in the philosophy of empowerment is the enablement of others and the provision of freedom and responsibility. Individual schools and educational groups must be freed to make their own decisions and to implement the common goals. Decentralization of authority must be real. Delegation by the superintendent will create trust, respect, and confidence and will also help develop effective leadership skills at the local level.

Each dimension of the educational system must fully experience its unique role and responsibility. While accountability always remains, freedom and autonomy are integral to real empowerment. Again, the image is the wheel. The superintendent is not at the top of a hierarchical structure; rather, s/he is at the center of a system that moves cooperatively toward the common goal of excellence.

Atmosphere and Environment

Implicit in many of the empowerment skills and practices is the atmosphere of freedom and responsibility. The superintendent must create an environment that encourages and nurtures cooperation, commitment, and creativity. Members of the school community must work together. Empowerment must breed commitment and dedication to the vision and goals. There must be active participation and a sense of ownership. This is the necessary *culture* of the effective school system.

Presence and Example

Finally, the superintendent can only empower others if s/he also is an empowered leader. The superintendent must lead by example. An effective superintendent practices what s/he promotes. Each day, the superintendent must be about the business of empowering and must present the image of an empowered leader.

Though perhaps a radical concept, the empowering superintendent might be a more effective leader without an office. His/her office should be the classrooms and corridors of the schools, the homes and meeting places of the community, the board room, and the playgrounds. After all, it is the people who are empowered. The superintendent must be visible to and interact with the people of the educational system and in doing so must constantly exercise his/her empowering power.

SUMMARY

Emowerment is transformational leadership in action. It is power sharing. It provides freedom, responsibility, and opportunity to fully participate in the vision and goals of the system. It enables those empowered to experience personal fulfillment, and, most importantly, it leads to excellence in education.

In a school system, the superintendent is the key empowering agent. S/he relates to the central office staff, principals, teachers, board members, and the community at large. S/he serves as the hub of the educational wheel, connecting the educational partners with the spokes of empowerment.

The empowering superintendent believes in the limitless potential of the people in the system. S/he empowers them to reach their potential and make their greatest contributions.

The superintendent carefully recruits and selects personnel who are competent, professional, open, and creative—people who are energized by his/her empowering leadership. The superintendent articulates a clear vision and goals. Empowering leadership allows all participants to own and celebrate this common vision and goals.

Critical empowering skills also include communications (speaking, listening, and networking), training and resources, delegation, and the creation of an atmosphere that encourages and nurtures cooperation, commitment, creativity, and risk taking. Empowerment directs all energy toward excellence.

The superintendent is the empowering leader and the empowered model. His/her presence and example witness to the reality that empowerment is not a strategy but a philosophy—a way of life. The superintendent has the power to empower, and the system has to empower to achieve excellence.

REFERENCES

Bloom, A. (1987). *The Closing of the American Mind*. New York, NY: Simon & Schuster.

Burns, J. M. (1978). *Leadership*. New York, NY: Harper & Row.

Gallup, A. M. and Clark, D. L. (1987). The 19th annual Gallup poll of the public's attitude toward the public schools. *Phi Delta Kappan, 68*(1), 17–30.

Lagana, J. F. (1989). Ready, set, empower! Superintendents can sow the seeds for growth. *The School Administrator, 46*(1), 20–22.

Peters, T. (1987). *Thriving on Chaos: Handbook for a Management Revolution*. New York, NY: Alfred Knopf.

Sergiovanni, T. J. (1989a). What really counts in improving schools? In Thomas J. Sergiovanni and John H. Moore (Eds.), *Schooling for Tomorrow: Directing Reforms to Issues That Count*. Boston, MA: Allyn & Bacon.

Sergiovanni, T. J. (1989b). The leadership needed for a quality school. In Thomas J. Sergiovanni and John H. Moore (Eds.), *Schooling for Tomorrow: Directing Reforms to Issues That Count*. Boston, MA: Allyn & Bacon.

Stimson, T. D. and Appelbaum, R. P. (1988). Empowering teachers: Do principals have the power? *Phi Delta Kappan, 69*(4), 313–316.

Task Force on Teaching as a Profession. (1987). *A Nation Prepared: Teachers for the 21st Century*. Washington, D.C.: Carnegie Foundation.

Zeigler, H., Kehoe, E. and Reilsman, J. (1985). *City Managers and School Superintendents*. New York, NY: Praeger.

CHAPTER 11

The Superintendent as Communicator

Communication is involved in more than 90 percent of a superintendent's work time and is used while on the phone, at meetings and appointments, while writing letters and reports, etc. Using his appointment book as the source, one superintendent analyzed his work for each of five years and found that, annually, he was involved in approximately 375 meetings and appointments. Communication was involved in all of these engagements. Thus, the superintendent as a communicator is a very important skill area.

As Kindred, Bagin, and Gallagher (1984) note, "Communication is a cooperative enterprise requiring the mutual interchange of ideas and information, and out of which understanding develops and action is taken" (p. 78). Thus, listening is also a part of communication.

In order to communicate effectively, a superintendent needs to know what, how, and with whom to communicate. This chapter is organized around these questions.

WHAT DOES THE SUPERINTENDENT COMMUNICATE?

The subject of the communication is dependent upon the need and the group. Because many systems employ hundreds and sometimes thousands of individuals who work with hundreds or thousands of students who come from a community of hundreds or thousands, communication is the link that holds the system together and keeps it moving. Those involved in the school system, as well as those in the community, must be kept abreast of the system's operation, including its plans, programs, personnel, etc. In addition, those within the system need to know about wages, benefits, and working conditions, and they also need to learn something about each other, especially if the system is large. Those in the community need to know about the goals, programs, services, and needs of the school system.

The linchpin of the communication function is the superintendent. Thus, it is the responsibility of the superintendent and staff to identify the communication needs of the various groups. This is done both by discussion and listening. After the needs are identified, the means to meet them and the persons to do so must be determined.

HOW DOES THE SUPERINTENDENT COMMUNICATE?

Verbal Communication

The superintendent communicates verbally in both oral and written form. Oral communication is done both formally and informally. Formally, the superintendent is often a presenter and, at times, the featured speaker at meetings, conferences, banquets, graduations, etc., in addition to often being asked "to make a few remarks" at different occasions. Informally, business is transacted on the phone and through casual conversation.

On those occasions when the superintendent is asked in advance to make a presentation, time is needed for preparation. This preparation often means doing some reading of current literature and making notes. It also means organizing the presentation, which involves developing an outline that presents the topic in a logical fashion. Writing, editing, and rewriting follow. It is helpful to have another individual, e.g., staff member, read and provide reaction to the concepts, presentation of the concepts, and format. The investment of time and energy in this effort says to the group to whom the presentation is delivered, "This subject is important, and you are important."

Even when the superintendent is asked to make a few remarks, it is important to make notes so that what is said is coherent and has some meaning. Beware of off-the-cuff remarks. They often become a trap that ensnares the superintendent. Think before speaking.

When making presentations, one might consider telling a story. Storytelling is increasing in use and was recommended earlier as one means of shaping organizational values. It can be used as a teaching tool, a vehicle to transmit the culture of the system, to illustrate a point, to provide an important segment of the system's history, or to reinforce values held as important to the system. Thus, in preparing a presentation, one might look for an opportunity to use a story for a specific purpose. If one is not accustomed to storytelling, s/he could take some time to learn the technique. In selecting a story, consider its purpose and, if appropriate, its adaptability to one's use. Once a story has been found, adapted, or developed, learn it so that it can be told with the right tone and inflections. Practice it! Make it your own. Over time, the superintendent could identify and learn several stories to illustrate points or convey aspects of the system. Used well, they can be attention getters and point makers.

The telephone is another important communication tool for the superintendent. The superintendent calls and is called by board members, staff, administrators, parents, business and community leaders, and many others. Much business is conducted via the telephone. Thus, one's choice of words and tone of voice, as well as the content, are critical for phone communication.

A suggestion regarding placing calls offered by a telephone company inservice person bears some consideration. It was suggested that one should place one's own calls, rather than place calls through a secretary. In this context, if the superintendent does the calling, it says to the person receiving the call, "You are important"; on the other hand, if the superintendent's secretary places the call and the superintendent gets on the line after the individual has been reached, that says to the person called, "I am more important than you, and my time is more valuable than yours." For the most part, people feel honored when receiving a call from the superintendent, especially when it's a direct call.

Another communication tool is the computer, particularly the personal computer equipped with a modem. This piece of hardware allows one to, via a telephone line, log onto a network and communicate throughout the network, between systems, across the state and nation, and around the world. Software programs are available to assist the superintendent in word processing, graphics, accounting, etc. Computer literacy is an important communication skill for today's superintendent.

Written communication is also a significant part of a superintendent's work time. There are letters to be written to a myriad of people, including administrators, teachers, parents, state agencies, community organizations, reports and proposals to the board, and newsletters to internal and external groups.

In order to meet the numerous written communication demands, a superintendent must have developed good writing skills. A poorly written communication, such as a letter, immediately creates an image of the superintendent as a less than professionally competent individual. Written communications must be thought out, organized, and clearly written. Sentences should be short and to the point and not compounded with several subordinate clauses. The vocabulary used should be understandable by the reader and should not include a lot of educational jargon. Finally, the communication should be neatly prepared. Computers and word processing software programs have made the preparation of written communication much easier.

Nonverbal Communication

The superintendent communicates nonverbally through body language and appearance; the positions one takes sitting and standing can convey attentiveness, laziness, or lack of concern. For example, sitting slouched in a chair with one's feet extended and crossed can be read as, "This is going too long. I'd better get comfortable." Facial expressions can be even more a display of one's attitude or feeling; a frown expresses displeasure, a smile acceptance. Eyes focused on the subject (person or action) indicate attentiveness, whereas eyes looking into the distance are often indicative of a lack of attention or concern or preoccupation with another topic.

Appearance is another form of communication. The superintendent should be dressed neatly and appropriately for the occasion. Neatness and appropriateness does not mean designer fashions. Grooming is equally important. Personal care conveys a message as well.

The superintendent's nonverbal communication, be it body language or appearance, should convey to those with whom contact is made that "this position is important and you are important." The superintendent, like it or not, is a model for others in the system.

WITH WHOM DOES THE SUPERINTENDENT COMMUNICATE?

In order to answer this question, it is necessary to understand the term *public* because the superintendent serves many publics and must communicate with them. The concept of public comes from the area of marketing and is defined as "a distinct group of people and/or organizations that have an actual or a potential interest and/or impact on an organization" (Kotler, 1975, p. 17). For our purposes, publics are classified as internal and external. Internal publics are those individuals who work for the organization, and external publics are those individuals outside the organization who have an interest in or impact on the organization.

Internal Publics

Internally, the superintendent communicates almost daily with the following groups:

1. Board of education, which is the legally constituted policy-making body of the system
2. Central office staff, which is or includes the system's top management team
3. School administrators who are the superintendent's links to and leaders of the system's schools
4. Teachers who are the front line staff in the teaching/learning process
5. Support staff who make the system function by their work as secretaries, custodians, janitors, food service personnel, classroom aides, etc.
6. Students who are the focus of the teaching/learning process

Special interest groups require a few added comments. Today, superintendents and boards are finding themselves confronted by "interest-group politics" (Crowson, 1992, p. 64). This is particularly true at the local level when several associations bind together into coalitions for the purpose of promoting or opposing issues, often single issues. Taxpayer groups from several districts in the area may coalesce around the issue of lowering the property tax or limiting its increase. Religious groups may gather together to prevent the introduction of, or to remove a particular family life or sex education program. The teacher association and athletic boosters may unite in an effort to oppose a change in or reduction of the extracurricular program. When such coalitions form, superintendents and boards may be "played off" against each other and, thus, will need to keep each other informed as to the status of an issue.

Crowson (1992) offers two perspectives for addressing school-community relations and politics. In the first, there is a distinction made between "the political environment and institution [system] recipient" (p. 91). From this perspective, he suggests the following questions for consideration (p. 83):

1. How do educators decode the political messages directed toward the schools?
2. How do the political messages become translated (converted) into educational policies and procedures?
3. How are the internal organizational structures of the public schools influenced by the external political environment?

In the second, "Both institution and environment are members of a single political community, more bound together by shared beliefs and common sentiments than separated by competing interests and powers in conflict" (p. 91). For this perspective, he offers these questions (p. 92):

1. How do educators perceive the political influences of the public schools on the community?
2. How do the internal organizational structures of the public schools influence the external political environment?

Thus, the system's core values are critical in addressing interest-group politics.

The superintendent communicates with these publics via many vehicles, such as newsletters, advisory committees, memoranda, and meetings, and for many reasons, such as recognition of accomplishments, involvement in planning, improvement of working conditions, and orientation.

The formal communication with internal publics should be planned, and such a plan should include the following:

1. The public to whom the communication is directed, e.g., administrators, teachers, or students
2. The information to be communicated, e.g., curricular program change, staffing changes or assignments, or new or pending legislation
3. The method of communication, e.g., newsletter, memo, letter, radio, or television
4. The communicator, e.g., superintendent, board president, principal, or community relations director

5. The timing of the communication and, if it is an ongoing communication such as a newsletter, the frequency

External Publics

Among those groups with whom the superintendent communicates outside the school organization are the following:

1. Parents who share their children with schools and are the coeducators of their children (The vehicle through which the superintendent often communicates is the Parent/Teacher or Home and School Association)
2. Governmental bodies such as the city or common council, the health department, fire and safety, public works, etc.
3. Civic organizations such as Rotary or Kiwanis who frequently have an interest in education and the community
4. Religious organizations that include churches, groups, clergy, etc.
5. Special interest groups who attempt to influence the school policy or organization
6. Advisory committees that are formed to address specific issues or concerns

The communication with external publics should also be planned, and the plan components are the same as those listed earlier for internal publics.

Finally, there is also another group, which sometimes has been labeled the *crazies*. These are individuals who are the self-appointed superintendents and system critics and evaluators. They are often frequent letter writers or phone callers to the superintendent, the media, or anyone who will read or listen. Also, they are usually single-issue people. Everything that happens has (or so they believe) some relevance to their issue. The superintendent must deal with these individuals. It's important to be courteous and helpful while, at the same time, being firm and conclusive.

SUMMARY

Thus, as can be seen, the superintendent is a frequent, if not constant, communicator and must develop effective communication skills. S/he must know what is to be communicated, with whom to communicate, and how to communicate. The superintendent's image is often judged on the basis of the type and quality of her/his communication.

REFERENCES

Crowson, R. L. (1992). *School-Community Relations, Under Reform.* Berkeley, CA: McCutchan Publishing Corporation.

Kindred, L. W., Bagin, D., and Gallagher, D. R. (1984). *The School and Community Relations* (3rd edition). Englewood Cliffs, NJ: Prentice-Hall.

Kotler, P. (1975). *Marketing for Nonprofit Organizations.* Englewood Cliffs, NJ: Prentice-Hall.

Superintendent Leadership Competencies: Professional (The Superintendent as . . .)

CHAPTER 12

The Superintendent as the Board's Chief Executive Officer

Successful superintendents must never forget that they are employees of the board of education. As such, the board of education is the boss.

The neglect of the simple truism stated above probably has been responsible for more superintendents losing their jobs than any other single cause. When a superintendent begins to think that, because one has spent a number of years in preparation for the superintendency and, thus, is eminently more qualified to determine the fate of the school district than a small group of noneducators, the road becomes steep and usually ends abruptly. When one begins to view the system as one's personal possession, the beginning of the end has begun.

If any complex organization is going to be effective in setting and achieving meaningful goals, the board of directors and the chief executive officer (CEO) must work well together. The board collectively and board members individually must have trust and confidence in the CEO. When this board/CEO relationship sours and when trust and confidence wane, the CEO is soon looking for another job.

Mr. Craig Gifford and Mr. Thomas Dickson provided the basic material for the section on "Board Expectations of the Superintendent." Mr. Gifford recently retired as executive vice president of the Ohio School Boards Association and served on a city board of education for eight years. He also has had experiences as a central office administrator in an urban system and a newspaper editor. Mr. Dickson recently retired as Director of Educational Services for the Ohio School Boards Association. He formerly was a superintendent for many years.

Mr. Darryl Graves provided material for the "Communicating with the Board" and "Board Meeting Procedures" sections. He is a superintendent.

Mr. Conrad Ott provided the basic information for the entire section on "Working with the Board of Education." He served as superintendent of the Akron, Ohio, City Schools for twenty-five years and currently is a board member.

The effectiveness one will experience as the top educational leader in the school system, the job satisfaction one will derive, and, in the final analysis, one's longevity in the superintendency will be determined by the extent to which one is able to build and maintain a strong relationship with the board of education. Therefore, this chapter on the superintendent as the chief executive officer of the board presents and discusses information that is extremely important to the professional well-being of anyone sitting in or aspiring to sit in the superintendent's chair.

In order to build a strong relationship with the board, one must know what the board expects of its superintendent. While there will be some variation between and among individual boards, certain common expectations of the superintendent can be identified that are shared by most board members.

The next section of this chapter identifies and discusses some commonly accepted board expectations of the superintendent and is followed by some insights into things superintendents can do to help develop and maintain strong relationships with their boards.

BOARD EXPECTATIONS OF THE SUPERINTENDENT

Personal Traits

No board will employ a superintendent unless s/he is perceived as an individual who has integrity and courage and is honest, fair, and open. Gaining a reputation as one who possesses these traits is accomplished over a number of years and constitutes an important part of one's value system. These attributes are not something one brings to the office and then discards on weekends. As a person's career progresses, a track record is continually being molded, and, by the time an individual is ready to assume a superintendency, his/her record has become quite well known in the profession. A single major faux pas in any of these areas can do major damage to a reputation that has taken years to build.

A board wants an individual who is able to keep one's ego under control. An ego running wild can create an individual who must always win. Every confrontation becomes personal and very competitive in nature. Winning becomes the primary goal as opposed to a resolution that is in the best interests of the students and school system. An overly egotistical individual cannot admit errors in judgment. The personal pronouns *I* and *my* are much used. The superintendent by her/his own admission is the root of all good things that occur within the school system, and s/he begins to refer to the employees as her/his employees and the school system as her/his system.

Superintendents can easily fall into the ego trap. Constantly being the center of attention can be heady business. Before long, instead of just taking the job seriously, the individual is also taking himself/herself seriously. Beware of the lurking ego trap, because superintendents who get caught in its web tend to disappear due to terminal pomposity.

A board wants a superintendent who will be the chief executive officer in fact as well as name. This means being strong in a crisis. It means keeping one's cool when others are losing theirs. It means resolving conflicts in a positive and constructive manner. It means a person who is positive and optimistic. One could go on with other examples. Suffice it to say that being the chief executive officer in fact, as well as name, means rising above the crowd and assuming a dynamic and positive leadership role.

Last but not least, a board wants a communicator. The board members especially want someone who will communicate with them, promote a positive image of the district, interpret the needs of the district to the public, and maintain positive relationships with the media. This important area is expanded upon in the chapter on the superintendent as communicator.

Roles and Relationships with the Board

The superintendent must work openly and cooperatively with the board in delineating the roles and responsibilities of each. The traditional policy/administration dichotomy provides a good starting point; however, in practice, this dichotomy is present only in the most general sense.

Mission statement development

The superintendent must work with the board, as well as with the other participants in the educational process, in developing a mission statement for the system that is acceptable to the board. This is a very important and difficult task for the superintendent because a mission statement that only the superintendent and board believe in will not get the job done. Thus, the superintendent is a catalyst, broker, and negotiator who provides general leadership and oversight in the development of a mission statement that is acceptable to all constituencies.

Vision statement

The vision statement for the school system emanates from the mission statement. An explanation of the crucial roles the superintendent and board members play in developing a vision is discussed in the next chapter on strategic planning.

Policy development

Once a mission and vision statements have been adopted, the superintendent must help the board develop general policy statements that will give the superintendent guidance in their implementation. During this whole process, the superintendent and board must work as a team with the usual give-and-take which takes place on an effective policy-setting team. When the team concept, or equilibrium factor, gets out of balance one way or the other, the board/superintendent relationship is in trouble. While some superintendents let their boards struggle by giving them very little guidance, a greater tendency is for the superintendent to assume too much of the board's responsibility. Appropriate board/superintendent equilibrium is very delicate and must be constantly discussed and monitored.

The reality of the superintendent/school board relationship is that both exert leadership and control in performing their respective roles. Leadership and control are not the domain of either party exclusively but, rather, are situation specific. That is, more often than not, the party exercising leadership and control is determined by the situation that is being addressed and the manner in which it is being addressed. Therefore, the key is not to designate leaders and followers on a permanent basis but, rather, to reach agreement on who has the primary responsibility for carrying the ball in a given situation. Moreover, in resolving a complex issue, the ball carrier may change several times during the resolution process.

Not only may the ball carrier change, but new ball carriers with different policy directions may arrive on the playing field. Weninger and

Stout (1989) did a historical study (1896–1986) of system governance in the Scottsdale, Arizona, School District. They tested the dissatisfaction theory of democracy using Iannaccone's (1983) TPEP (turning point elections period) process. This process has five stages (p. 162):

1. Changes in the underlying demographics of a community leading to rising voter discontent
2. A triggering election and subsequent elections in which a new school board majority assumes leadership
3. Realignment of the policy system, which may include the employment of a new superintendent
4. Articulation of a new policy mandate
5. A final test election, in which the new majority is returned to power

The results of their study indicated that (p. 170):

1. During a TPEP period, it was highly likely that incumbent board members would be defeated.
2. An indicator of voter discontent was the level of voter approval of bond and tax override elections.
3. The rate of involuntary superintendent turnover increased.
4. An important indicator of the struggle by an emerging majority to impose a new political mandate is the level of acrimonious debate among school board members.
5. All of this political and administrative turmoil produces a significant change in policy.

Informed board members

Board members want to be kept informed. If something of significance has occurred within the system, they need to hear about it from the superintendent first, not from one of their constituents or via a phone call from a reporter or, in the worst case scenario, read about it in the paper or see it on the evening news. In some instances, the superintendent calls each board member personally. In others, a member of the staff calls, or the superintendent calls the board chair who, in turn, contacts the other board members.

A number of superintendents send a written communication to their board members each week, apprising them of recent and upcoming items of interest within the school system. These communiques can often be used to get board members thinking about issues that the superintendent will be bringing before them two or three months down the road.

Board meeting agendas are a very important means of communication with the board. The agenda should be thorough, nicely organized, and accompanied by appropriate supporting material. All board members should be asked for items they wish to have included on the agenda, and, in most instances, the superintendent and board chair will cooperatively develop the agenda. The entire packet (agenda and supporting materials) should be delivered to the board members with enough lead time prior to the board meeting so that they will have adequate time to study the materials and contact the superintendent if they have any concerns or questions. Board members should be informed of anything that will be discussed at the meeting. They should never be surprised by the superintendent. Likewise, the superintendent should never be surprised by the board.

On occasion, an individual board member will call the superintendent to inquire about a situation that has come to his/her attention or to request information of some nature. In these instances, the superintendent obviously should be as cooperative and helpful as possible; however, the job may not be complete when the inquiring board member has been satisfied. It is important that all board members have access to the same information and that they all be treated as equals. Thus, it very well may be necessary to inform the other board members of the information provided to one or several board members.

Implementing and supporting board policies

The superintendent is expected to enthusiastically implement and support board-adopted policies in an equitable manner. This goes even for those policies in which the superintendent may not be in total agreement. In doing this, one may, on occasion, have to protect, defend, and/or speak up on behalf of the board. Under no circumstances should the superintendent indicate that something is being done only because the board asked or mandated that it be done. At times, the superintendent must stoically take some "heat" over board policies. Openly disagreeing with them is not an option. If the superintendent cannot ethically or educationally support a policy or directive of the board and is not able to work with the board to arrive at a mutually acceptable resolution, then resignation is the appropriate alternative.

Collective bargaining participation

Collective bargaining is a very important part of the superintendent/board relationship. The board, with input and leadership from the superintendent, must determine its bargaining priorities. The board must give guidance to its negotiating team by making decisions on such things as: Where can compromises be made? What are the top figures for increases in salaries and fringe benefits? What items are worth taking a strike over? The superintendent, in addition to providing accurate information to the board on these matters, must also take a leadership role in keeping things in perspective. For instance, it sometimes is easy for a board member to sit in executive session and indicate that "they can walk before we'll give in on that one." In a situation like this, the superintendent must make sure that the board member(s) really understands all the ramifications of a strike.

It is important that the superintendent, as the leader of the board's negotiating team, be given some latitude in making decisions at the table; however, it is equally important that the board be kept continuously informed of the progress in negotiations. The members need to know what the priorities of the union are, items where agreement has been reached, items that are proving troublesome, etc. They must have a "feel" of how negotiations are proceeding. As the give-and-take of negotiations continues over a period of time, it may be necessary for the superintendent to recommend that the board reconsider some of its previously established negotiating priorities. It will be easier for the board members to understand and accept such a recommendation from the superintendent if they have a sense of the negotiating dynamics that have transpired.

Budget development

The board should be allowed and encouraged to actively participate in budget development. The budget document is the vehicle by which the board's priorities are funded; it speaks to what the board really believes is important. The board should be given help by the superintendent in understanding the importance of the budgeting process and the implications that budgetary decisions have for the school system. Once the budget has been adopted by the board, the superintendent should be allowed to administer it as long as s/he operates within accepted legal and ethical parameters. The board should be kept apprised of expenditures and encumbrances through appropriate monthly reports and explanations.

Responding to board requests

On occasion, the board will direct the superintendent to do something on its behalf. As long as the request is not illegal or immoral, the superintendent is expected to do as any good employee would do, which is to carry out the board's directive to the best of one's abilities. Hopefully, the number of board directives issued without reaching prior agreement with the superintendent will be limited to a few; however, there will be some. If the superintendent feels the directive is inappropriate, s/he can fulfill the request and then possibly use it as a springboard for entering into a dialogue with the board so that it does not recur in the future. A superintendent cannot make a big issue out of every infringement on the administrative domain, as the board should not do so each time the superintendent infringes on its domain. There are tolerable limits within which the board and superintendent must constantly strive to stay.

Requests for special or additional information by the board should be attended to by the superintendent in a timely and thorough fashion. The same advice is true of information requested by an individual board member. However, if an individual board member is constantly requesting information or if several board members make personal requests in an uncoordinated fashion, it may be necessary to discuss the situation with the board chair or the entire board. Sometimes, agreement can be reached where individual board member requests will be channeled to the superintendent through the board chair. This will serve to better utilize valuable staff time and will help ensure that all board members are treated equally.

Respecting privileged communication

The superintendent should respect the confidentiality of privileged conversation with the board and individual board members. This is crucial to maintaining their trust and confidence. However, a word of caution is in order. Entering into privileged communication with individual board members has the potential to silence the superintendent on matters that should be shared with the board. It is also possible that, when things shared in confidence become public, as they are prone to do, the superintendent may be accused of withholding important information.

Respect for board members

Board members have a right to be treated with respect. They are the representatives of the community. Sometimes, it is difficult to follow this advice when one is being berated by a board member in something less than a respectful manner. However, reciprocating in kind only brings the superintendent down to the level of the berating board member. Two wrongs don't make a right.

New board member orientation

One of the toughest aspects of the superintendency is dealing with the constant turnover of board members. It usually takes about two years for a board member to obtain sufficient knowledge and appreciation of board member roles and responsibilities to be an exemplary board member. Thus, it is very important that the superintendent provide orientation programs for new board members. Many board members have campaigned and got elected as special interest advocates, perhaps to fire the superintendent. Often, they have had no prior experience in providing leadership to a large complex organization. Once elected, they can easily become overwhelmed by the situation. They also realize for the first time that an individual board member has no legal authority to hire or fire anyone. The superintendent must help the new board members to function effectively during this on-the-job learning period.

Board member constituencies

Last but not least, the superintendent must realize that every board member, whether elected or appointed, has a constituency. There is a human tendency for people with a perceived problem to want to go straight to the top to get it resolved. Thus, board members will constantly hear complaints, concerns, gossip, rumor, and even a little factual information about the school system. A good board member will learn to use discretion in handling the concerns of individuals. S/he will not find it necessary to share everything with the superintendent.

A new board member will learn, probably the hard way, that there is usually more to a complaint than is initially presented. S/he will learn not to jump to conclusions and make promises based on incomplete and perhaps inaccurate information. It is during this learning process that the superintendent must be understanding, but firm, in dealing with board member pressures. If a board member(s) is responding inappropriately or, perhaps, is even encouraging inappropriate comments, such as from staff members, the superintendent should professionally address the situation with the board member(s) in a manner that allows the individual(s) to save face. The board chair should be kept informed of such problems.

Providing Leadership to the School Organization

This portion of the chapter addresses the expectations the board has of the superintendent in implementing its policies within the school system. It does not address how the policies should be implemented because this aspect is addressed in other chapters.

The superintendent is expected to be a child advocate. Other staff members will have vested interests, and, often, the board will be preoccupied with financial, business, or personnel concerns. It is the responsibility of the superintendent to keep the students on the front burner.

A strong instructional program is expected. Boards tend to rely heavily on superintendents in this area, because instruction usually is the area in which they feel least competent. Instructional items should be a prominent part of each regular board meeting. Board members need to know and be able to explain to others the good educational things that are taking place in the school system.

A fiscally sound operation is a sine qua non. Inappropriate expenditures, even of a minor nature, can quickly discredit the school system and superintendent.

A strong personnel evaluation system should be in place. Accountability is here to stay. With respect to personnel evaluation, the board should have a formal procedure whereby the superintendent is evaluated at least annually. A mid-year progress assessment is gaining popularity.

Strong and supportable decision-making is crucial. The superintendent is expected to be open and objective in the decision-making process. S/he is expected to consult appropriate specialists, i.e., lawyers, psychologists, state department of education personnel, etc., in garnering information, and the rationale for such decisions should be thoroughly explained to the board.

It is expected that conflict will be handled in a positive manner. The overall objective is to motivate employees to work toward the achievement of organizational objectives. Conflict resolution and motivation are difficult under the best of circumstances. In a collective bargaining environment, they become even more difficult. Sometimes, board members have difficulty in understanding that the superintendent does not directly control a number of activities within the system. At times, the superintendent may be asked to do more than s/he can deliver. Open and continuous communication with the board is necessary to alleviate this type of expectation.

WORKING WITH THE BOARD OF EDUCATION

General

The board as a filter

A filter of any type, by definition, serves as a separator. It lets through only that which satisfies predetermined criteria; that which does not satisfy the appropriate criteria is withheld. Depending on the nature of what is being filtered, much or very little original input may make it through the filter.

Each individual has a filter, an immediate boss or a board of directors, through which one's ideas have to be processed. In the case of the superintendent, the board of education serves as the filter. All of the great thoughts, perspectives, imperatives, and recommendations that a superintendent may have go absolutely nowhere if they aren't processed and accepted by the school board.

Every recommendation presented by the superintendent to the board for filtering must have a dividend for the filterers, the board members. Seldom is a board member interested in something that reflects well only on the owner, the superintendent. If the filtering process is not working properly with respect to a particular recommendation, the recommendation probably should be withdrawn and repackaged by the superintendent so that there is a better match between the package and the filtering criteria established by the board.

If a superintendent views the board of education as a filter, the questions and concerns board members have with respect to a particular recommendation can be kept in better perspective. It is more incumbent upon the superintendent to find the right filtering combination than it is upon the board to suspend its filtering process for the benefit of the superintendent.

Understanding the splinter

There is an adage that, if you don't understand the splinter, you won't understand the tree. A superintendent has to read signals very clearly with respect to the school board, administrators, teachers, and citizens. While going around like an Indian scout with one's ear to the ground, it is important to remember that others are doing the same thing. You, in turn, are being read. The processes are reciprocal.

In the superintendency, one must search for and understand the implication of everything. Nothing is insignificant that comes to the superintendent. Even the errant and anonymous postcards received complaining about the lousy bus schedule can be splinters. One can gain infections from splinters if they are not given proper attention and removed, if at all possible. Constantly striving to be aware of the thoughts and feelings of many publics is a very draining type of commitment that the superintendent accepts; however, this commitment is essential for the well-being of the school system and the survival of the superintendent. Nothing is too insignificant to be given attention. Each splinter constitutes a part of the network of a tree, and if the splinter is ignored, one may be felled by the tree.

Knowing the board members

There is a need to have both an extensive and an intensive knowledge of the likes, dislikes, and motivations of each board member. It is necessary to know something about the age, employment, economic status, children, grandchildren, vacation plans, clothing likes, hobbies, etc., of each one. All of this information goes together to help the superintendent understand why they vote as they do.

Many times, the superintendent is positioned with people who don't particularly care for his/her stance on a given matter. The superintendent is placed in the situation of facing an antagonist on the board who often opposes that which the superintendent is proposing. At this point, the superintendent has to search for reasons. What does the board member have in mind in opposing something that you, as the superintendent, believe is in the best interest of the children? You know s/he likes children as well as you like children—why is s/he doing this? In an attempt to answer these questions, the superintendent calls up the mental log on the board member and begins to sift through it for answers. What does the board member like, dislike, eat, not eat? Is his/her job in danger? Is s/he in good health? Is his/her spouse and/or mother all right? Is s/he grandstanding for the paper? Is s/he grandstanding for the other board members? Have you as superintendent done something to irritate her/him? Is this retribution or retaliation? What does this all mean? This litany of mental interrogations may take a tenth of a second but often will provide clues to the board member's motivation.

The sooner the superintendent can define the reason for the board member's reaction, the better off s/he will be. In order to do this in a public meeting, it is essential that the superintendent have a wealth of information in mental storage. In essence, it is necessary to keep a *mental* book on each board member. Indeed, each board member is doing the same on the superintendent. Again, the process is reciprocal.

Changes in superintendent/board relations

The state and national school board associations are telling school board members to do their own homework and to protect themselves from various and sundry liabilities that may arise. Board members are elected by the public and have a constituency to serve. Sometimes the decisions of the superintendent and staff are not politically appealing ones. For these reasons and probably a host of others, board members are much more questioning today. They are less apt to accept a superintendent's recommendation at face value. They are asking: How do you know that? Where did you gain that impression? What is your source of data? How did you reach that conclusion?

As a result of the extensive questioning received from board members, it is no longer enough for superintendents just to make a recommendation. They must communicate the steps, reference sources, and individuals involved in deriving the recommendation. This is a very time-consuming process but an essential one in light of the increased interest in the rationale behind recommendations.

Everybody wants to ask the hard question that makes the superintendent bleed, or at least sweat heavily. If the superintendent can show that, in addition to his/her questioning, the assistant superintendent, an attorney, several parents, children, and other knowledgeable persons are also being questioned, the superintendent's view becomes much more persuasive. The superintendent's opinion alone is no longer looked upon as superior to the opinions of others.

The superintendent and staff are no longer automatically supported by board members out in the community. Instead, board members are quicker to say let's sit down and talk about it. As a result, the superintendent receives a call from a board member wanting to know if s/he can bring a parent(s) in to talk about a problem. To inform the board member that the parent has bypassed several steps in the resolution process is no longer acceptable. The result is that a meeting is held with the superintendent, appropriate staff, the parent(s), and board member in attendance. The board member tends to be an observer during the meeting, a sort of informal arbiter, making mental notes about how adequately the superintendent and staff support their decision. If the superintendent is able to make a case for a well-researched and -reasoned decision, the board member probably will be less quick to request such meetings in the future. However, most board members have to go through this trial by fire before they become convinced that the superintendent's decisions are worthy of their support.

The superintendent's decisions, more and more, are refined judgments based on information gleaned from a number of sources. The superintendent must become an astute consulter of specialists. This role has become so important that a subsequent chapter has been devoted to it exclusively.

Relationships with the Board as an Entity

Communicating with the board

The manner in which a superintendent communicates with the board varies with the size of the district and the leadership style of the superintendent. Most superintendents communicate in writing with their board at least once a week. This is often done on Friday via a memorandum with attached supporting materials that is sent to all of the board members. The object of the communique is to give the board a general update on the week's activities of a nonemergency nature within the school system, to notify them of important events in the forthcoming week, and to set the stage for items that the superintendent intends to bring before the board in the future. Figure 12.1 is an example of such a communique.

It is preferable to have information provided to board members by the superintendent and staff, rather than by the media, angry parents, or some group calling them. In providing information to board members, always let them know whom to contact if they wish to pursue it further. Often, their choice will be to call the superintendent, but this does not have to be the case. Depending on the size and competence of the superintendent's staff, individuals other than the superintendent can be listed as the contact persons. This conserves the valuable time of the superintendent, gives the appearance of a competent administrative team, and gives board members options for obtaining their information.

For the team concept to work in responding to board members, the superintendent must have a great deal of confidence in both himself/herself and the staff. There must not be a feeling that somebody is going to upstage somebody else. A trust level must exist that has been earned through a number of experiences. The team approach also implies that any one of several individuals can respond on behalf of the superintendent to important system concerns. This does not just happen. It takes a considerable amount of meeting time daily to arrive at common understandings and approaches.

In summary, communicating with the board is a time-consuming and terribly important process, and, thus, a team approach is suggested.

Superintendent expectations of the board

Probably the greatest expectation a superintendent should have of the board is that they let him/her speak. A superintendent should have the opportunity to express his/her thinking, feelings, and perceptions. S/he should not filibuster but should have the opportunity to speak uninterrupted about the rationale for a recommendation. Given this

FRIDAY WRITTEN COMMUNIQUE TO ALL BOARD MEMBERS

FROM: Jane/John Superintendent   **DATE: November XX, 19XX**

1. *Winter sports coaches nominations*—attached (pink) please find the employment rationale for the winter sports individuals you will be hiring at the November board meeting.

2. *Equity and adequacy*—attached (green) please find an in-depth update on the court case being tried in the Upbeat County Common Pleas Court.

3. *Mr. Perennial Problem*—attached (lilac) please find the suspension notification given to Mr. Problem. There is a good possibility that this will be grieved and go to arbitration.

4. *Special education update*—attached (yellow) please find an update from our special education coordinator indicating the progress we have made with our special education needs.

5. *Teacher development funds*—attached (blue) please find the response I have received from my letter to the State Department of Public Instruction concerning teacher development funds.

6. *Electric power at Ace Elementary School*—we have been having power shortages at Ace. Attached (salmon) please find a proposal from Crazy Consulting Services to study this problem and provide recommendations.

7. *Counselors*—the high school has been examining the counselors' work load in an attempt to ascertain what changes can be made to increase services to students. Attached (cream) please find a computer summary of the activities in which our counselors are engaged.

8. *Computers*—attached (goldenrod) please find a summary of the writing lab utilization at the high school.

9. *Miscellaneous*—There are three items that we must find time to discuss: 1) next levy campaign, 2) total quality, and 3) administrative salary schedules.

10. *My calendar for next week*—Monday: meeting of joint vocational school superintendents; Tuesday: lobby legislators on pending voucher legislation; Wednesday: termination hearing; Thursday: county superintendents meeting on sharing technology.

FIGURE 12.1. Sample Weekly Written Communication with the Board.

opportunity, the board should then have the opportunity to question the superintendent.

It is important for the superintendent to keep in mind that the board, many times, does not understand where s/he is going or why. What the board members understand on one given day in terms of organizational direction may become hazy in three days. The superintendent has to constantly reestablish his/her bearings with the board. They must be given a directional reading frequently.

Board member orientation

There is general agreement that not enough work is done in this area at the local level. State associations have a number of meetings on boardsmanship, and good publications are available on a host of topics. These are all very important; however, the highest priority for board member orientation at the local level is to establish a feeling of openness with and access to the superintendent and administrative staff. There are many ways this can be done. One successful method is to establish an open lunch period several days a week, at which time any board member knows that s/he can stop in and see the superintendent and/or members of his/her staff. If a board member cannot come in at this time, s/he knows the superintendent and staff are available for phone calls. The same concept can be used on Saturday mornings. Whatever the strategy, it is imperative that the board members come to believe in all sincerity that the superintendent and his/her staff are available to discuss any topic of interest to them.

Involving board members in committee work with staff members is a good way for board members to gain expertise and to establish a personal working relationship with staff. Standing committees can include such things as facilities, finances, employed personnel, student personnel, legislation, etc. Ad hoc committees can be used effectively to study such items as discipline policies and grading policies. These committees should be established for a specific purpose and for a specified period of time.

An offshoot of the committee approach is to have specific staff members develop special relationships with individual board members. These relationships can be very positive factors in the communication process. Again, trusting relationships must exist between the superintendent and staff for this approach to work effectively.

Importance of secretaries

A capable superintendent's secretary is almost an assistant superintendent, in terms of what s/he knows about school operations and how s/he interacts with people. This individual has to be proficient in the usual secretarial types of tasks; however, the most important attribute is that s/he knows how to work with the public. Often, a board member would rather talk initially with the secretary than with the superintendent. S/he may feel more comfortable in conveying a request to the secretary or in venting dissatisfaction. The secretary can channel a request to the appropriate staff member or help calm down an irate individual, both of which can save damaged feelings and enhance communication between the superintendent and board.

The same trust should exist between a superintendent and his/her secretary that exists with the professional staff. If the secretary is to function effectively, s/he must be as fully informed as any professional staff member.

Superintendent evaluation by the board

Superintendents are usually evaluated formally once a year. If the formal evaluation process is working properly, mutually agreed-upon goals and objectives for the superintendent and school system will be established, and the evaluation will focus on the degree to which the goals and objectives have been met. These goals and objectives can be used as guides for personal time allocation and for time allocation at board meetings. How individual acts by the superintendent and board further one or more of the goals or objectives should be a constantly asked question.

The reality of the evaluation situation is that it is never quite as clear and concise as that depicted. Instead, the superintendent is being evaluated daily by board members. Every time a board member reads the paper or talks with a constituent, some type of impression is being made. Every time the superintendent makes a presentation to a senior citizens' group, to the board of realtors, to the Chamber of Commerce, etc., s/he is being evaluated. Every time a board member sends a note or makes a call, the superintendent is being evaluated. Perceptions developed informally in these ways by board members will be reflected in the formal evaluation.

The tenor of board meetings can be an indicator of the informal evaluations being formed by board members. Recommendations that are constantly running into trouble, public and private expressions of concern about the school system, or comments such as "I thought we put that one to rest six months ago" are revealing with respect to informal board member evaluations. An alert and perceptive superintendent who is attuned to the nuances of the informal evaluation process should never by surprised by the contents of the formal evaluation.

Relationships with Individual Board Members

Communicating with individual board members

The desire to respond to the concerns of individual board members and, at the same time, not provide individual board members with privileged information is a dilemma faced by superintendents. An approach to this dilemma that usually works is as follows. When an individual board member calls to request information relative to a particular concern, ask the board member if s/he cares if you share the concern with the other board members and staff. Usually, there will be a pause, and then the board member response will be, "Yes, you probably should." At this point, involve appropriate staff members in collecting data and formulating a response.

Always put the response in writing. In addition to stating the specific concern and the formulated response to the concern, also 1) indicate that the letter will be shared with the other board members, 2) name the staff members who were involved in formulating the response, 3) indicate the number of staff hours required to formulate the response, and 4) indicate that, if the response is incomplete, any of the board members should feel free to contact the superintendent or any of the listed staff.

Board member infringement upon superintendent prerogatives

A board member becoming overly concerned and involved with employment practices or the general day-to-day operation of the schools is, at one time or another, a problem for every superintendent. If the superintendent disagrees with the action of a board member, s/he has to find a way to let the board member know that s/he is uncomfortable with the situation. A good first approach usually is to let the board member know that you respect what s/he has to say, but that s/he is only one-fifth or one-seventh of the board, and that her/his concerns should be brought before the entire board for their consideration. Beware of deal making with individual board members. This type of action has resurfaced to haunt many a superintendent.

If the board member persists at a board meeting, the superintendent should request the opportunity to respond without interruption to the issue. The superintendent's response may not dissuade the dissident board member, but other board members expect the superintendent to rise to the occasion and respond logically to his/her criticism. Thus, on occasion, the superintendent will have to stand up and be counted, an unpopular situation where feelings can get bruised. But to do otherwise means that you allow yourself and/or your staff to be 1) subverted, 2) intimidated, or 3) completely neutralized when you are being paid to be a leader.

In dealing with a problem board member, the telephone sometimes is not the best means to resolve a disagreement. Although much communication takes place on the telephone, it usually is not a good instrument of persuasion. In a problem situation, there is more credence in open discussion, where everyone has a chance to speak and to listen. In this forum, reconciliation is apt to come from another board member. Or another board member can provide a cooling affect by saying, "Hey, this conversation has degenerated. Let's see if we can't find a resolution." If another board member has a good suggestion, don't hesitate to recognize the suggestion as such. This places the dissident board member in the position of going along or being isolated.

Of course, informal and amicable means for working out disagreements represent the preferred route; however, there will be times when this is not possible. The superintendent needs to make plans for handling these situations.

Board member criticism of the superintendent in the media

One should go to great lengths to avoid a debate through the media. After a board member unloads on the superintendent via the media, the superintendent should first search his/her mental file in an attempt to ascertain the real reasons for the outburst. Trusted staff can also be very valuable in this effort. Second, if the superintendent is contacted by the media for a response, s/he should state the rationale for the decision or position but not criticize the board member. Third, contact the board member and let him/her know that this type of behavior benefits neither of you and that perhaps the two of you should have a debate at an open board meeting. Usually, the board member will respond that his/her real intent was not conveyed by the reporter. Sometimes this can be used as an entree for a discussion on how items can be handled differently in the future.

If a board member persists with media criticisms, s/he should be again reminded that s/he is only one-fifth or one-seventh of the board and will be looked upon as such. At this point, it is important to get a good reading of the other board members. As discussed earlier, one must make sure that what one thinks is a splinter is not, in reality, a branch, a trunk, or a whole tree. Nothing should be taken lightly. Avoid at all costs a confederation of board members aligned against something the superintendent is doing because, ultimately, the superintendent will lose. Other board members often are the most influential in bringing a recalcitrant board member back into the fold.

Facility visitation by board members

Most board members visit facilities upon invitation. Usually, the superintendent will receive an invitation also. When this is the case, the superintendent or a member of the staff should make a concerted effort to be in attendance.

If a board member drops in unannounced at a facility, the principal should be prepared to take things in stride. S/he should inform the superintendent of the visit. This is particularly true in smaller systems or if the board member has raised some questions, questioned the cleanliness of the building, or in other ways has expressed dissatisfaction about a particular facility. Unannounced visits tend to be more common today than in years past.

Socializing with board members

There are varying opinions with respect to socializing with board members; however, a good rule of thumb is to keep the superintendent/board member relationship pure and professional. Socializing with individual board members and their spouses tends to distract from the overall picture. The spouses may not get along or may say something that is questionable, at least. In addition, there is always the possibility that perceptions will emerge within the community that a particular board member(s) is in the hip pocket of the superintendent or vice versa. Neither perception is desirable.

Of course, there will be social occasions where the entire board, the superintendent, and spouses will be in attendance. This is a part of the superintendency and a part in which the superintendent's spouse plays a vital role.

Board Meetings

Agenda

The superintendent usually takes the lead in putting together an agenda for a board meeting. Often, the board chair is consulted prior to finalizing the agenda. If the board meeting is on Monday, the agenda should be in place by Wednesday of the preceding week and hand delivered to the board members on Thursday. This gives them a chance to review the materials and, if need be, ask for clarification or suggest additional item(s) for the agenda.

Many formats are available for organizing the board agenda and its supporting materials. Whatever the format, the agenda should have a logical organization, be clear and concise, and be cross-referenced with supporting material.

There are differing opinions as to how much supporting material should be provided with the agenda. Some superintendents feel that too much supporting material tends to overwhelm board members to the point where they either do not read the material or else become confused by it. However, the prevailing feeling is that it is better to err on the side of providing too much information. If a board member does not study all of the material at one time, s/he should be encouraged to develop a filing system so that reference may be made to any number of topics throughout the year. Some superintendents help their board establish a personal filing system for the benefit of consistency. When this is done, supporting material should be coded as to its file.

Procedures

Many board meetings are held in the evening; however, there is a trend to schedule more meetings in the late afternoon. Afternoon meetings have been criticized for being at a time of day that limits citizen participation, but attendance figures at board meetings do not seem to support this. People make the meeting regardless of the time. For some unknown reason, evening meetings tend to lend themselves to more distractions and deviations.

A good board meeting should last no longer than two hours. Robert's Rules of Order should be followed as the board moves through the agenda. (A good superintendent will be intimately familiar with Robert's Rules.) In addition, there should be guidelines as to how additional items may be added to the agenda. Some boards are very strict, allowing no new items to be added to the agenda during a meeting. Others take a more lenient approach and will address concerns from the audience at the end of a meeting. If there isn't time, the item is placed first on the next meeting's agenda. It is important to note that discussing a concern does not mean that action has to be taken on it. In fact, in most instances, it would not be wise to do so without time for reflection.

Some superintendents like to give each board member the opportunity to give regular reports at board meetings. The subcommittee format can be used for this. This enables the other members to share "air time" with the superintendent and board president, and it also allows them to become more familiar with a particular aspect of the school operation and the school personnel who have responsibility for that operation.

At times, it is necessary and prudent to bring items before the board for discussion purposes. This helps create public confidence and gives each member the opportunity to express his/her views in public. As is always the case, the board members should have been provided with ample background information prior to the meeting.

Most boards and superintendents establish a policy of *no surprises*. If and when the superintendent and/or board gets surprised at a meeting, action should be postponed if at all possible. Hasty and poorly researched judgments make for bad decisions.

Seating arrangements at board meetings are a personal preference; however, a case can be made that the superintendent should sit next to the board chairperson because they may be communicating throughout the meeting. A word of caution is in order. The superintendent must take precautions to ensure that the board and audience perceive that the board chairperson is actually in control of the meet-

ing. Seats on coasters make it easier for the superintendent to unob-
trusively confer with staff or other board members during the meeting.

Executive sessions should be held only when absolutely necessary.
As most states have some type of "sunshine law" that indicates when
and for what purposes a board may go into executive session, a thorough knowledge of applicable laws is imperative. When it is necessary to have an executive session, there is merit to holding it prior to
the regular board meeting. This establishes an ending time for the
session, and sensitive items will be discussed before fatigue sets in.
The superintendent should provide the board members with all relevant background information in advance of the executive session. An
added benefit is that the regular meeting tends to run in a more
orderly fashion with less sensationalism once the tension has been
released in the executive session.

Last, but certainly not least, the superintendent and board president
must set the tone for a board meeting by modeling appropriate demeanor, respect for others, and decorum. In a nicely run board meeting, a friendly, yet businesslike, atmosphere prevails.

Citizen participation

Every board should have a policy and guidelines addressing citizen
participation. Most guidelines require the individual wishing to address the board to submit his/her name and topic to the board office
at a specified time prior to the board meeting. If a group with a common interest will be in attendance, the group is asked to designate a
spokesperson. Often, a time limit per speaker of three to five minutes
is established.

Boards often are reluctant to limit the number of presenters or curb
the length of presentations. It is at these times that the superintendent,
in conjunction with the board chairperson, must intervene. If the
issue is a contested one, the superintendent or board chair may say,
"We have heard three pros and three cons. I think we understand the
issue. We will study the issue and formulate a written response." The
worst way to handle the situation is to ask, "Does anyone else wish to
address the board?" Following this question, individuals who had no
intention of addressing the board will be moved to try their hand on
center stage.

Sometimes an individual will be permitted to address the board
with a concern directly related to school operations. In such a situa-

tion, the superintendent should resist the urge to chastise the individual for not giving the staff a chance to work on the problem. The superintendent should take matters as they are and proceed from that point.

If citizens wish to address the board with a common concern, the board, after hearing representative concerns, should attempt to have these individuals meet with the superintendent or staff member. In this way, the staff will work with the group. At times, the board may need to be reminded that a board meeting is held to allow the board to conduct business *in* public, not *with* the public.

In recent years, there has been a tendency for more and more individuals to address the board. The media loves this action. It is much more exciting than the purchase of textbooks, toilet tissue, and supplies. At times, the media will blow a rather mundane circumstance out of proportion.

Citizen participation at board meetings is another sliver that should not be ignored. Once their concerns have been made public, some type of response from the superintendent's office is required. Often, much staff time is necessary to adequately respond to these concerns.

Leadership role for the superintendent

In addition to presenting the recommendations and giving background information, the superintendent must rise to the occasion as critical situations emerge during board meetings. As Jack Kennedy said, "It is amazing what one person can do in a critical moment to turn things around." That one person could be the superintendent.

Board members should be recognized by the public as independent thinkers. They do perform yeoman duty and deserve credit for their civic contributions; however, in moments of crisis during board meetings, they usually turn to the superintendent to carry the ball. There is the expectation that the superintendent should put the figurative noose around his/her neck and then adroitly work his/her way out of it. Every superintendent worth his salt must noose himself/herself occasionally. This is part of being a real leader.

SUPERINTENDENT/BOARD LEADERSHIP TEAM EVALUATION

A great deal has been written about evaluation of the superintendent by the board of education. This is appropriate, for as the chief executive officer of the board, it is important that the superintendent receive an annual evaluation.

However, it also is increasingly important for a board to go beyond the traditional annual superintendent evaluation and include itself as part of a comprehensive superintendent/board leadership team evaluation. Under this leadership team evaluation concept, the superintendent and board are looked upon as the top leadership team in the school district, and the school district leadership accomplishments and shortcomings are viewed as team successes and failures.

The rationale for this superintendent/board team approach to evaluation is well grounded in the leadership literature. Successful organizations have 1) a compelling vision of what they can and should become and 2) a driving motivation to get there. Research has indicated that strong leadership at the top must exist if these two traits of successful organizations are to become a reality. In a school district, strong leadership at the top can exist only if the superintendent and board function as a team. As a team, they must lead the way by exhibiting Kouzes and Posner's ten commitments of leadership that were discussed in the chapter on transformational leadership.

During the nineties and into the first decade of the next millennium, the face of education will probably change more than it has in the past 100 years combined. Client choice, individualization of instruction, and technology will be the change catalysts.

Organizationally, school systems will become more decentralized. Individuals at the school level will be empowered to make many of the decisions that historically have been the prerogatives of central office personnel. Teachers will be the primary recipients of school-level empowerment. In this organizational environment, the board and superintendent must provide the overriding vision for the school system and motivate the empowered decision-makers to be committed to the achievement of this vision. Without this vision and commitment, the school organization becomes a system of schools, rather than a school system.

The strategic plan is the vehicle for achieving the vision. A strategic plan to which school personnel are committed sets the stage for the superintendent/board leadership team evaluation process. The amount of progress that has been made on the various components of the strategic plan is the overall evaluation yardstick. If the system has fallen short in an area(s), the superintendent and board must assess the reasons why. Were there extenuating circumstances? Was the leadership team deficient in one or more of the transformational leadership areas? If this was the case, what can the superintendent/board leadership team do to rectify the situations? *In the final analysis, student accomplishments that have been achieved in an ethical, legal, and caring manner provide the ultimate evaluation for the superintendent/board leadership team.*

In conclusion, the traditional superintendent evaluation schemes will continue to provide useful information because they evaluate some important superintendent activities and traits; however, they do not assess the effectiveness of the superintendent/board leadership team. A new evaluation scheme must be put in place to evaluate this leadership concept that will be required during the remainder of the nineties and into the twenty-first century.

CONCLUDING COMMENT

The superintendent/school board relationship is the leadership keystone for the school system. Thus, it is appropriate that this discussion constitutes the longest chapter in this book.

REFERENCES

Iannaccone, L. (1983). Community education and turning point elections. In D. Schoeny and L. Decker (Eds.), *Community Educational and Social Impact Perspectives,* Lanham, MD: University Press of America.

Weninger, T. A. and Stout, R. T. (1989). Dissatisfaction theory: Policy change as a function of school board member-superintendent turnover. *Educational Administration Quarterly, 25*(2), 162–180.

CHAPTER 13

The Superintendent as Strategic Planner

INTRODUCTION

What Is Strategic Planning and What Is a Strategic Plan?

Strategic planning is "a disciplined effort to produce fundamental decisions and actions that shape what an organization . . . is, what it does, and why it does it" (Bryson, 1988, p. 20).

A strategic plan is the map that provides direction to the school system. Specifically, it

1. Identifies the mission of the system (Who is it and why is it in the education business?)
2. Puts forth a "vision" for the system in the environment in which it will be functioning in six to ten years
3. Includes action plans for posturing the system to successfully compete and function in the envisioned future

Why Develop a Strategic Plan?

A school system without a strategic plan is like a ship without a rudder. Either the waters are completely still and the ship goes no-where, or the waters contain currents that carry and toss the ship to and fro at random. The authors suggest that the latter scenario will be the plight of a school system without a strategic plan. As Hamilton (1991) states, "Planning permits administrators to anticipate events, prepare for contingencies, establish directions, and define activities for organizational improvement" (p. 22).

Tichy and Devanna (1990) indicate that the first act in transforming an organization is recognizing the need for revitalization. There are numerous signs that K–12 educational constituents are demanding a revitalization of the educational institutions. For instance, client (parent/pupil) choice is sweeping the nation. Many K–12 educational organizations are, or will be, in competition with each other.

Some states are giving top priority to eliminating the "Carnegie Unit" at the high school level. This brings into question the entire time-honored K–12 grade structure. If the Carnegie Unit is abolished, the need for traditional grade levels will be greatly diminished, and instruction will become highly individualized.

Technology is beginning to drastically alter educational delivery processes. No longer do students have to learn within the confines of school buildings, nor is learning restricted to the traditional school hours. Instead, the world is at the students' disposal at any time of the day or night and from an unlimited number of locations. The role of school organizations and their employees will be significantly impacted.

When changes of the magnitude suggested above occur, it is clear that school systems must be proactive in shaping their futures. They must take the initiative in revitalizing their organizations. The development of a strategic plan is the vehicle a superintendent may use to take the initiative and be a proactive leader in preparing his/her school system to successfully meet future educational demands.

Purpose of the Chapter

Strategic planning is not a neat, logical, and orderly process; it takes place over an extended period of time (usually at least a year) and it involves many people. This chapter gives an overview of the complex strategic planning process. An understanding of the process will enable superintendents and board members to make enlightened decisions on whether, or to what extent, they should seek outside help.

Throughout the entire strategic planning and implementation process, the superintendent and board must function as visionary and transformational leaders, as well as divergent thinkers. These important functions have already been addressed in Chapters 3, 7, and 8, respectively, and will not be dwelled upon in this chapter. Rather, the remainder of the chapter will present a detailed description of the strategic planning process. It is organized around the three major components of a strategic plan as put forth in the opening paragraph of this chapter.

THE MISSION STATEMENT

A mission statement is "a declaration of organization purpose" (Bryson, 1988, p. 104). It answers the questions "Why educate?" and "What are we about?" and it usually grows out of a discussion of the following questions (Bryson, 1988, p. 105):

1. Who are we?
2. What are the basic needs we exist to fill or problems we exist to address?
3. What do we want to do to recognize or anticipate and respond to these needs or problems?
4. How should we respond to key stakeholders?
5. What is our philosophy, and what are our core values?
6. What makes us distinctive or unique?

Every school system has a mission statement; however, for the most part, these statements are collecting dust and are retrieved only when accrediting agencies make their periodic visits. Individuals involved with a system (board members, administrators, teachers, students, and parents) are not familiar with the contents and certainly do not use them in guiding curriculum and instructional decisions.

If a viable strategic plan is to be developed, the mission statement must become a living document that accurately reflects school system priorities and goals. Historically, little thought has been given as to why things are included in the curriculum. In many instances, the best explanation for their inclusion is that they have always been included. This must change. Curriculum content and instructional decisions must be guided by the mission statement. Everything in the curriculum must contribute in some manner to the achievement of the mission statement. When viewed in this manner, the mission statement becomes a living document that must be understood by the educational community and to which the community members are committed.

One might find such beliefs as the following in a mission statement. Upon graduation, a student should have

1. The ability and motivation to get along with others
2. A concern for the welfare of others
3. A willingness to accept and appreciate both cultural and individual diversity
4. An appreciation of the importance of family
5. A concern for the environment
6. The ability and desire to contribute to the general welfare of society
7. A knowledge and appreciation of the culture and values of our society
8. The ability to positively participate in a democracy
9. A positive and accurate self-concept
10. The ability and motivation to accept responsibility for one's personal actions
11. A knowledge and appreciation of a global society
12. An ability to express oneself (communicate) via a variety of media

In summary, the mission statement provides guidance for the entire strategic planning and implementation process because it puts forth what the school system is trying to accomplish. It is central to creating the system vision that is discussed in the next section.

CREATING THE VISION

On the opening page of the American Society for Training and Development's document, *How to Develop a Vision,* a Peter Drucker quote is provided and reads, "The best way to predict the future is to create it" (ASTD, 1991, p. 1). The piece also notes that "visioning begins with the future, not the present: It focuses on the end state . . ." (ASTD, 1991, p. 2).

Joel Barker (1990) has put forth four key components in developing a good vision. First, the vision must be leader initiated. The leader interacts with the "vision community" and takes their input into consideration when molding the vision. Second, the vision must be shared and supported by the vision community. Third, the vision must be comprehensive and detailed. Last, the vision must be positive and inspiring.

It is important to note that Barker's first component is that the vision must be developed by the leader. In a school situation, this can be expanded to the superintendent/board leadership team. The concept of a leader-developed vision runs counter to some strategic planning processes that advocate comprehensive community involvement in formulating the vision. The result of the community involvement approach is usually a vision that represents incremental extensions of the present, rather than a real vision for the future. The masses cannot create a viable vision statement.

It is extremely difficult for individuals to divorce themselves from the present when thinking of education. Perhaps this is because the basic educational delivery system has changed little during the past century. Barker (1989) refers to this phenomenon as the "paradigm effect," in which individuals have a tendency to discount any idea as counterproductive that does not "fit the mold." He further states that "paradigm paralysis" or the inability to see past what is currently happening is a terminal illness.

It is extremely important for superintendents and school boards to develop a vision that seriously takes into account the dramatic educational changes looming on the horizon. One should not assume that educational futures will be incremental extensions of the present. As Fiske (1991) states, "Trying to get more learning out of the current system is like trying to get the Pony Express to compete with the telegraph by breeding faster ponies" (pp. 14–15).

The school system leadership team must proceed through a two-step process in developing a viable vision statement. The first step is to acquire a knowledge base by listening to the vision community and by reading about projected futures at the global, national, state, and local levels. (An educational vision cannot be developed independent of projected societal and world changes.)

The second step is to attend and actively participate in an intensive two-day retreat at an out-of-district location. The elements of the vision statement will be developed at this retreat. A skilled facilitator familiar with the use of "futures techniques" can be a great asset during these intense two days.

Many good visionary ideas will emanate from the two-day retreat. These ideas must be organized into a comprehensive vision statement. In doing this, the vision statement can be broken down into specific subdivisions or spheres of emphasis. Figure 13.1 shows a schematic of a comprehensive vision having seven spheres of emphasis.

FIGURE 13.1. *Spheres of Visionary Emphasis.*

Furthermore, if necessary, an individual sphere of emphasis can be further subdivided. For instance, client learning could have the following subdivisions.

1. Accountability/assessment
2. Life-long learning
3. Role of the teacher
4. Concern and appreciation for others
5. Curriculum scope and content
6. Individualization of instruction

Each of the subdivisions would have vision statements. For example, vision statements for life-long learning could be

1. The divisions between high school and post-secondary education will become blurred.
2. Life-long, systematic, and continuous learning will be the norm.
   • The public schools will routinely serve one to five year olds.
   • Community and adult education programs will be incorporated into the mainstream of the school system.
3. There will be greater use of facilities as both school and community educational needs are served.
4. Magnet schools will be available.
5. Instructional settings will routinely include individuals of all ages.

In developing the vision, one should not be concerned about having too grandiose a vision. It is much easier to tame a wild idea than to invigorate a tame one. Also, it is commonly accepted that the way to have good ideas is to have a lot of them. In the final process of molding a comprehensive vision statement, individual vision suggestions can be merged and/or discarded.

After formulating a comprehensive and detailed vision, the superintendent and board must develop detailed plans for articulating and communicating the vision to the vision community. This takes a lot of effort, communication, and transformational leadership by both the superintendent and board. It is extremely important that each board member become actively involved in this process. The vision community must understand that the board believes in the vision and plans to use it as a guide in making future curricular and fiscal decisions.

DEVELOPING ACTION PLANS

What Are Action Plans?

As Joel Barker (1990) states,

Vision without action is merely a dream;
Action without vision just passes the time;
Vision with action can change the world.

Therefore, action plans are the maps that guide a school system toward the achievement of its vision statement. They describe in specific terms a series of activities that must take place in order for the preferred future, or vision statement, to become a reality. Specifically, an action plan consists of

1. An objective that must be attained if a vision is to become a reality
2. A time line of specific activities that must take place in order to achieve the objective

Using Figure 13.1 as a reference, multiple action plans will be developed for each of the seven spheres of emphasis. In this particular example, the client must always remain center stage. Therefore, the work of the action planning subcommittees on staff development, involvement and communication with external constituencies, extramural funding, facilities, organizing for effective and efficient educational delivery to clients, and technology must support that of the client learning subcommittee. In addition, the work of each subcommittee must be coordinated with the work of each of the other sub-committees. As can be seen, action plan development is a time-consuming and intricate process.

A Process for Developing Action Plans

Now is the time for intensive involvement of school staff and community. The school board and superintendent should have exerted considerable time and effort to communicate and sell the vision statement to all constituents.

While there are a number of ways that one can go about developing action plans, a process that has been successfully implemented is presented in this subsection. A school system can take the process and modify it as needed to fit its own needs. For the sake of brevity, a listing format is used.

1) The superintendent and board should select an action planning committee chair and co-chair from the community for each sphere of emphasis. Interest, commitment, and leadership potential should be used in selecting these individuals. This will be the only time that the school's leadership team will be involved in selecting the membership of the action planning committees. However, these leadership positions are crucial to the process and cannot be left to chance.

2) The superintendent appoints a staff liaison to each planning committee. This liaison person is the link between the planning committee and the superintendent's office. S/he will be responsible for obtaining information and data for the committee as requested.

3) The chairs/co-chairs, liaison persons, individuals who attended the retreat, and union presidents (if appropriate) will form the action planning steering committee. This committee will meet at least once a month. At each meeting, the planning committee chairs will share the progress of their respective planning groups with the entire steering committee. Problems and concerns will be jointly discussed and resolved.

4) An inservice meeting for all members of the steering committee must be held. (It is very important that the board members participate.) Important items to cover at the meeting are

- Board members expound upon their interest in and commitment to the strategic planning process in general and the mission and vision statements in particular.

- The mission statement and strategic vision are reviewed in detail. The means by which these documents were developed and their importance to action plan development should be discussed.
- The leadership responsibilities of the chairs and co-chairs are discussed.
- The action plan development process is described and discussed.
- The role of the staff liaison individual is explained.
- The "Action Plan Forms" (Figures 13.2 and 13.3) are distributed and discussed.
- Time lines and dates for future meetings are established.

5) Invite all school employees and citizens to an open meeting to discuss the strategic planning process. The format for the meeting

ACTION PLAN FORM

SPHERE OF EMPHASIS: _____

Objective: _____
_____
_____

Activity Identification:
 1994–1995: _____
 _____
 _____

 1996–1997: _____
 _____
 _____

 1998–2000: _____
 _____
 _____

Effect of Objective on Other Spheres of Emphasis:
 Client Learning:
 Staff Development:
 Involvement and Communication with External Constituencies:
 Extramural Funding:
 Facilities:
 Organizing for Effective and Efficient Educational Delivery to Clients:
 Technology:

FIGURE 13.2. Action Plan Form.

SPHERE OF EMPHASIS: Client Learning (Accountability/Assessment)

Objective: There will be an increased emphasis on continuous and individualized learning and a de-emphasis on letter grades.

Activity Identification:

19__-19__: A series of inservice sessions should be conducted for the purpose of educating teachers, administrators, and community members on strategies to implement continuous and individualized learning. These strategies will be routinely used in the classroom by all teachers.

19__-19__: A committee consisting of teachers, administrators, and community members will assess the strategies. Concurrently, the committee will investigate the format for student evaluation. This will become an ongoing process.

FIGURE 13.3. Example of an Objective and Accompanying Action Plans for the Client Learning Sphere of Emphasis.

will be basically the same as the one used for the steering committee. At the conclusion of the meeting, those in attendance can choose an action planning team on which to serve. The general session ends, and the action planning committees convene with the chairs and co-chairs to establish meeting dates and discuss their charges.

6) The action planning committees do their work. Ideally, their plans should be developed within a four-month period of time. After this period of time, the committee members may begin to lose their enthusiasm and focus.

7) After the action planning committees have completed their work, the board holds highly publicized open hearings, at which time each committee presents its plans to the board and responds to questions from the board and audience. The board formally accepts the work of the committees.

8) The superintendent and staff prioritize the plans submitted by the committees and put together a draft of a coordinated and comprehensive strategic plan. The draft is then presented to the steering committee for its edification and eventual approval.

9) The board formally adopts a strategic plan. This is the final act in the strategic planning process. The board and school staff now move into the implementation phase.

IMPLEMENTING THE STRATEGIC PLAN

As the plan will be providing direction for the school system during the next decade, it should be given the publicity it deserves. Through a variety of communication techniques, the staff and public should be thoroughly informed on the plan contents and on its intended usage by the superintendent and board.

The responsibility for implementing and evaluating each action plan should be assigned to a staff member with expertise in the area. The superintendent should serve as the coordinator of the implementation efforts.

The board should monitor the progress that is being made in the implementation of its strategic plan at least semiannually. The progress must be evaluated in relation to the occurrence of unexpected events, changing priorities, and available fiscal resources. In addition, the board and staff must constantly be environmentally scanning in a continuing effort to update the strategic vision.

A strategic plan is a living plan, and strategic planning is an ongoing process. The strategic plan should be revised annually as dictated by the monitoring and evaluation processes. The action plans should then be adjusted accordingly to reflect the revisions in the strategic plan.

REFERENCES

American Society for Training and Development. (1991). *How to Develop a Vision* (Info-Line). Issue 107, Alexandria, VA: ASTD.

Barker, J. (1990). *The Power of Vision*. Burnsville, MN: Chart House International.

Barker, J. (1989). *Discovering the Future: The Business of Paradigms*. Burnsville, MN: Chart House International.

Bryson, J. M. (1988). *Strategic Planning for Public and Nonprofit Organizations: A Guide to Strengthening and Sustaining Organizational Achievement*. San Francisco, CA: Jossey-Bass.

Cook, B. (1988). *Strategic Planning for America's Schools*. Arlington, VA: American Association of School Administrators. (Four videotapes and a video leader's guide are also available.)

Educational Leadership. (1991). Contains a strategic planning subsection (eleven articles). *48*(7), 4–43.

Fiske, E. B. (1991). *Smart Schools: Smart Kids.* New York, NY: Simon & Schuster.

Hamilton, D. N. (1991). An alternative to rational planning models. In R. V. Carlson and G. Awkerman (Eds.), *Educational Planning—Concepts, Strategies, Practices,* pp. 21–47, New York, NY: Longman Publishing Group.

Hay, R. D. (1990). *Strategic Management in Non-Profit Organizations: An Administrator's Handbook.* New York, NY: Quorum Books.

Kaufman, R. and Herman, J. (1990). *Strategic Planning in Education: Rethinking, Restructuring, Revitalizing.* Lancaster, PA: Technomic Publishing Co., Inc.

Malphurs, A. (1992). *Developing Vision for Ministry in the 21st Century,* Grand Rapids, MI: Baker House.

Pearson, G. J. (1990). *Strategic Thinking.* New York, NY: Prentice-Hall.

Tichy, N. M. and Devanna, M. (1990). *The Transformational Leader.* New York, NY: Wiley.

CHAPTER 14

The Superintendent as Negotiator

In the current era, there is probably nothing that has a greater impact on the day-to-day operation of a school system and staff morale within the system than the collective bargaining process and the formal collective bargaining agreement. In some states, the collective bargaining agreement is so prominent that its contents take precedence over state law. It is obvious that a process and document that collectively exert such a great influence on a school district must be of primary concern to the superintendent. It is imperative that superintendents give careful thought to the role they can best serve in the collective bargaining process.

The purpose of this chapter is to explore the pros and cons of the three primary roles the superintendent can play in the collective bargaining process. The first two roles are options within the traditional adversarial bargaining process; i.e., the superintendent will be either the chief negotiator for the board, or s/he will serve in a coordinating and data-gathering capacity while an individual employed from out-

Mr. Leigh Herington, Esq., provided the basic material for the "Public School versus Private Sector Bargaining" and the " 'Hired Gun' as Spokesperson" sections and contributed material for the "Collaborative Bargaining" section. Mr. Herington is an attorney who is employed by numerous boards of education to serve as their spokesperson in the traditional bargaining process and as a facilitator in the collaborative process. He also has served as a board of education president.

Ms. Martha Motsco contributed material for the "Collaborative Bargaining" section. Ms. Motsco is an assistant superintendent and an attorney.

Dr. Norman Sommers provided the basic material for "The Superintendent as Spokesperson" section. He was a superintendent of schools for over twenty years and served as the chief spokesperson for the board during his entire tenure. He also conducts workshops and has published articles relative to the superintendent as spokesperson.

side the system serves as the board's spokesperson. The third role is an emerging one that is evolving with the increased use of collaborative bargaining. There is no *right* answer regarding the role a superintendent should play. The situation and individuals involved are the determining factors.

The chapter begins by identifying some differences between public sector and private sector bargaining. The second section presents a case for employing an outside negotiator. This section also discusses the role of superintendent when someone else is serving as the chief spokesperson. The third section presents a case for the superintendent serving as the board's chief spokesperson. The fourth section discusses the collaborative bargaining process. The chapter concludes with some suggestions for the superintendent that are applicable regardless of the bargaining process used.

PUBLIC SCHOOL VERSUS PRIVATE SECTOR BARGAINING

When negotiations take place between a labor union and a for-profit company, the results are different than when they take place between a labor union and a publicly funded organization. In the private sector, by keeping a dollar away from the employees, a dollar has been saved for stockholders. In the public school context, the result is a delicate balance between prudent expenditure of public funds and appropriate wages for employees. Determining a prudent expenditure of public funds for employee salaries is a difficult dilemma. Generally, communities have a desire to pay their teachers well; however, individual community members also have a desire to pay as little in taxes as possible.

Public school negotiations actually become a negotiation with the community, as well as the school staff. The board's negotiating team attempts to determine an appropriate salary and benefit package that is within the confines of what the community is willing to accept. The correct determination of this package will have a significant bearing on whether the community will support the schools in the future and will be instrumental in determining future relationships between the school staff, administration, and board of education.

The achievement of the correct balance for the salary and fringe benefit package can also have a lot to do with how good the school district feels about itself. Teachers tend to be more productive when they perceive that they are paid appropriately and that they work in a community that appreciates its schools.

The other critical difference in public school negotiations is the potential for various nonmonetary issues to cripple the administration's ability to promote and require good education and good teaching. Items such as just cause for nonrenewal, limitations on teacher transfers, restrictions on reductions in force, and restrictive evaluation procedures can negatively curtail the ability of a school system to provide quality education.

"HIRED GUN" AS SPOKESPERSON

Why Hire an Outside Gun as Spokesperson?

There are six reasons for employing an individual from outside the school system to serve as the chief spokesperson for the board. Each reason is presented and discussed below.

An understanding of and feel for the process

Negotiating is a dynamic and strategic process. The art of negotiations is one for which there are no specific ground rules or guidelines. It is unlike a court of law, in which there are established rules of evidence and procedure. Although techniques are important in negotiations, there are no rules that are required to be followed when two parties meet at the negotiating table.

Often, the negotiations' context and the dynamics of the process are much more important than the subject matter. For this reason, whoever is responsible for the coordination of the negotiations for the board must be responsible for a vision of the entire process. This vision starts with the perceived end result and moves backward to the initial contact. The strategies involved in the development of this process are very important. A professional negotiator is more attuned to the nuances of the process and more skilled in developing a strategy that will lead to positive results.

Initial positions need to be handled very carefully. Often, presentations and reactions at this stage are as important as any future developments. It may be that the initial contact requires very aggressive behavior from the management team. Other circumstances require a cooperative approach. Strategy for the initial presentation and reaction to proposals are difficult points in the process. A professional negotiator can be very helpful in the decision-making process during this aspect of the negotiations.

An important dynamic of negotiations is that the parties begin to build bridges through the process so that a feeling of mutual trust and respect can evolve. The development of this type of climate often is identified as the reason for a successful negotiating process. Developing this climate in a confrontational environment takes a special skill that is developed by participating in the negotiations process on a continuing basis.

An understanding of contract language

Regardless of whether or not the teachers' association uses a professional negotiator as its spokesperson, the association always receives assistance from professionals in formulating the language used in proposals. The nature of contract language and the board's response are important. Unless the board's team has a full understanding of language implications, the participants could inadvertently agree to problematic language that appears harmless but is actually very harmful. For instance, if the board agrees to language that was presented by the staff but was actually developed by the union professionals, at some later date, the union could bring in its professionals in a language dispute to give their interpretations of the intent of the language. Because they (the union) wrote the language, their testimony would be persuasive.

Also, it is important to have knowledge on how contract language will be interpreted by a court of law, an arbitrator, or a neutral third party.

A board negotiating team that is led by an in-house spokesperson often is very reluctant, as it should be, to enter into signed agreements on language that has been recommended by the teachers' association. As a result, negotiations can be delayed for as much as a month or more because of the insecurity and reluctance on the part of the board's team to reach agreement on language.

In contrast, a professional negotiator is expected to immediately understand the significance of the language and to advise management on any language-related problems. A professional negotiator should also be able to present counterproposals in appropriate language without unnecessary delay. An ability to quickly analyze language and respond appropriately can be a big asset in bringing negotiations to a productive conclusion.

Very few negotiations are completed without some self-imposed deadlines that result in zero-hour marathon bargaining sessions. Under these conditions, analysis and immediate response abilities are invaluable. The professional negotiators earn their keep under such conditions. A capable professional negotiator can assure that last-minute decisions and language agreements do not contain undetected hidden costs and/or problematic language.

An ability to separate the wheat from the chaff

The individuals in charge of the negotiations need to have the ability to understand what is important, when it is important to settle certain issues, and when to stand firm on others. Early negotiation strategies and settlement of minor issues become very important to the overall progress of negotiations. The more time that is spent on an item, the more important it becomes; therefore, it is important not to let a minor item for the board get blown out of proportion. The professional negotiator, in part, is paid for knowing when to resolve certain items and when to resist settlement.

Professionals dealing with professionals

Professional negotiators for the board and the teachers' association constantly come in contact with and negotiate against each other on the circuit. Thus, no one particular negotiating session is so important that one party is going to ruin his/her credibility with the other party for future negotiating sessions. Even though each party is forcefully representing the interests of his/her side, over time, a mutual respect and understanding develops between the two negotiators. As a result, there is less of an inclination to take advantage of the individual on the other side or to offer language that a professional will be unlikely to accept. Unreasonable positions may not be held as tenuously as might be the case with an in-house negotiator.

Ability to devote an appropriate amount of time to the negotiations process

Superintendents and other administrators are required to spend extremely long hours providing general leadership to the school district.

Negotiating in and of itself is a time-consuming process, often lasting months. To add the role of spokesperson to the superintendent's already overcrowded agenda would present an untenable time commitment. Something would have to give. Either the schools would be lacking in leadership during the negotiating period, or the negotiations process would receive inadequate attention and preparation. Neither alternative is an acceptable one.

Preserving the superintendent's relationship with the board

The importance of the relationship between the superintendent and the board of education is a major reason the majority of superintendents should not attempt to go through the negotiations process without professional assistance. The first obstacle is preparing the board for negotiations. Traditionally, boards begin the negotiations process by being very aggressive. They believe that the board's negotiating team should have very little latitude in the negotiating process. It is important that the board members be made to understand that this is not an appropriate attitude. They must understand that negotiating is a dynamic give-and-take process. If there is to be a satisfactory conclusion, compromises must be made along the way. An outside professional negotiator can often be more direct in addressing the board relative to these matters.

As negotiations progress, it is likely there will not be unanimity among the board members on strategy, what concessions must be made, the presentation of final offers, etc. As a result, some will probably be unhappy with decisions reached. If this unhappiness is directed at the superintendent, it could impair relationships long after the contract is settled.

By being actively involved in the negotiating process, but not as the spokesperson, the superintendent avoids much of the unpleasantness at the table that could have long-range implications on his/her staff relations. If the negotiations go well, the superintendent can receive a lion's share of the credit; if they prove troublesome, the hired gun can take the brunt of the criticism.

The Role of the Superintendent

The most important thing that a superintendent can do for the negotiations process is to work continually toward the development of a positive labor relations climate. How the staff feels at any given time will have a major impact on the problems and language that come to the table. For instance, a contract that has resulted in few grievances and questions of interpretation will mean a smaller new package with fewer changes brought to the table by the union.

The attitude taken by the staff when they come to the table is also affected by the general labor relations climate within the system. The superintendent must be certain that the spokesperson is fully aware of the labor relations dynamics that have transpired in the district since the last negotiations.

The superintendent as the chief executive officer of the board must always be in control of the negotiations. S/he must advise the spokesperson on such things as the goals of the board, what management would specifically like to see accomplished, and the attitude to be displayed by the board's team during negotiations.

The superintendent must be the leader in the development of the board's proposals and counterproposals. In providing this leadership, s/he must coordinate the thoughts and efforts of the board, other administrators, and the spokesperson. After the proposals have been developed, the superintendent must work with the spokesperson to jointly determine the strategies that will be used in presenting and defending the proposals at the table.

Once the negotiations begin at the table, the superintendent should be available at all times, preferably at the table, to monitor progress and to make certain the board's goals are being met. If there is a variance from the strategies previously developed, the superintendent must work closely with the spokesperson to alter plans appropriately. The superintendent must then inform the board of these changes and continuously keep the board informed of the progress and dynamics taking place during the negotiations.

It is essential that the superintendent keep the communication lines open during negotiations. S/he must obtain information from a number of sources relative to the dynamics within the staff, community, and board. The potential pressures exerted by one side on the other are central to the negotiations process. The superintendent must have a good barometer to accurately perceive the ebb and flow of feelings. S/he must share these perceptions with the spokesperson and board.

A key role of the superintendent is to oversee the analysis of financial data and the development of the board's financial proposals and counterproposals. These analyses and proposals must be accurate because they determine the financial parameters within which the board must negotiate. A mistake in either direction can have a negative impact on the district for years.

In summary, the superintendent plays a crucial role in the negotiations process, even when a hired gun is used as the spokesperson. S/he has a major responsibility in helping the board establish viable negotiating goals, and s/he also retains responsibility as the ultimate decision-maker during the day-to-day negotiating process.

THE SUPERINTENDENT AS SPOKESPERSON

Traditional Assumptions

Conventional wisdom in educational administration has dictated against the superintendent serving as the spokesperson for the board during negotiations. This time-honored position has generally been supported by three assumptions. First, the superintendent will somehow destroy her/his ability to provide leadership to the district if s/he becomes involved in the confrontational activities of collective bargaining. Second, it takes a tremendous amount of time and energy to negotiate. This is time and energy taken away from the other important activities of the superintendent. In general, the negotiation process will tend to overshadow all of the other activities. Third, the superintendent is probably not an expert in negotiations. Thus, a skilled outside professional negotiator will do a better job.

Each of these bits of conventional wisdom can be challenged. The dangers of losing educational leadership ability because of confrontation can be challenged on two fronts. The first is that no successful leader has ever led without some confrontation. Being able to lead in the face of and in spite of confrontation is a sign of a good leader. The second is that serious confrontation is not necessary in the negotiation process. A good negotiator can reach agreement successfully with a minimum of real confrontation (real as opposed to the usual theatrics inherent in the playing out of roles by the participants in the game).

The second assumption is that the amount of time and energy taken away from other more important activities in a superintendent's life places the negotiation of an acceptable contract much too low on the superintendent's priority list. However, in the contemporary setting, one of the most important things a superintendent can do is negotiate a good contract. All the excellent work done on curriculum, academic achievement, staff relations, community relations, etc., will be for naught if the negotiated contract does not permit the superintendent to effectively lead the school district.

The contract is binding on all who work in the system. It can be the single most important document in the working life of the staff and management. It sets salary, working conditions, and the parameters within which the staff, administrators, superintendent, and school board will relate to each other. As superintendent, one cannot afford to leave such an important piece of work in the hands of an outsider who will leave as soon as the contract is settled. Also, in all likelihood, the professional negotiator will not be an educator and will not fully comprehend the nuances inherent to an educational organization.

The third statement that the superintendent is not a negotiations expert and does not work at it every day assumes that a superintendent cannot become a good negotiator. In reality, all superintendents negotiate every day. Successful negotiations is an ongoing process that is carried out daily with every contact the members of the management team have with the other employees in the district.

Advantages Gained by Serving as the Spokesperson

If a superintendent is to advantageously use the negotiations process as a management tool, then the process must take place year-round. The psychological preparation, the planting of ideas, and the analysis of current operations and attitudes must be done daily throughout the year. All of these things have a bearing on what takes place at the negotiating table. They must be used advantageously at the table to achieve optimal contract language. An outside negotiator cannot do this because s/he is not in the system on a daily basis.

Everything that affects the staff affects negotiations. Thus, everything the school board, superintendent, and principals do affects negotiations. These daily activities establish the atmosphere and tone that will prevail at the table.

Another key to successful negotiations is trust. This seems so obvious that it need not be mentioned, but, unfortunately, it is often not present at the bargaining table. Trust is an elusive element that is somewhat mercurial in nature and has many forces working to drive it away. It takes daily effort over a long period of time to achieve, and yet, a single incident by someone unfamiliar with a situation can destroy it immediately.

Trust can be built at the bargaining table. As an example, on one occasion, a union put a proposal on the table asking for less sick leave and lower severance pay than they already had. This was an obvious mix-up, but under the rules at the table, it was irretrievable. The choices for the superintendent were clear: accept that part of the proposal as written and get three years of less sick leave and lower severance pay or gently let the union save face. The board's decision to go with a timely rejection of this proposal along with a suggestion that sick leave and severance pay be brought back to the current level achieved two things. First, it prevented bitter feelings and resentment that would have been forthcoming on the part of the union leaders when they realized that the superintendent had embarrassed them by capitalizing on their mistake. Second, it made the superintendent look more competent and caring about the staff members than the union. This did nothing but enhance the positive psychological image of the superintendent with the staff.

The third primary key is the achievement of a "we win" attitude at the conclusion of negotiations. This is not to be confused with the win-win process of negotiating. Win-win can be used advantageously, but it is a process. We win is a state of mind that can be achieved via a variety of mechanical processes. We win is essential to successful, nonconfrontational negotiations. One can have things come out the way one wants and still not antagonize the staff. This takes a conscious effort and involves looking at things from the other person's point of view. It does not mean giving in to all union demands.

We win means simply that, when the collective bargaining process is over, both sides will feel good about the settlement. There will be few settlements in which both parties are completely satisfied with the agreement, but a feeling and sense of satisfaction must be there for both.

Self-Assessment

In order to capitalize on the advantages outlined above, the spokesperson for the board must possess the appropriate personal traits and mind-set. A self-assessment of these items is in order to aid one in making the decision to serve as the spokesperson. By both formal and informal means, one needs to obtain answers to the following questions: How do I lead? What is my dominant leadership style? What is my dominant decision-making style? What makes me react? What is my value system? It is important to develop a personal profile of this nature in order to get a handle on how one is likely to react in the role of spokesperson.

The union members will be making judgments of their own, relative to the superintendent's personal traits. They will attempt to use these traits to their advantage during negotiations. For example, if the union perceives the superintendent as an impatient person, it may prolong negotiations in the hopes of obtaining more concessions from the superintendent who wants the negotiations to progress at a more rapid pace and is eager to bring closure to the entire process. If it perceives the superintendent as a combative, reactive sort, it will attempt to goad him/her into personal confrontations and rash reactions. If the superintendent has great pride in being fair, the union will couch its demands in terms of fairness; e.g., it is only fair that no teacher should have more than twenty-five students in a class because some teachers have classes with as few as fifteen enrolled. Or, if the superintendent likes to be perceived as a very logical individual, the union may present its class size argument in terms of logic, e.g., smaller classes are bound to enhance the learning environment because there will be fewer disruptions and fewer papers to grade, the students will receive more individualized attention, etc.

If the self-analysis process uncovers some factors that could be detrimental to one's effectiveness as a spokesperson, one must make some decisions relative to the severity with which they will impact on the spokesperson's role. It also is necessary to assess the level of motivation one has to learn and practice new and more appropriate behavior patterns. While there is some debate on the issue, there is evidence that one's behavior patterns can be changed if there is a commitment to do so.

The mind-set one has toward the bargaining process is the second factor that must be addressed when making a decision on serving as the board's spokesperson. If one looks upon collective bargaining as a big game—a big game that makes poor use of valuable time—this attitude will quickly become evident at the table. If one does not feel comfortable entering into personal and intense give-and-take for hours at a time, serving as the spokesperson will be a very trying experience. In fact, if one dreads the thought of bargaining for whatever reasons, the spokesperson's role will not be a positive experience. It has been said that, if one does not envy the role of a trial lawyer, then one will probably not enjoy negotiating. One has to look forward to and enjoy being a participant in the process.

Under no circumstances should one agree to be the chief spokesperson at the table unless one has observed and participated in a contract negotiation in some capacity. There is a feel for the process that is difficult to put into words. Negotiations is a game, a serious one, but a game nonetheless. Like all other games, it has rules, both written and unwritten. The written rules come from collective bargaining law and procedures, and the unwritten rules come from the process, psychology, and strategy. To use an analogy, in poker, the written rules say a flush beats a straight, and three-of-a-kind beats a pair. An unwritten rule says never draw to an inside straight. Winning poker players have learned both the written and unwritten rules. They know when to raise and when to fold. They know how to read other players. A good spokesperson is like a good poker player.

In the final analysis, if one decides to take on the role of spokesperson, this responsibility will be in addition to the other negotiating responsibilities discussed earlier in the chapter. The superintendent must still be the general overseeing the negotiation process and, in addition, now will be serving as the platoon leader.

COLLABORATIVE BARGAINING

While the collaborative bargaining concept has been around for several years, it is just beginning to be recognized as a viable alternative to the traditional adversarial across-the-table bargaining. It is an emerging concept, and, as such, the participant roles are not well defined.

As school organizations become more threatened by external factors such as student choice, citizen and legislative discontent, and negative media coverage, the leaders within the school organization, including the union leaders, are coming to the realization that the ranks must be closed and a united front presented. Collaborative bargaining seems to be a viable alternative to help with this effort.

In another scenario, school systems that have had bad experiences with traditional bargaining (low employee morale, a nasty strike, many grievances, etc.) are looking for a viable alternative. Collaborative bargaining is often the alternative to which these districts are turning.

Differences between Collaborative and Traditional Bargaining

Traditional bargaining is reflective of two distinct teams, i.e., management and labor. In contrast, the collaborative process requires that the board/administration and the teachers' association work together as one team. This team looks at the interests of the parties and seeks solutions that meet their respective needs.

Communication in traditional bargaining is usually through a single spokesperson for labor and one for management. But the collaborative approach encourages *all* participants to take an active role in the process. All participants are considered equal members of the team, and they have the responsibility to share their insights and perspectives during open discussions on the issues.

Traditional bargaining usually takes place in a formal environment where lengthy discussions sometimes arise regarding such minor details as table and seating assignments. The collaborative approach is much more informal in design. Participants are encouraged to sit in alternating seats (administrator, teacher, administrator, teacher, etc.) so that the outward effect is that of an integrated team. Refreshments are often enjoyed during the sessions, with the board and teachers' association jointly picking up the cost.

Traditional negotiations typically focus on problems facing the school district. In contrast, the collaborative model focuses on solutions. The team is taught to brainstorm ideas and to use problem-solving techniques to identify and evaluate appropriate solutions.

Traditional bargaining is characterized by the exchange of written proposals and counterproposals; however, written proposals are seldom, if ever, exchanged in the collaborative process. Instead, the concentration is on issues, interests, and joint problem solving that occur at the bargaining table.

Compromise is expected in the traditional approach, while consensus is sought in the collaborative model. Caucuses typify traditional efforts, but they are discouraged, if not prohibited, in collaborative bargaining.

Traditional negotiations are often adversarial, fostering a "we-they" attitude, which has a negative impact throughout the organization. A collaboration problem-solving approach focuses on trust and cooperation. It fosters a "we" attitude among team members, which can evolve into a positive working environment well beyond the negotiations process.

Factors to Consider before Changing to the Collaborative Approach

If collaborative negotiations are to be successful, the superintendent and the top association/union leadership must be committed to change. The administrative and union leaders must be personally involved in promoting the process. Not everyone will be sold on the idea. A collaborative selling process must take place.

There has to be some evidence of successful labor/management cooperation during the term of the existing contract, and there has to be a willingness on the part of both parties to fully share bargaining information. Along with this cooperative/sharing attitude, a willingness to forego the use of power to secure outcomes must be present. The absence of clearly divisive issues also is very helpful.

The participants in the process must have an understanding and acceptance of the process. To this end, they must agree to participate in team-building training and collaborative process techniques. Also, there needs to be enough time remaining prior to contract expiration to allow for effective participant training to occur and for the collaborative process to be used effectively. In general, the participants must realize that collaboration takes time.

The Collaborative Bargaining Process

While there are a number of collaborative approaches to bargaining, a process offered by the Federal Mediation and Conciliation Service called "Interest Based Bargaining" (IBB) will be explored. The IBB problem-solving cycle is as follows:

1. Agree on a list of issues: Sometimes each participant is asked to write a sentence addressing his/her concerns. Through discussion and consensus techniques, issues of mutual concern are identified.

2. Discuss interests on one issue: It often is discovered that many interests on the issue are mutual to both parties. It is building upon mutual interests that can further facilitate the process.

3. Generate options on the issue: A number of techniques such as brainstorming, force fitting, story boarding, etc., are available to help generate options. It is important that all participants feel free to offer options at this stage without criticism and without anyone taking a position regarding the options offered. In this manner, many more options will be offered, and creativity becomes the norm.

4. Establish and apply standards: The standards are applied to the options in an effort to decide which one(s) represents viable solutions. The standards, such as cost-effective, fair, legal, manageable, and mutually beneficial, are reviewed to see if the options meet the standards. If so, then the parties can review the options that meet the criteria to determine if the parties can reach consensus. If consensus cannot be reached at that time, the parties can always set the matter aside for further discussion and review with other articles. If a settlement is not reached in this manner, as a minimum, everyone is aware of others' interests.

5. Reduce the solutions to appropriate written language: It is important that this be done as soon as possible and brought back to the group for consensus on the final language.

Additional Factors in Successful Collaborative Bargaining

1. The key participants on both sides must
   - be trained *together* in the collaborative problem-solving approach
   - be committed to the process
   - understand the issues confronting the organization
   - have realistic expectations for the process
   - recognize that collaboration and change takes time! All participants must be patient as they work together to build relationships and seek mutually satisfying solutions to identified areas of concern. Participants must also understand that some of their constituents may not buy into this process.

2. There should be open access to all information—including financial data—required by the team. Openness and honesty are key elements in the process.

3. If possible, the team should begin with easily solvable problems

and then move toward more challenging issues after several smaller successes.

4. Team members should communicate with their respective constituents throughout negotiations. This is especially important in an organization where many individuals are still skeptical about the collaborative approach.

5. The whole effort should be based on partnership, cooperation, and trust.

6. Follow-up is key. In order to have the greatest impact on the organization, the collaborative process should become an integral part of the school system's operation. This is typically accomplished through a systemwide committee, often referred to as a "communications forum" or labor/management committee. The forum, or committee, should be comprised of teachers and administrators who focus on significant areas of system concern, such as communication, student discipline, or teacher evaluation. Temporary committees should also be formed to address selected topics, and building-level advisory groups should be empowered to settle building-level issues. In other words, collaboration should not be limited to formal negotiations. Instead, the collaborative process should become a dynamic part of the system so that mutual trust and cooperation are reflected in the day-to-day operation of the school system.

The importance of the development of mutual trust and cooperation cannot be overstated. The greatest benefit is that educational quality and effectiveness increase when all members of the school system are enthusiastically working together to implement a strategic plan.

Additionally, the number of formal grievances decreases. This is significant because it results in both time and monetary savings for the school system. Processing a formal grievance demands the personal attention of the superintendent, as well as other administrative personnel, and represents a cost factor in employee time and the employment of an outside consultant skilled in grievance processing, usually an attorney. The further the grievance proceeds through the resolution process, the greater is the cost to the system in terms of both time and money.

If a grievance reaches the arbitration stage, which is the final stage of most grievance processes, the costs to the system in time and money are considerable. An arbitration hearing is much like a court proceeding, in that there are opening statements; the presentation of evidence, witnesses, and arguments; cross-examinations; and summation statements (American Arbitration Association, 1993, p. 16). There are a few superintendents trained and skilled enough in this proceeding to adequately represent their system. Thus, the employment of legal counsel is usually an imperative. The superintendent will be responsible for doing all the data collection, which can be considerable. This means that much superintendent and staff time will be diverted from other tasks. Finally, an arbitration hearing involves the union, in addition to the individual filing of the grievance, and is a very divisive process. It has the potential of destroying in a short period of time the mutual trust and cooperation that may have taken years to build.

Role of the Superintendent

The superintendent is expected to participate in the collaborative bargaining process. While participating, s/he is but one among equals. No concessions are made to position power. The strength lies in the unified decision-making of the group. Interestingly, the superintendent's position is somewhat analogous to a board of education member whose only formal power is through the collective action of the board.

The peer role is one in which the superintendent seldom finds himself/herself within his/her school system. It is very important for the superintendent to play this role well, for one impatient or intolerant outburst can put a damper on the entire process. S/he may need preparation and practice in fulfilling the role effectively. It is somewhat ironic that, while the superintendent is only one among equals in bringing the collaborative process to a successful conclusion, s/he is capable of severely impeding the process in a few seconds with an untimely remark.

Role of Outside Agents

The role of outside agents is very different in collaborative bargaining. In traditional bargaining, the "hired guns" have had a significant role in the presentation of their parties' positions. In collaborative bargaining, the outside agents become equal members of the process. No one is more important than anyone else. The outside agents must have the skill to assist in the facilitation of the process and to look for ways in which the group can be creative in its problem-solving techniques.

A very important role of the professional in this process is to work with the other side in developing language that meets the needs of all participants. The parties may agree or understand in concept what is desired, but appropriate language must be drafted that will reflect these agreements and understandings.

PSYCHOLOGY OF NEGOTIATING

Regardless of the bargaining process used, a knowledge of psychological/motivational theories and their applications can greatly enhance the quality of both the process and the outcomes. Some insights into the psychology of negotiating follow.

Most books on collective negotiations deal with things like the law, labor board rulings, unfair labor practices, arbitration, and language. These are all things in which a negotiator should be well versed, but the real secret of negotiation success resides in the psychological dimension. As a basis for the discussion of the psychology of negotiations, Maslow's hierarchy of needs and Herzberg's motivation-hygiene theory, as explained in the chapter on motivation, are used.

Much of what is negotiated is at the first two levels of Maslow's hierarchy, the physiological and safety-security levels. Such things as salary, fringe benefits, tenure, fair dismissal, and working conditions fall into these categories. According to Herzberg, satisfaction of needs at this level will keep productivity from decreasing but will not bring about increased productivity.

In reality, the alleged physiological and safety-security factors identified in the preceding paragraph may be symbols for something else. For instance, teachers' salaries are at a point where, under ordinary circumstances, their basic physiological needs are satisfied. Likewise, the education profession enjoys safety-security provisions like few other professions due to tenure laws, and, in a number of states, strong retirement systems. If this is the case, what psychological needs are being fulfilled by the negotiation of these factors? There is some evidence that these things are not only important in and of themselves but also represent a tangible way of comparing oneself with other professionals. In other words, a higher order need, esteem, is involved. How am I valued in relation to my colleagues in other districts?

A good example of this phenomenon is illustrated in the case of two adjacent school districts of similar size and resources who were negotiating at the same time. The teachers in system A had agreed among themselves to settle for a salary increase of 4.5 percent. However, before this amount could be formalized at the table, system B agreed to a 5 percent salary increase. Immediately, the teachers in system A raised their ante to 5.2 percent. The end result was a bitter strike. It is quite clear from this scenario that ego and esteem were much more the issues than the monetary amount.

Physiological and safety-security needs cannot be ignored, for they must be fulfilled before the staff moves up to higher order needs. However, if it can be assumed for the moment that physiological and safety-security needs are being addressed reasonably well in most situations, what about the next higher need level on Maslow's hierarchy, the social need level? It is human nature for people to want to belong to a group(s) that will give them a sense of belonging and identity. This is the reason high school students buy school jackets and class rings. This same approach will work with the staff at very little expense to the board. Such things as staff athletic teams, TGIF parties, picnics, breakfasts, coffee mugs, key rings, caps, tote bags, etc., can be provided at minimal cost. The superintendent should be ever alert to ways in which loyalty to a school building and/or the school system can be promoted. Individuals who have a strong sense of being a part of the district team or the school family are less likely to have a strong militant bond with the union. Loyalty tends to follow identity. The cost and time involved in promoting a sense of identity away from the table is very minimal when compared to the price that likely will be paid at the table.

The goal of the superintendent should be to fulfill the lower order needs on Maslow's hierarchy so that as much time as possible may be spent at the esteem level. At this level, the individuals value being perceived as competent responsible professionals. Satisfaction of needs at the esteem level falls into Herzberg's motivation category, which means that productivity within the system can be increased by negotiating at this level.

At the esteem level, inclusion in decision-making processes and assumption of responsibilities for outcomes become important items.

The information contained in the chapter on empowering is crucial to fulfilling needs at the esteem level.

Esteem needs vary by individual. Thus, more creativity and innovativeness must be used in the negotiation process. However, a simple two-letter word used both at the table and on a daily basis can do wonders in this area. This two-letter word is *we*.

When the superintendent says to the union representative or whoever the significant other is, "We have a problem. Please help me solve it," the ownership of the problem has been shared. It has become our problem to solve; therefore, we must work together to arrive at our solution. The significant other now has a partial ownership of the problem, as well as a partial ownership of the solution. This approach gives the superintendent the chance to get in some positive strokes. It also provides the opportunity to give the significant others credit at an appropriate time.

It is important not to ruin others' esteem at the table. This means that no matter how serious the problem, the superintendent should seldom, if ever, leave the union with no acceptable way out. Individual(s) who are about to lose prestige with their peers become desperate and act in strange vindictive ways. It is never out of fashion to permit the union to save face.

Finally, the negotiation process deals with people more than situations. Thus, one must address people first. The people must be separated from the problem(s).

REFERENCES

American Arbitration Association. (1993). *Labor Arbitration Procedures and Techniques.* New York, NY: American Arbitration Association.

Barrett, J. (1991). *P.A.S.T. Is the Future: A Model for Interest-Based Collective Bargaining That Works!* Falls Church, VA: Barrett and Sons Publishing Company.

Buckingham, G. (1993). *Interest Based Bargaining: A Brief Orientation to the Process as Offered by the Federal Mediation & Conciliation Service.* Cleveland: FMCS.

Fisher, R. and Ury, W. (1993). *Getting to Yes: Negotiating Agreement without Giving In.* New York, NY: Penguin Books, Viking Penguin, Inc.

Williams, G. (1981). *A Lawyers Handbook for Effective Negotiation and Settlement.* Washington, D.C.: The Legal Education Institute.

CHAPTER 15

The Superintendent as Business Manager

The business management area is large and diverse. For example, Hill et al. (1982) list the following nineteen business management task areas, which are applicable to any school system, regardless of size or location:

1. Financial planning
2. Accounting
3. Debt service and capital fund management
4. Auditing
5. Purchasing and supply management
6. School plant planning and construction
7. Operation of plant
8. Maintenance of plant
9. Real estate management
10. Personnel management
11. Permanent property records and custody of legal papers
12. Transportation of pupils
13. Food service operations
14. Insurance
15. Cost analysis
16. Reporting
17. Collective bargaining
18. Data processing
19. Board policies and administrative procedures as related to fiscal and noninstructional matters

Over the years, providing leadership and oversight to these functions has become increasingly more complex; however, the basic task areas have changed little. Books have been written about each of the areas. Thus, skill development in the business management area is beyond the scope of this chapter. Rather, this chapter discusses how a superintendent must relate to the business management area and identifies some business management knowledge that a superintendent must possess.

A "MACRO" VIEW OF THE SUPERINTENDENT AS BUSINESS MANAGER

The business management area is probably the area in which most new superintendents feel the least competent. Perhaps it is no coincidence then that it is also the area that gets many superintendents into trouble.

Board members and citizens have a keen interest in the business management area, and there are several reasons for this interest. The first is historical in nature. Chapter 1 indicated that citizen involvement in education and in the superintendency itself has its roots in the business management area. Thus, there is a longstanding belief that business management should receive close oversight by the local citizenry. Second, business management task areas are tangible in nature. They represent things that can be counted, added, multiplied, bought, sold, etc. Third, money is a scarce educational resource. Many school systems receive a substantial portion of their financial support from local revenues. As a result, the citizens view the school board and superintendent as spending their money and, consequently, display concern that it be spent frugally and appropriately. Fourth, everyone has business management experience of some kind. There are personal budgets to be managed and purchases to be made. There are local businesses to be run. It is little wonder then that business management concerns tend to occupy the major portion of many board meetings and receive extensive media attention.

In a small school system, the superintendent will be required to personally perform much of the business management detail work, with some help from principals and secretaries. In larger systems, professional help in the form of an assistant superintendent for business affairs, a business manager, and/or a treasurer will be available to perform the detail work. However, by whatever means the work is performed, the superintendent must understand the various components well enough to use them appropriately in decision-making; make explanations to the board, media, and citizens; and procure appropriate information for planning and reporting purposes. Foulups in the business management area will not be tolerated by the public. It is usually the superintendent's head that rolls in such instances.

The superintendent is the planning leader for the school system. At some point, all planning gets reduced to dollars and cents. Thus, if a superintendent does not understand the nuances of fiscal management and budgetary development, s/he, in essence, has delegated the planning function to those who do understand them.

The same can be said of decision-making. If the superintendent has to ask someone if funds are or can be made available to hire additional teacher aides, repave the parking lot at the high school, or send some teachers and a principal to an educational conference, s/he has said to this someone, "Please make this decision for me." In the final analysis, the individual who makes the fiscal decisions also makes the educational decisions.

The trend toward empowering others to make significant educational decisions also means empowering them to make budgetary and expenditure decisions and causes interesting dilemmas as to how a superintendent empowers and still maintains appropriate systemwide fiscal accountability. The development of some innovative fiscal practices will be called for, and it is difficult to be fiscally innovative if one does not understand basic budgetary and accounting concepts.

The business management area poses a paradox for the superintendent. Seldom are superintendents hired primarily for their business management expertise, and seldom are they expected to spend a significant portion of their time on business management tasks. They are employed to be educational leaders, to raise student achievement scores, to improve school/community relations, etc. Business management tasks are but means to these ends and, as such, do not merit a lion's share of the superintendent's time. However, business management concerns tend to have an urgency about them and, consequently, often do occupy much of a superintendent's time. Thus, it becomes imperative that a superintendent develop personal knowledge and skills in the business management task areas so that s/he can use them as they should be used, e.g., as support areas to the planning and educating functions. S/he must not become personally immersed in them to the extent that they become ends in and of themselves.

A "MICRO" DISCUSSION OF THE SUPERINTENDENT AS BUSINESS MANAGER

In this section, eleven selected business management task areas are discussed as they relate to the superintendency.

Financial Planning

The budget of a school system should reflect the educational goals of the district. This responsibility rests with the superintendent. S/he must be sure that the allocations to the various budget categories and line items do, in fact, reflect a proposed financial plan that supports and promotes the goals of the school system. This type of financial planning should take place on a strategic long-range basis, as well as on an annual basis.

The superintendent is responsible for budget control. This means not just being sure that the system is living within its budget but also that expenditures are being made that reflect the system's goals. For instance, if a new math curriculum is being implemented, then a series of expenditures by a principal in the English area should at least be questioned.

Accounting

It is imperative that a superintendent know specifically what funds are included in each budget category and how these funds may be spent. It is also important to know how funds may be legally shifted between and among accounts. As emergencies and unforeseen needs appear throughout the year, the superintendent must be in a position to determine which needs take priority and to make decisions as to how these priority needs will be covered within the budget.

The superintendent must know the capabilities of the accounting system used in his/her system and devise ways to get maximum utilization from it. How can monthly revenues, expenditures, and encumbrances best be displayed for comparative and planning purposes? When does the system receive payments from the state foundation program, and when does it receive its local property tax, sales tax, or income tax payments? How sophisticated is the accounting system with respect to the capability to calculate per instructional unit costs? If the superintendent knows the answers to these questions, s/he will have enhanced her/his decision-making capabilities.

A knowledge of how revenue flow correlates with expenditures will enable the superintendent to invest idle funds. Sometimes the investment of these funds for just a weekend can be worthwhile. The prudent short-term investment of funds is impressive to the board and community in addition to generating much needed revenue for the district.

Is the district taking advantage of discounts available for early payment of invoices? Having to pay an extra 5 percent because a payment is made two days late is an expenditure of funds that cannot be justified.

Purchasing and Supply Management

A district can save a great deal of money with good purchasing and supply management procedures. Are complete specifications being developed prior to bidding? Are products tested prior to purchasing to make sure that they conform to specifications? Is bulk purchasing being optimally used? Could additional savings be rendered by joining with other systems in cooperative purchasing efforts? Are inventory procedures in place to ensure that supplies are being appropriately allocated and used? It is the superintendent's responsibility to see that someone is monitoring and trying to improve the purchasing and supply management process.

School Plant Planning

Determining facility needs is extremely important. This entails performing demographic and student enrollment studies and then applying the results of these studies to determine the best utilization of existing facilities. It is disastrous to close and sell a school facility and then have to go to the community five years later and ask for money to build a new one because enrollments have increased. On the other hand, it is difficult to justify keeping facilities open that are only partially filled because the per student cost of operating such facilities becomes inordinately high.

In situations calling for either facility renovation or new construction, it is important that educational specifications be developed prior to employing an architect. It is also important that the educational specifications be adequately communicated to the architect. The superintendent should insist on several schematics from the architect. Revising plans that the architect has used on another project seldom results in substantial financial savings to the district and often results in a design that does not adequately address the educational specifications.

The architect is the key to successful construction or renovation. Thoroughly check an architect's background. What other educational facilities has s/he done? What other projects does s/he currently have underway? Who will actually be doing the work on your project? Does the architect have a history of change orders? Does s/he adequately monitor the construction process? Too often, an architect is employed without a thorough background check.

Plant Operation and Maintenance

The appearance of the school facilities and grounds is very influential in how the community views the schools. Windows broken and unpainted, bushes untrimmed, and litter around the grounds show a lack of pride. In addition to the enhancement of school-community relations through good operation and maintenance practices, some effective schools research has indicated that these practices are also correlated with higher student achievement levels.

The operation and maintenance personnel need to be inserviced so that they complement the educational program. Their schedules should be adjusted to the program and not vice versa. They should be treated as important people within the school organization.

When funds are tight, it often is maintenance that gets postponed. Roof and parking lot repairs, painting, and preventive maintenance activities can be postponed for one more year. Sometimes it is necessary to be these things; however, this is often penny-wise and pound-foolish. For instance, roof and window replacements that resulted from deferred maintenance are much more costly than the preventive maintenance would have been. Sometimes decisions not to postpone maintenance are very difficult ones, particularly when the teachers are pushing for raises and funds are not available.

Personnel Management

Records are extremely important in this area. Accuracy and currency are a necessity. This is an area in which the superintendent probably will spend little personal time but one in which s/he will pay a big price if there is a mistake.

The appropriate selection, training, and supervision of noninstructional staff is often not given the attention it deserves. In addition to providing important services, these individuals can be very effective goodwill ambassadors for the schools.

Pupil Transportation

Policies, rules, regulations, and procedures are very important in pupil transportation. Parents get very concerned over such seemingly minor things as changing the pickup or dropoff location for their child by a block or several hundred yards.

A superintendent of a small district can find himself/herself devoting much of his/her personal time to transportation. Problems in this area can have significant negative public relations consequences and, thus, cannot be ignored or delegated carelessly.

One may be called upon to make recommendations on contract versus district-owned equipment. There are pros and cons to both sides. A very thorough investigation should be performed before any recommendations are made.

Food Service Operation

In many school systems, the number of school lunches served on any given day surpasses the total number of meals served in all the restaurants in town. An operation of this magnitude obviously must be well managed fiscally. In addition, lunchroom workers who are rude to students, a shortage of food, inappropriately prepared food, and more can cause public relations problems.

Most systems have a goal of making the cafeterias self-supporting. Sometimes the cafeteria managers take pride not in just breaking even financially, but in making money. The superintendent must make sure the food service operation is fiscally sound, provides nutritious and tasty meals, promotes a good image of the school, and is also looked upon by the food service personnel in a proper perspective. In other words, the food service operation is for the benefit of the students and the educational program and does not have entrepreneurship as a primary objective.

Insurance

It is necessary for school systems to purchase a number of insurance policies. This is a complex and costly endeavor. There must be constant monitoring to assure that the coverages are appropriate and that they are being purchased for the best possible price.

As mentioned, insurance has become very complex. It is necessary to get the advice of specialists both in determining insurance needs and in analyzing policies. Chapter 17 addresses the important, but difficult, task of working with specialists.

Collective Negotiations

Directly negotiating with noncertified personnel has become as big an issue in many systems as negotiating with certificated personnel. One must be careful to maintain educational flexibility in negotiating a contract with noncertified personnel. The educational program should not be curtailed because of contract limitations in such areas as working hours, job responsibilities, supervisory authority, etc.

In all negotiations, it is important to have accurate and timely information. It is important that the cost of any proposal put on the table be accurately projected. Any hidden costs should be identified. Again, the superintendent may not have the direct responsibility for doing the projecting, but s/he will be the one who will bear the brunt of any miscalculations.

Data Processing

This is the last selected task area to be discussed, but perhaps it is the one that presents the greatest decision-making difficulty for the superintendent. With computer hardware available that can store vast amounts of data and perform an almost unlimited number of calculations in an unbelievably short time, the superintendent is faced with a number of crucial decisions. One of the most difficult is to determine the system needs. Due to advancements in both hardware and software, a vast array of data-analyzing alternatives are available that heretofore were nonexistent. Even with the help of specialists, it is difficult to get a handle on all of the possibilities.

When system needs have been determined, hardware decisions have to be made. Should some activities, such as payroll, be contracted out? Should hardware be purchased or leased? How actively should the system get into developing its own software? Decisions on these matters are not cast in granite. However, due to substantial capital outlays and extensive personnel training necessitated by decisions in this area, a school system is bound by its decisions for a period of years.

CONCLUDING COMMENTS

To be an effective educational leader, a superintendent must also be an effective business manager. It is through the business management task areas that the school organization is made to function efficiently and funds are appropriated and expended in such a way that the achievement of the system's goals is optimized.

The business management area can be a source of frustration for a superintendent. It is a diverse and complex area that must be handled accurately and astutely and, consequently, can become very demanding on a superintendent's time. However, it is a support area to the educational leadership function and must be treated accordingly. It is essential that a superintendent constantly monitor the allocation of his/her time between business management activities and other vital educational leadership-related demands.

The size of the school system generally determines how much business management detail work the superintendent personally must perform. However, in any system, the superintendent must be familiar with the many and sundry aspects of business management and use them innovatively and advantageously in the educational leadership process.

In preparing for a superintendency, one should seek opportunities for exposure to the business management side of school operations. No internship in the superintendency should be devoid of such exposure.

In conclusion, a superintendent must not be overwhelmed by the business management aspects of operating a school system. Providing leadership for educational planning and effective instruction should always be the top priorities.

REFERENCE

Hill, F. W., et al. (1982). *A Special Committee Report Sponsored by the ASBO Board of Directors on the Qualifications and Responsibilities of the School Business Administrator* (Bulletin No. 21, third edition). Park Ridge, IL: The Research Corporation of the Association of School Business Officials.

CHAPTER 16

The Superintendent as Lobbyist

One can no longer be an effective superintendent by just minding the store at the local level. One must work to become influential in educational matters at the state level and, on occasion, at the national level. With many public school districts receiving over 50 percent of their funds from the state and with all districts being directly subjected to state control via state-level legislation and administrative mandates, it is extremely important that a superintendent work to exert influence at the state-level in a way that will benefit education in general and one's own district in particular.

Often, superintendents who do make an effort to be influential at the state level confine their efforts to executive branch bureaucrats because these individuals develop the guidelines for implementing newly enacted legislation. However, to focus one's efforts in this manner ignores a co-equal branch of government, the legislature. It is in the legislature that basic policy affecting education is forged. It is in the legislative arena that superintendents are finding it increasingly necessary to be active. In other words, superintendents must now be competent lobbyists on behalf of education and their school systems. Quite simply, lobbying has become one of the most effective ways of fulfilling one's system's needs.

The lobbying effort is performed as an individual on behalf of one's local system and, at times, as part of an educational coalition with

Mr. Warren Russell provided the basic material for this chapter. Mr. Russell served many years as a full-time lobbyist for the Buckeye Association of School Administrators, a state association for school superintendents. He currently is employed as the Director of Legislative Services for the Ohio School Board Association. He is viewed by legislators as a very reliable and effective lobbyist on behalf of education.

mutual interests. The larger the represented group, the greater is the power base.

Being an effective lobbyist presents another dimension to the superintendency. Lobbying means interacting with noneducators who often will have divergent ideas about what is good for education. Partisan politics and competition with competing interest groups become a reality. The legislative process itself is complex and difficult to comprehend. Foes one day will be allies the next. Legislators will shift their stances on issues overnight. One could go on with the interesting and, at times, frustrating vagaries in the life of a lobbyist. It is a process with which most superintendents have had limited experience. Thus, the object of this chapter is to identify some basic guidelines to start one on the route to becoming an influential lobbyist. It should be noted that these guidelines are just the beginning, because becoming an effective lobbyist is a time-consuming and ongoing task.

In the interests of brevity, much of the information that follows is presented in list form.

CONTACTING LEGISLATORS

General Guidelines

When communicating with your legislator, the following general guidelines will be helpful:

1. Provide factual information on the subject that supports your position. Do not do such things as demand support, make threats, present unfounded allegations, become emotional, or express indignation. Emotional responses are usually not heard.

2. In explaining the problem or issue, remember that the legislator is probably not an educator; thus, avoid the use of educational jargon. Such language will confuse—not impress—your legislator.

3. Honor any reasonable request made by your legislator for information that s/he may need on educational issues. Respond in a timely and concise fashion.

4. Express your views promptly on any pending legislation so that your position will be considered along with the other opinions that your legislator will receive.

5. Do not concern yourself with the legislator's party affiliation. Most legislation that directly affects the public schools will be decided on its merits, as opposed to party line philosophies.

6. Know your legislator. What are your legislator's outlooks, aspirations, and problems? Formulate your arguments, and arrange and present your facts accordingly. Often, a cost/benefit ratio is an approach worth considering.

7. Remember that legislators try to represent all their constituents. Recognize the fact that there are legitimate differences of opinion that will necessitate the legislator's compromising or contradicting your position on occasion. Therefore, when formulating your reaction to a situation, try to understand the motivations and thinking of others who do not agree with your position.

8. Be sure to thank and commend your legislator for the helpful things s/he does. Let your legislator know that you are aware of and appreciate the work and support s/he has put forth on behalf of your position.

9. Maintain contact with your legislators throughout the year. Do not contact them only when you need their help. Keep them informed. Invite them to tour your schools.

10. If a certain legislator has been particularly helpful, give your support in his/her effort to gain reelection. This help can be either monetary or a volunteering of your time. Superintendents typically remain aloof in reelection campaigns. Of course, there are legitimate arguments for not becoming involved in some partisan campaigns. However, do not remain noncommittal on the sidelines while a particularly effective legislator for education gets defeated.

11. Usually, it is best not to ask legislators to introduce legislation. Coalitions and professional associations are usually more effective at this. There may be an occasion when your association asks for your assistance with your legislator regarding the introduction of legislation.

Personal Contacts

A well-planned personal conversation with a legislator is almost always the preferred course of action. During the legislative session, legislators are extremely busy, so make the most of the opportunity to meet with your legislator, however brief it may be.

1. The first step is to get an appointment. You can try for a personal appointment; however, you will probably have to go through an appointment secretary. Appointment secretaries have a tremendous amount of influence over who gets to see the legislator. Getting to know the appointment secretary is usually time well spent.

2. When attempting to get an appointment, give your name, indicate if you are a constituent, indicate your primary interest in meeting with the legislator, and offer two or three alternative times you are available for a meeting.

3. Unless you are a personal friend of the legislator, address a representative as *Mr./Ms.* and a senator as *Senator*.

4. It is often advisable to take a colleague along to the meeting.

5. Be prepared when you arrive. Know the bill you want to discuss and what you want to say about it. Have accurate facts to support your position. Offer a solution to the problem that is win-win for both you and the legislator.

6. After the meeting, send a thank-you letter. If you promised to furnish the legislator with some written information, now is the time to do it.

Written Correspondence

If you are not able to contact your legislator personally, letter writing is the next best approach. By following a few simple guidelines, it can be an effective approach.

1. Always correspond with your legislator and the appropriate committee chairperson. As a matter of courtesy, your legislator should be copied on all correspondence sent to other members of the legislature. On federal matters, limit your letters to members of your state delegation in the U.S. Congress and Senate and write your representative and senators first. As a matter of Congressional courtesy, all letters written by nonconstituents are referred to the proper congressman for a reply. It usually is advisable to copy your professional association on any correspondence with legislators at either the state or federal level.

Address correspondence to any legislator at either the state or federal level to *The Honorable John/Jane Doe*.

Correspondence with legislators should be sent to the following addresses:

U.S. Senator	*U.S. Congressman*
United States Senate	House of Representatives
New Senate Office Bldg.	House Office Bldg.
Washington, D.C. 20515	Washington, D.C. 20515
State Senator	*State Representative*
(Name of State) Senate	(Name of State) House of
(State Capitol), (State)	Representatives
(Zip Code)	(State Capitol, (State)
	(Zip Code)

2. Be sure your letter is timely. Preferably, write just prior to committee hearings that will address your area of concern and, again, just prior to a vote on the issue.

3. Avoid form letters. They are easily recognized by legislators and have little impact. Letters expressing your own thoughts in your own words are what legislators want to read.

4. Some specifics of letter writing are as follows:
   - Clarity and conciseness are essential.
   - Type the letter and use your own or your district's stationery.
   - Identify yourself and briefly state your purpose for writing.
   - Limit your letter to one specific subject; indicate what the issue is; and identify the bill by author, number, and subject.
   - Make your point in the first paragraph. Use the remainder of the letter to explain and support your view.
   - Personalize your argument. Give examples to illustrate your point and how the legislation would affect your school district.
   - Always provide accurate information.
   - Indicate that your district serves x number of the legislator's constituents.
   - Be polite. Reason works better than coercion. Don't demand his/her vote. Ask for it.

5. Say "Thank you" when it is deserved.

TESTIFYING AT LEGISLATIVE HEARINGS

Testifying before a legislative committee can be a very rewarding experience; however, if you are unfamiliar with the hearing process, the following suggestions will be helpful:

1. The first requirement is that you be completely familiar with the bill currently being discussed. Know what the opponents, as well as the proponents, of the bill are saying.

2. Learn something of the district represented by each committee member. This will assist in anticipating questions and in understanding each member's frame of reference when asking questions.

3. It is necessary to register with the committee before you testify. The committee chair will have witness slips available for completion.

4. When beginning your testimony, acknowledge the chair and committee members as follows: "Chair (name) and members of the (name of committee) committee."

5. Identify yourself and your mission in the following manner: "My name is (name) and I am testifying in support of (or opposition to) House Bill (or Senate Bill) (bill number). I am the superintendent of the (name of school district)."

6. If at all possible, do not read from a written statement—summarize and paraphrase. Take no more than seven to ten minutes to present you testimony. Highlight the key issues in your testimony. Describe your positions, issues, and concerns clearly and succinctly. Don't duck the issues. Make a concise statement describing central problems and your expert proposal for resolving them.

7. Use accurate data and examples to illustrate your points where appropriate. If you have charts, graphs, or other complex data to present, pass out copies before you testify.

8. If you wish to refer to particular parts of the bill, do so by line number(s).

9. If you wish to distribute written copies of your testimony, it is usually best to do so after you have testified.

10. Following your testimony, the committee members may question you. Respond only to those questions for which you have

answers, experience, knowledge, or considered opinions. Do not be reluctant to say, "I don't know." Don't try to fake it.

11. Don't interrupt a committee member when s/he is asking a question or making a statement.

12. Don't argue with a committee member. If you disagree, courteously indicate such, state your case, and say no more.

13. Speak slowly, distinctly, and loud enough to be heard by all committee members.

14. Don't be alarmed if legislators leave the room during your testimony. Often, many committees meet at the same time, and legislators frequently have to move from one committee to another.

15. At the close of your testimony, thank the chair and the committee members for the opportunity to testify.

16. Immediately follow up with any additional information that you may have agreed to furnish the committee.

POTPOURRI OF LOBBYING TIPS

Some specific pointers have been put forth in the preceding sections relative to contacting legislators and testifying at legislative hearings. This section includes a score of general suggestions for improving your lobbying effectiveness. Some of the suggestions will be more apropos for you than others. Use those that can benefit you.

1. Know how a bill becomes law. You must know the process before you can effectively use it to your advantage.

2. Be current on issues that interest you. When the legislature is in session, professional associations usually publish a weekly status update of pending legislation that could potentially affect education. Loiter around the legislative halls and listen more than you talk. Legislators like to talk; take advantage of this trait. You need all the information you can obtain.

3. Usually, the best thing you have to offer a legislator is information; thus, *be prepared*. Do your homework.

4. Always be objective and tell the truth—all of it. Learn to say, "I don't know, but I'll find out." Once personal credibility is lost, the return road is a long one. In the final analysis, the essence of lobbying is credibility. Don't lose it!

5. Don't mix facts and personal bias without explaining which is which. Along this same line, don't operate on assumptions, and don't get caught up in too much speculation.

6. Always be on time with material. Provide sufficient background information. Legislator knowledge of important background information cannot be assumed.

7. Identify your priorities. Identify one or two major issues and pursue them diligently. Don't confuse minor issues with major ones.

8. With any issue, know what you are willing to settle for. Understand the art of compromise, trade-offs, and coalitions.

9. Deal with issues, not personalities. Personalizing is dangerous. Your adversary today very likely may be your ally tomorrow.

10. Some people in the legislative process at any given time will be more important to you than others; however, don't burn any bridges. In this day and age, legislators and aides tend to be around government in various capacities for a long time.

11. Relate to legislators from both political parties.

12. Whenever possible, form coalitions. The larger the constituent base you are representing, the greater is your power.

13. Recognize the politics of issues. Remember that legislators have a number of different constituencies.

14. Know as much about key legislators as you can. Study their voting records. What are their basic philosophic beliefs? Who are the prominent constituent groups in their districts? Who contributed money and time to election and reelection efforts? What kinds of advice are the legislators receiving from their aides?

15. Maintain consistent contact with your legislators and other key legislators. Provide assistance whenever possible.

16. Always follow through on a promise.

17. Don't leave a legislator hanging by switching positions on an issue.

18. Always try to share the glory with a legislator. Never embarrass one or make a member of his/her staff look bad.

19. Never bad-mouth another legislator.

20. Always remember to say "Thank you." Put it in writing.

CONCLUDING COMMENTS

Develop your own unique lobbying style by integrating the suggestions in this chapter with your personal strengths and experiences. Being an effective lobbyist is no longer an occasional concern for a superintendent. It has become an integral part of the superintendency. Learn how to lobby well and also have fun while doing it. No matter what happens in one legislative session, another one will follow.

CHAPTER 17

The Superintendent as Consulter of Specialists

Beginning with the passage of the Occupational Safety and Health Act of 1970 and the National Environmental Policy Act of 1970, state and federal regulation of safety, health, and environmental practices has proliferated. Currently, virtually every aspect of a private employer's safety, health, and environmental practices is controlled.

In recent years, a very clear trend of increasing governmental regulation of the public employer has developed. As a result, public employers now are subjected to a number of federal environmental regulations, such as Title III of the Superfund Amendments and Reauthorization Act (SARA–Title III), the Underground Storage Tank (UST) Regulations, and the Asbestos Hazard Emergency Response Act (AHERA). Public sector regulation in the health and safety areas has moved more slowly; however, this may be short-lived because major public sector unions are giving high priority to the passage of safety and health legislation. They also are pushing to have safety and health provisions included in collective bargaining agreements.

All of the areas mentioned in the preceding paragraph require the superintendent to work with specialists. Additional examples of the impact of specialists on the school system are numerous. For instance, the various types of insurance coverage schools must purchase have become complicated enough to require the advice of specialists. If one is renovating or constructing new facilities, one must rely on the recommendations of engineering firms and architects. It is a rare school system that does not have a lawyer on retainer. The recommendations of school psychologists have become very influential in the special education arena.

The list of specialists with whom the superintendent must interact on a daily basis is lengthy. Unless handled properly, these specialists will, in fact, become the decision-makers for the school system. Their recommendations will supplant the decision-making of the superintendent and his/her staff. Then, the specialists become substitutes for superintendent leadership. However, it is possible to interact with these specialists, assimilate and use their information, and still retain the leadership and decision-making reins of the school system. The purpose of this chapter is to offer suggestions for how this can be done.

The next section addresses positive ways to interact with specialists. This is followed by a section on the appropriate use of consultants. The superintendent has complete control over whom s/he employs as a consultant, which is not the case with other specialists with whom the superintendent must interact. Thus, selection of the most appropriate consultants and the conditions of their employment are factors that can and should be controlled by the superintendent.

INTERACTING WITH SPECIALISTS

The objective of using specialists is to get them to serve the school system but not to control it. The first rule of thumb is to confine the specialists to their areas of expertise. There is a tendency for specialists to go beyond their areas of expertise and offer personal opinions under the guise of professional advice. For instance, a lawyer, instead of informing you regarding what the law specifically allows or does not allow, will offer an opinion as to what s/he believes your decision should be. The lawyer may indicate that a student should be given another chance, not because the law indicates that the student is entitled to another chance, but because s/he personally believes it would be a desirable thing to do. In other words, instead of providing you with a set of viable options, s/he has attempted to make a decision for you.

To avoid having specialists substitute their judgment for that of the superintendent, one should decide a desirable course of action and, then, using the example of the attorney, say to him/her, "This is what I want to do; how can I do it?" instead of asking him/her "Can I do this?" There are always reasons why something cannot be done. Teach the school staff to interact with specialists in a similar manner. Other wise, the staff members will allow the specialists to make decisions for them and, in the process, for the superintendent and the school system.

If a law or policy is being put forth as the basis for a specialist's recommendation, ask for a copy of the law or policy in question. Study it. What does it really say? Assign staff members the responsibility for becoming knowledgeable in specific speciality areas. Ask questions, ask questions, and then ask some more questions. What if we do this? Why do things have to be done this way? What would prohibit us from taking another course of action?

Some government bureaucrats who are imposed on the schools will probably resist this probing at first by using verbal intimidation tactics, but a calm unemotional pursuit of the issue will bring results. However, it must be added, this can be a delicate situation, particularly with local officials with whom you must interact on a continuing basis or who might be politically influential. These situations call for exceptionally good interpersonal relations skills, as well as persistency.

Check with other superintendents about advice they have received and how they have dealt with similar situations. The superintendent should not feel that s/he has to rely solely on a specialist's advice.

In summary, if specialists know that the superintendent is going to be inquisitive and do homework on his/her own, one generally will receive more thoughtful and reliable advice from them. No professional likes to appear unprepared in his/her area of expertise.

THE APPROPRIATE USE OF CONSULTANTS

The term *consultants* refers to individuals that a superintendent employs to perform a specific task(s) because s/he has a special need for their expertise. A plan outlining the appropriate use of consultants can be very helpful to a superintendent. When a superintendent has a problem with a consultant, it is usually because enough thought and effort did not go into defining the need for the consultant, the selection of the consultant, and/or the conditions of employment. Thus, each of these important aspects will be addressed individually in the sections that follow. The superintendent has complete control over both who is employed as a consultant and the conditions of employment. S/he should take full advantage of these options.

Need for a Consultant

A superintendent should first determine with the staff and the board the specific problem(s) that needs to be addressed. For instance, if facility utilization appears to be a problem, information on student and community demographics, enrollment projections, and facility analyses must be obtained. Decisions must then be made on which of these things can be done in-house and which, if any, call for the services of a consultant.

Once a problem has been identified, the decision regarding the hiring of a consultant usually depends upon the expertise available on staff, the time available for staff members to devote to the problem(s), and/or the credibility that might be gained by receiving a report from an unbiased outside source.

If expertise is not available on staff, then, obviously, some form of outside help is needed; however, often, expertise is available on staff, but time to devote to the problem is not. For instance, a good demographic study requires a considerable amount of time and effort. If all of the central office administrators are over-committed already, to ask one of them to take on the task would mean that other important leadership responsibilities would be put on hold. Often, it is not in the best interests of the school system to reallocate administrator time to address the problem. Lastly, changes in facility utilization policies usually mean some students will be transferred to other schools. This, in turn, means that a number of parents are going to be upset and that the motives and wisdom of the superintendent and board will come into question. An outside consultant can add credibility to data that are generated and can help to take some of the heat as well.

Consultant Selection

As with the employment of any personnel, there is no substitute for time spent performing a thorough background check. Competent individuals that one wants to hire as consultants have an established reputation. Check their record. Do their projects come in on time? Are their reports meticulously done, and do they provide supporting data to back up conclusions, recommendations, and alternatives? Do they display good interpersonal relations skills when working with the staff and community? And, most importantly, do their projections and conclusions withstand the test of time? In other words, do they have a history of success?

Do not be bashful to ask consultants to submit copies of reports generated for other jobs. Check with other systems who have employed them for work similar to what you want them to do.

Be sure that it is known who will actually be doing the work. Will assistants or, in the case of university personnel, graduate assistants, be the ones actually collecting the data? How many other projects will the consultants have in progress at the time your job is being done? Will they have an ample amount of time to devote to your project?

After all the background and reference checks have turned out positive, there still is an element of art in the final selection. The superintendent should feel comfortable with the consultant. A certain positive chemistry should exist, and if it doesn't, be wary about employing the individual(s).

There are two situations that should raise a red flag. First, beware of the indispensable consultant. A good consultant should phase out of a project. Second, do not allow a situation to develop where a consultant may realize a personal monetary gain as a result of a particular recommendation. For example, a case can be made that the attorney who recommends that a school system pursue a resolution to a problem through the courts should not be the attorney who will represent the system in court. The recommendation to go to court may be a solid one and made in good faith, but a doubt still lingers if the recommending attorney stands to receive a healthy fee for representing the school system in the court proceedings.

Contracting with a Consultant

It is essential to clearly communicate to the consultant the type of report desired and the things that should be included in the report. For instance, facts should be clearly differentiated from opinions and projections. Background information and assumptions upon which projections and recommendations are based should be included in the report. It also is important, when feasible, to ask the consultant to present a list of alternatives with the pros and cons of each alternative listed. This approach leaves the superintendent and board with the final responsibility for selecting a course of action, which is as it should be.

After the details have been agreed upon with the consultant, a written contract should be developed. The contract should be detailed and specific, in writing, and approved by the board. Memories are short on the specifics of employment. As time elapses, disagreement can arise over the specifics of the services to be rendered. A detailed written contract greatly decreases the probability of such a misunderstanding. A clear contract is helpful to both parties.

A contract can be very legalistic in nature, but it does not have to be. More importantly, it should include the specific objectives of the consulting project, the responsibilities of the employing school system, the responsibilities of the consultant, a timetable for completion of the project, the project cost, and method of payment. A sample contract of this nature follows.

A PROPOSAL TO PROJECT STUDENT ENROLLMENTS AND PROVIDE FACILITY UTILIZATION ALTERNATIVES FOR THE A-ONE SCHOOLS

I. GENERAL COMMENTS AND ORGANIZATION OF PROPOSAL

This proposal is submitted at the request of the board of education and superintendent of the A-One Schools. Its general purposes are to collect and analyze data and, subsequently, to formulate enrollment projections, determine facility capacities, and provide facility utilization alternatives. The proposal is organized as follows:

A. Objectives of the study
B. Responsibilities of the A-One Schools
C. Responsibilities of the project director
D. Timetable for completion of the project
E. Project cost

II. OBJECTIVES OF THE STUDY

The proposal is designed to address the following objectives:

A. Determine the educational design capacity and general condition of each facility
B. Project student enrollments through 2005
C. Provide alternatives for housing the anticipated student enrollments

In order to fulfill the objectives put forth above, the project director will use on-site visitations; interviews with appropriate educational, community, and business leaders; and data provided by school personnel, city officials, and other agencies in the city. The assumptions and methods of data analysis used in formulating each projection or alternative will be presented.

III. RESPONSIBILITIES OF THE A-ONE SCHOOLS

The A-One Schools will provide the following data to the project director:

1. Schematic drawings of each facility and addition
2. Construction dates for each facility and addition
3. Interior space usage information for each facility, i.e., number of classrooms and offices, average square footage per classroom, etc. (Forms will be furnished by the project director.)
4. Site data, i.e., acreage, restrictions, drainage problems, etc.
5. Map(s) showing the current school attendance boundaries
6. Data on any special instructional programs currently housed in any of the facilities, i.e., nature of the programs and number enrolled
7. Enrollments by grade level by school for the past nine years. Any changes in attendance areas during this period of time should be identified. (Forms will be furnished by the project director.)
8. Number of tuition students by grade level in each facility for the current year
9. Data on students attending private or parochial schools, i.e., number, grade level, and attendance areas in which residing
10. Data on students attending school(s) in another district
11. Current board policy for the assignment of students to schools
12. Current board policy on class size
13. Itemized operating and maintenance costs for each facility for the last five years
14. Itemized listing of major capital expenditures for each facility for the last ten years by year and dollar amount
15. Copies of any studies performed relative to student demographic and/or enrollment trends or facility utilization
16. Copies of any documents containing data relative to city demographic trends

IV. RESPONSIBILITIES OF THE PROJECT DIRECTOR

In order to accomplish the objectives of the proposal, the project director assumes the following responsibilities:

1. Gathering of all information relevant to the proposal, except that outlined in the preceding section
2. Analysis of all information
3. Development of relevant projections and alternatives
4. Compilation of a written report

5. Providing the board and superintendent with fifteen copies of the written report
6. An oral presentation of the written report to the board and superintendent
7. Travel costs
8. Data analysis costs
9. Costs associated with producing the written report
10. Costs of additional professional help that the project director may deem necessary for the successful completion of the project

V. TIMETABLE FOR COMPLETION OF THE PROJECT

Upon adoption of this proposal by the board of education, the project director will provide to the board and superintendent fifteen copies of the written report on January 30, _____, if the information in Section III is made available by September 1, _____. The oral presentation to the board and superintendent will be made at this time or, at the discretion of the board, will be made on a mutually agreeable later date.

VI. PROJECT COST

The project will be undertaken as presented in this document for a total cost to the A-One Board of Education of X dollars ($ X). Y dollars ($ Y) will be due on November 1, _____. The remaining Z dollars ($ Z) will be due when the fifteen copies of the written report are submitted to the board and superintendent.

The above amounts are payable to the project director, Connie Consultant, at the following address:

> Connie Consultant
> Honorarium Ave.
> Demographic City, Any State 99999

Respectfully submitted,

Connie Consultant
Project Director

PART THREE

Preparing for, Obtaining, and Departing a Superintendency

Aspiring to and learning about the superintendency are academic exercises unless one is knowledgeable about the processes of preparing for and obtaining one. This part addresses these key processes.

After one has "superintended" for a number of years, a feeling of being trapped in the position sometimes sets in. Professionally viable alternatives to the superintendency do not seem to be available. Also, with the advent of earlier retirements, many individuals wish to remain professionally productive and active but are at a loss as to how to do so. This part addresses this career change dilemma that superintendents are experiencing with greater frequency.

CHAPTER 18

Preparation for and Initiation into a Superintendency

An individual's preparation for and initiation into the super-intendency is both formal and informal and occurs both prior to and after assumption of the position. The formal and informal preparation and initiation processes are grounded in socialization theory. Thus, the chapter begins with a brief review of socialization literature in order to set the stage for the discussions on formal and informal preparation and initiation that follow.

SOCIALIZATION THEORY

Socialization is the process by which a role aspirant learns the values, norms, requisite work skills and abilities, and required behavior for a specific role (Clausen, 1968). According to Baldwin (1969), the principal components of socialization theory are internalization, identity, significant others, role learning, and process. A brief discussion of each of these components follows.

With respect to the first component, it is important that one identify and internalize the values and norms that are shared by those in the group to which one aspires or has joined and which are expected for a particular role (Spencer and Inkeles, 1976). This belief does not mean that the individual has to blindly accept all standards and may never question them.

Second, during the socialization process, one assumes an identity—in this case, the role of superintendent. The aspirant begins to take on the values, norms, and behavior of a superintendent and develops an identity with it. Internalization and identification occur together.

227

The third integral component is what Mead (1934) calls the "signifi-cant other." Significant others are those persons "who have great in-fluence because of their frequency of contact, their primacy, and their control over rewards and punishment" (Brim and Wheeler, 1966, p. 8). The significant other may be a group, as well as an individual, and is sometimes referred to as the socializing agent. Mentors and sponsors are examples of significant others. It is the role, behavior, at-titudes, and values of the significant others that are taken on by the one being socialized.

The fourth component is role learning. A role, according to Sarbin and Allen (1968), "is an organized set of behaviors that belongs to an identifiable position, and these behaviors are activated when the posi-tion is occupied" (pp. 545–546). Thus, to perform the superinten-dent's role satisfactorily, the aspirant must know what is expected and be willing to meet those expectations.

The superintendency role expectations are the specifications estab-lished for that position by the individual occupying it and by others who interact with it. Those expectations "define the limits or range of tolerated behavior" (Sarbin and Allen, 1968, p. 501) and comprise "the rights and privileges, the duties and obligations, of [that position] in relation to other positions" (p. 487) in the educational and com-munity structure.

Another type of role learning is modeling. A role model is an in-dividual whose "behaviors, personal styles, and specific attributes are emulated by others" (Shapiro, Haseltine, and Rowe, 1978, p. 52). Ac-cording to Bandura (1977), "Most behavior is learned observationally through modeling" (p. 22). In modeling, an individual observes be-havior, mentally codes it, and later recalls it for performance use. An important plus of modeling is its multiplicative power because a sin-gle model can transmit behavior to several individuals.

Before leaving this discussion of role learning, it is important to note that cultural learning is also important. Culture applies to the or-ganization or institution. "An organization . . . has a personality of sorts, often referred to as an organizational culture . . . [which] con-veys important assumptions and norms governing membership, values, activities, and aims" (Louis, 1980, p. 232). The new superintendent, then, must learn who's who and what's what in the system and community in order to function effectively.

The fifth and final element of socialization concerns the process. The socialization process is continuous and interactional. It is a two-way process involving the socializee and the socializer(s). An individual is not socialized for a role that is then performed unchangingly. There is interaction with others, and that interaction contributes to the continued socialization.

The socialization process is divided into two principal types, primary and secondary, and these are further segmented into formal and informal. Primary socialization is that socialization an individual experiences in childhood and through which one becomes a member of society. Secondary socialization "is any subsequent process that inducts an already socialized individual into new sectors of the objective world of his [/her] society" (Berger and Luckman, 1967, p. 130).

Distinguishing factors between formal and informal socialization are the role of the learner and the material to be learned. Greenfield (1985) notes that "in formal socialization . . . both the role of the learner and the material to be learned are specified . . . [whereas in] informal neither . . . are specified in an explicit, formal sense" (p. 100). Formal socialization processes are found in seminaries, military training, medical schools, and graduate schools. Informal socialization includes that which Wolcott (1973) calls "conventional wisdom," i.e., the verbal and informal transmission of an oral literature accumulated through years of experience and passed on to succeeding generations primarily by the peer group.

Socialization also occurs in two stages, before and after assuming the role. That which takes place before role assumption is labeled anticipatory, and the learning that occurs after role assumption is called encounter.

FORMAL PREPARATION AND INITIATION

Formally, a person aspiring to the superintendency is expected to secure state certification for the position. While the specific requirements differ from state to state, there are three general requirements: 1) satisfactory completion of specified graduate coursework and/or degrees (usually a minimum of a master's degree is required), 2) satisfactory completion of one or more internships or a practicum, and 3) evidence of satisfactory performance in another administrative position within a school system. Upon satisfactory completion of the above requirements, the state department of education issues the applicant a provisional certificate for a specified number of years.

Usually, graduate coursework and/or other professional development activities are required for renewal of the certificate.

In graduate school programs and courses, aspiring superintendents are exposed to the relevant knowledge, skills, and thought processes, as well as to the expected norms and behavior, that are associated with the superintendency. They also begin to develop an image or understanding of the role and its demands.

One or more internships or a practicum is required for certification. Today, most states have increased the intensity and/or duration of the internship or practicum during which the individual is expected to devote at least a semester, and often a year, working under the supervision of a practicing superintendent and university professor. Here, one assists in many of the superintendent's tasks and is gradually given responsibility for some of them. In this way, the person begins to make the transition from theory to practice and gets a feel for the position.

Following employment, a new superintendent is engaged in a second and somewhat less formal socialization process, which consists of an orientation program introducing the individual to the system. The content of the program usually includes an introduction to or review of the system's philosophy, objectives, mission statement, and organization. There is also an introduction to the central office staff, building-level administrators, faculty, support staff, and key community leaders.

INFORMAL PREPARATION AND INITIATION

As noted in the theory section, there is an informal socialization process, the passing on of conventional wisdom and role modeling. This informal process may be even more influential than the formal process discussed in the preceding section. It is a process that does not stop with the acquisition of a superintendency. In fact, many of the informal socialization processes continue uninterrupted as one makes the step from an aspiring to a practicing superintendent. As such, the informal socialization of aspiring and practicing superintendents will be treated together.

Practicing superintendents and professors with superintendency experience share their experiences with aspirants and newcomers. It is not uncommon for new superintendents, and even experienced ones, to call a valued peer and/or professor to discuss a difficult situation or seek some advice regarding an existing challenge. Often, then, it is this discussion or advice that significantly influences the superintendent's behavior in a particular situation or challenge.

Role modeling is another socialization practice that greatly affects the behavior of superintendents, particularly new ones. These individuals have invested several years in education prior to assuming a superintendency. They have been teachers, school-level administrators, and, frequently, central office administrators. In each of these roles, and particularly in their administrative capacities, they have observed one or more superintendents in action. They noted how those superintendents worked with their boards, unions, parents, and communities. They observed their communication skills and leadership styles. These observations were mentally noted and recalled later for application to their own situations. It should be noted that modeled learning can also give one clues on how *not* to act. In other words, while some learning is observed, noted, and emulated, other learning is observed, noted, and discarded. In the latter case, the behavior of the model is considered to be inappropriate for the situation or role. For example, an aspiring or new superintendent may have observed a superintendent who had poor relationships with the community or board and noted that such behavior was not conducive to being an effective chief administrator. Or perhaps the model superintendent exhibited an authoritarian leadership style in inappropriate situations. Again, the observer noted that such behavior was not suitable.

PREVENTING DERAILMENT

Sorcher (1985) estimates that failure rates for senior executives are as high as 33 percent, and the Center for Creative Leadership found a 50 percent involuntary turnover during a five-year period for high-potential managers and executives (Lombardo and Eichinger, 1991). Why do so many high-potential leaders, such as individuals making steady progress toward a superintendency, get derailed, and what are the characteristics of the individuals who overcome these derailment(s) to get back on the fast-track? This section addresses these questions and presents some steps one can take to avert serious derailment.

It is important to note that many top executives have been derailed at least once along the way. In fact, successful managers have reported more failures and mistakes than the less successful (McCall, Lombardo, and Morrison, 1988). However, somehow they have been able to overcome these derailment(s) and get back on the fast-track while others have not. What is it that separates these individuals from the others?

Performance standards change as one moves upward within an organization. Lower level administrative positions tend to have more task-oriented demands that can be accomplished independent of others. As one moves up the organization, motivating others to work toward the accomplishment of organizational goals becomes more important than individual achievements. It becomes more important to see that things are done rather than doing them. Higher level administrative positions require more interpersonal, team-building, and conceptual abilities and less task orientation.

Derailed managers fail to realize that personal strengths that led to early promotions can later become weaknesses. They continue to exhibit the same behaviors that brought them success in the past. They don't learn from their mistakes. McCall (1988) indicates that having an experience is not a guarantee that new learning will occur. Only effective managers added new leadership behavior patterns. To do this, one must overcome comfortable and successful past habits and make the transition to newer more appropriate ones. In studies across a number of organizations, three major effectiveness factors were found to reflect these changing leadership behaviors. The more effective leaders were, according to Lombardo and Eichinger (1991),

1. More adaptable to change, dealt better with ambiguity and complexity, and learned more quickly from a variety of experiences
2. Able to build teams in a variety of circumstances with many different types of people
3. Characterized by respect for self and others. They sought out feedback, delineated their strengths and weaknesses, likes and dislikes. Knowing themselves enabled them to both appreciate others and develop compassion for the inevitable limitations both they and others had.

In other research McCall, Lombardo, and Morrison (1988) found that some combination of the following three factors differentiated successful from derailed executives.

1. They gleaned useful feedback on their performance, largely from reflecting on their job-related successes and failures.
2. They faced a greater variety of leadership challenges.
3. They were, or were helped to be, avid learners of new management behavior which could lead to a more balanced perspective.

This research offers several helpful insights to individuals preparing for the superintendency. The first is that one must be constantly assessing the reactions that one's personal behavior elicits from others. In the early stages of one's career, one may be so intent on accomplishing the task demands of the position that s/he tramples on and is inconsiderate of others. He/she does not see this as a problem because s/he is getting good strokes from the school organization for task accomplishment. The poor human relation skills and inconsiderateness of others do not become derailing factors until one has advanced to higher levels in the organization. Thus, it is important to start making efforts early to assess and improve these skills and not wait until they become derailing factors.

Research performed by the Center for Creative Leadership (Lombardo and Eichinger, 1991) concluded that confronting a variety of leadership challenges in tough, high-stakes, pressure situations played a significant role in differentiating the successful leader from the derailed one. Interestingly, only some of the developmental jobs that fit this description were also promotions. This means that seeking a breadth of experiences in high-risk situations might, at times, supersede the opportunity for a promotion and that one may need to make a parallel move instead. For example, a parallel move perhaps could become beneficial after one has served several years in an assistant superintendency or directorship in the central office. While these are important positions, they tend to be focused roles in which one is exposed to a narrow range of experiences in reduced risk situations. Thus, while one will gain a greater appreciation for addressing concerns from a systemwide perspective, a position of this nature can also become an inhibiting factor.

When a board of education is in the process of selecting a new superintendent, it is vitally concerned with how one performs when the "heat is on." The ability to be "street smart" in applying one's knowledge and experience to the resolution of tough practical situations is the bottom line (Wagner, 1987).

If the apparent nationwide trend away from certification continues, boards of education will have to rely more heavily on their own leadership skill assessment of superintendency candidates. By utilizing the suggestions put forth in this section, individuals aspiring to a superintendency can establish a track record of leadership effectiveness and, by doing so, increase the probability of obtaining a superintendency and of being successful after obtaining it.

ACCESS TO THE SUPERINTENDENCY

After preparing oneself for the superintendency and becoming certified, how does one get in the right position to receive consideration for the real thing? The significant others that one is able to call on at this point become very important. For instance, the professors one had in the graduate administration program, the superintendent under whom one completed an internship, and one's mentor, if the aspirant has one, are often the individuals who can open the doors to a superintendency and who are frequently called upon for recommendations.

Janice Maienza studied some of the characteristics of access to the superintendency and used Kanter's structural elements of an organization as her focus. Those elements, according to Maienza (1986), are

> Opportunity . . . [is] the state of being in a place where one can be noticed by others in the organization. . . . Power . . . [is] the ability to gather resources, to reallocate and use those resources effectively, and get things done. . . . Relative Representation . . . [is] the degree to which one individual is represented in the organization by others like him or herself. Persons represented in the organization by high relative numbers are a part of the "in" group. (p. 61)

Opportunity translates into being visible to those in top positions in one's own system or another system and having one of those individuals act as a sponsor for career advancement. Power means that one should volunteer for and accept assignments that will demonstrate one's administrative knowledge and abilities. Relative representation means becoming an accepted member of the chief administrator's group.

Mentoring is an important part of opportunity. Many individuals, both men and women, move into the top position because of a mentor. A mentor is an influential person who helps one achieve his/her goal, which, in this case, is a superintendency. The mentor invites the protégé into the upper echelon world, introduces the person around, shares knowledge, offers criticism, sponsors the individual for important assignments or key positions, and, most importantly, imparts his/her blessing, indicating that "this is my choice." Mentors frequently identify and nurture their own protégés, but it is not uncommon for protégés to seek out mentors. In the latter case, the person identifies what one needs to learn and a list of possible mentors who could assist in this learning. Then, the protégé seeks to become one of those individuals' understudies. In doing this, it must be clearly understood that the foundations of mentoring are trust and sharing. The individuals involved must be willing to trust each other and share their knowledge and expertise.

Mentoring, in general, is becoming more important in accessing a superintendency, and it is particularly important for women and minorities aspiring to the position. Thus, those currently serving as superintendents can assist women and minorities through their willingness to serve as mentors. In addition, women and minorities should actively seek out model superintendents to serve as their mentors.

CONCLUDING COMMENT

The socialization of a superintendent begins prior to assuming the role and continues during the performance of the role. Individuals who anticipate seeking a superintendency, as well as those who are already practicing, should understand that their socialization does not stop. They must continue to seek challenging and diverse opportunities, pursue new knowledge, and develop new skills to meet new job demands. The role expectations, their own as well as those with whom they interact, are often in the process of revision. New significant others enter their lives. All of these changing socialization components result in changed role performance.

REFERENCES

Baldwin, A. (1969). A cognitive theory of socialization. In D. A. Goslin (Ed.), *Handbook of Socialization Theory and Research,* pp. 325–345, Chicago, IL: Rand McNally & Company.

Bandura, A. (1977). *Soical Learning Theory.* Englewood Cliffs, NJ: Prentice-Hall, Inc.

Berger, P. L. and Luckmann, T. (1967). *The Social Construction of Reality.* Garden City, NJ: Anchor Books.

Brim, O. G. and Wheeler, S. (1966). *Socialization after Childhood: Two Essays.* New York, NY: Wiley.

Clausen, J. A. (1968). Socialization as a concept and as a field of study. In J. A. Clausen (Ed.), *Socialization and Society,* pp. 3–17, Boston, MA: Little, Brown, & Company.

Greenfield, W. D. (1985). The moral socialization of school administrators: Informal role learning outcomes. *Educational Administration Quarterly, 21*(4), 99–119.

Lombardo, M. M. and Eichinger, R. W. (1991). *Preventing Derailment: What to Do before It's Too Late.* Greensboro, NC: Center for Creative Leadership.

Lombardo, M. M. and McCauley, C. (1988). *The Dynamics of Management Derailment.* Greensboro, NC: Center for Creative Leadership.

Louis, M. R. (1980). Surprise and sense making: What newcomers experience in entering unfamiliar organizational settings. *Administrative Science Quarterly, 25,* 226–251.

Maienza, J. G. (1986). The superintendency: Characteristics of access for men and women. *Educational Administration Quarterly, 22*(4), 61.

McCall, M., Lombardo, M. and Morrison, A. (1988). *The Lessons of Experience.* Lexington, MA: Lexington Books.

Mead, G. (1934). *Mind, Self, and Society.* Chicago, IL: University of Chicago Press.

Phillips-Jones, L. (1982). *Mentors and Proteges.* New York, NY: Arbor House.

Sarbin, T. R. and Allen, L. (1968). Role theory. In G. Lindzey and E. Anderson (Eds.), *The Handbook of Social Psychology, Vol. 1,* Reading, MA: Addison-Wesley Publishing Company.

Shapiro, E. C., Haseltine, F. P. and Rowe, M. P. (1978). Moving up: Role models, mentors, and the "patron system." *Sloan Management Review* (Spring), 51–58.

Sorcher, M. (1985). *Predicting Executive Success.* New York, NY: Wiley.

Spencer, M. and Inkeles, A. (1976). *Foundations of Modern Sociology.* Englewood Cliffs, NJ: Prentice-Hall, Inc.

Wagner, R. and Sternberg, R. (1987). Tacit knowledge and managerial success. *Journal of Business and Psychology, 1*(4), 301–312.

Wolcott, H. F. (1973). *The Man in the Principal's Office: An Ethnography.* New York, NY: Rinehart & Winston.

CHAPTER 19

Obtaining a Superintendency

The last chapter addressed the things one does to prepare for a superintendency. This chapter discusses the process an individual must go through in obtaining one.

There are a number of good general publications available on such things as résumé writing, interviewing, and dressing for success, and there are also a number of good publications on the specific process of applying for a superintendency. As one prepares to apply for a superintendency, these publications should be read. This chapter is not an attempt to recreate existing publications but, rather, to highlight specific pointers that may prove helpful in the application process and to identify pitfalls to avoid.

Before discussing the "nitty-gritty" of applying for a superintendency, it is necessary to emphasize that the most important thing to do in posturing oneself as a serious superintendency candidate is to do a good job in the position one currently occupies. Decisions must be made that are appropriate for the current position and situation, not for how they might further one's superintendency aspirations. Decisions made for the wrong reasons generally are poor decisions. If each position is approached as the most important thing in one's professional life at the time, the enthusiasm and dedication so engendered will be a great asset in climbing the organizational ladder. In the contemporary setting, there is too much happening for anyone to attempt to use impact on career advancement as a factor in decision-making.

While this chapter will probably be of the greatest help to an aspiring superintendent, it is surprising to note how often seasoned superintendents who are applying for another superintendency make the same mistakes. Thus, if one is a practicing superintendent but has not changed positions in several years, much of the material in the chapter will serve as helpful reminders.

GETTING IN THE STARTING BLOCKS

It is necessary for the superintendent aspirant to sit down with his/her family and make some very basic decisions before completing the first application. Things such as the type of district and community in which the applicant and his/her family can function and live comfortably must be addressed. Professionally, if one has been an urban dweller all one's life, it will probably be very difficult to function effectively as a superintendent in a very rural setting or vice versa. If both spouses are enthusiastic about a move and view it as a challenge, families can enjoy almost any situation; however, an unhappy spouse has caused more than one superintendent to make a move at a less than opportune time.

How geographically mobile is the family? It's easy in the excitement of contemplating a move for the spouses to agree that there will be no geographic restrictions, but when the aspirant is actually offered a position and moving becomes a hard reality, hesitations begin to mount. The children cry, it seems more necessary to remain close to elderly parents, the good times one has had in the area are recalled, etc. If one goes through the application process, is offered the superintendency, and then turns it down because the community is not appropriate or the family has balked at the move, it will be many years before this stigma is removed. Those who promote and screen individuals for superintendencies don't like to be embarrassed in this manner. It must be added that making a decision not to accept a superintendency for these reasons is not to be confused with legitimately refusing a position because of extenuating factors that surface during the interview process.

Once a decision has been made to "go for" a superintendency, there are several things that should be done. First, let others know that you are interested in making a move. These others could be college professors, associations and individuals who perform superintendent searches for school boards, college placement offices, professional friends, relatives, and one's current superintendent. A good lead can come from anywhere. As a word of caution—at times, one must use discretion in informing one's current superintendent; however, fortunately, most superintendents are anxious to help their subordinates advance. At any rate, before one is offered a superintendency, the board will check with the current employer. Thus, it is only a matter of time until one informs his/her superintendent—not whether.

Start a placement file at a university placement office. If you already have one, make sure that it is current. Ask individuals who should know about your job performance to write recommendations for inclusion in your placement file.

A brief discussion relative to obtaining appropriate references is in order because obtaining references is an ongoing process throughout one's professional career. First, always extend the courtesy of asking an individual if it is okay to use him/her as a reference. Second, make it easy for an individual to complete a reference for you. Briefly, and in writing, describe the job for which you are applying and some suggestions as to what might be addressed in the reference. Provide the individual with a copy of your résumé and a stamped envelope appropriately addressed. Always waive your right of access to the reference. Any reference in which this right is not waived or any reference that the applicant provides is always suspect.

Periodically, significant others in your career retire or move to other jobs. Obtain references from these individuals for your university placement file at the time of their departure. This is true even if you are not in the job market at the time. Also, your university placement file should be reviewed periodically to be sure that it is current and that it reflects the type of position for which you are currently applying. Usually, university placement officers or professors are willing to do this for you. While they will not relate the contents of the recommendations in the file to you, they will suggest additional references that would be helpful and identify references that perhaps are dated or inappropriate.

A résumé needs to be developed and kept current. Most university placement offices offer excellent seminars in résumé writing. Take advantage of them. Not only do they provide some good advice, but they also offer the chance to have your résumé critiqued. This is extremely important even if you are an old hand at résumé writing, because it is seldom that suggestions cannot be made for improvements.

It is through your résumé that you will be judged first. Individuals screening candidates for a superintendency vacancy will be scanning the résumés of thirty to 100 candidates. The word *scanning* is stressed. At the preliminary screening stage, the screeners will not be pouring over the résumé of each applicant in great detail. Instead, they will be attempting, rather quickly, to identify candidates who look as if they deserve further consideration. Therefore, your résumé needs to be both scannable and complete. This is not an easy task, but it can be done.

A résumé must look neat and be consistent in style, and it should not have a cluttered appearance. Don't put as much information as possible on a legal size page and then reduce the page. The résumé must be pleasing to the eye. The different subdivisions in the résumé should be easy to identify, and the contents of the subdivisions should be chronologically arranged and easily read. One work of caution is in order. It is possible to make a résumé look too slick or too much like a Madison Avenue product, and this practice often leads to skepticism on the part of the screeners and board members.

A résumé should be designed for a particular superintendency. This is particularly easy to accomplish in the current age of personal computers and word processors. Put first things first. That is, include the things that you believe will make you an attractive candidate early in the résumé. Items of lesser importance should be included toward the end of the résumé.

Be concise but complete with the contents of your résumé, and, above all else, be honest. Don't make yourself out to be someone you are not. As a rule of thumb, do not include anything on a résumé you wouldn't want to be made public. On the other hand, do not leave gaps. For instance, in presenting your employment history, do not leave some years unaccounted for. This will raise questions as to what you were doing during this time and why the omission exists. In the final analysis, when one is done reviewing your résumé, will s/he have a feeling for the real you?

RUNNING THE RACE

Your preliminary work is completed, and you have let it be known that you are in the market for a superintendency. It is spring, and you are receiving notices of superintendent vacancies. You have already determined what type of system you wish to superintend, so you have been prioritizing the vacancies. Now you check out the top vacancies in a little more depth. Why is there a vacancy? Is the current superintendent retiring, moving to a bigger job, or has s/he been fired or asked to leave? What type of individual does the board seem to be seeking? Is it a split board? Usually, answers can be obtained via informal contacts. If an individual or association is doing the initial screening for the board, either will be glad to respond to these types of questions.

You have selected your vacancies of preference, and it is now time to make application. Follow the application instructions precisely. If special reference forms are provided, see that your references receive these forms. If a copy of your superintendent's certificate is to be included with the application, be sure that it is included.

Spend time completing the application. It is advisable to make a copy of the application form and complete a draft first. Honestly and forthrightly complete everything asked for on the application. Do not say, "Please see résumé" or make such statements as, "This is the ideal school system and community for me." If you are anxious and prepared to assume a superintendency, then this will suffice as a reason for applying. Make sure that the application form submitted is neatly typed; a handwritten application is always a no-no. There should be no grammatical and/or spelling errors and few typing corrections. If your typing skills are not good, get someone to do it for you.

Ask the university placement office to forward your file to the appropriate place. If you are serious about the position, do not leave it to the screeners to request your file from the placement office. *You* make sure that they have it. Make it easy for your credentials to be reviewed.

Now that your application packet has been completed, you are ready to compose a cover letter. Make it short. Do not try to restate the information contained in your résumé and application form in the cover letter. One page is usually sufficient. Include the purpose of the letter (you are applying for the superintendency); perhaps briefly call attention to a couple of your experiences that are particularly germane to this position; indicate that your placement file containing transcripts, certificates, etc., is being forwarded; provide both home and work telephone numbers; and indicate a willingness to provide any additional information that may be needed. Do not be arrogant by including a statement like, "I am the ideal person for your job." The cover letter should be on personal, not school, stationery.

At this point, you have done about all you can do except wait. It is usually not appropriate at this time to have individuals calling the screeners on your behalf.

Boards usually will select from four to ten candidates to be interviewed. Round two of the application process begins. The second round becomes much more intense and personal. You are now going to have the opportunity to present yourself and your views to the board and other individuals such as citizens, teachers, classified personnel, and perhaps even students. This is possibly your first educational interview in which your fate will be determined by noneducators, the board. The questions and concerns will be different than those you experienced in interviews with educators for lesser positions. If possible, have some associates put you through a mock interview.

Now is the time to do your homework in earnest. Most boards, at this time, will send you a packet containing basic information on the school system and community. Study this information and request additional information if necessary. Learn the names and backgrounds of the board members. What are the current concerns and issues of importance to the board, community, teachers, etc.? What is the history of the system? Often, a visit to the community prior to the interview is helpful. Perhaps a review of the board minutes for the past year will be revealing. Another source of information is the local newspaper. One can find current and back issues in the local library. This source can identify current and recurring challenges facing the system, and it can also identify the paper's position regarding the schools.

Anticipate interview questions. What are some ideas you have about the superintendency in general and about resolving certain system problems in particular? (Never be critical of current practices or individuals.) What are some of your strengths? What are some of your weaknesses, and how are you going to compensate for them? For instance, if you have never served as the spokesperson in negotiations, have you had other positive negotiating experiences, and have there been other situations in which you have served as the spokesperson for a group? Why do you want the job? You will not anticipate all of the questions, but you should be able to anticipate a number of the important ones.

Be on time for the interview at all costs. Arrive in town in sufficient time prior to the interview so that you will have the opportunity to relax and collect your thoughts. Perhaps arriving the night before the interview will be helpful. Don't be hesitant about spending some of your own money for travel and lodging. Use some free time to talk with the local people about the system. They can provide you with views that may not otherwise be available.

Dress appropriately for the interview. This may go without saying, but a pair of shoes not shined or a rip in the seam of a suit coat can make a difference. You need every edge you can get.

During the interview, listen closely to the questions. Do not anticipate a question and start responding before the inquisitor has had a chance to completely voice his/her concern. After the question has been posed, look the individual in the eye and give your response. Respond to the question courteously, concisely, and with no more explanation than necessary. This means more than a yes-no response, but it does not mean entering into a long rambling dialogue. It is possible to talk yourself out of a job.

Anticipate some of the dynamics that may take place during the interview process. Sometimes one or two board members will dominate the interview, even to the extent of cutting short questions from one or more of the other board members. Remember that each board member has one vote. Therefore, you must tactfully return at some point to the concern of the less assertive board member(s). Some antagonistic questions may be posed, perhaps by design, to see how you react under pressure. Never, under any circumstances, lose your cool.

Some board members may get into byplay or chiding among themselves in an effort to ease the tension during a slow time in the interview or perhaps before the interview starts. It is best not to become involved in interactions of this sort.

It is good to have several questions of your own to ask the board at an appropriate time, usually toward the end of the interview. Such questions as "What are you particularly proud of in your system?" "What are some of your aspirations for the school system?" or "What are you looking for in a superintendent?" are relevant types of questions. Materialistic types of questions, such as salary and fringe benefit concerns, are not appropriate at this time. If you have done your homework, you will know the general parameters the board is operating within with respect to these items. The second interview is the more appropriate time to discuss specific details of this nature.

Usually, every candidate that the board has selected to interview is capable of effectively fulfilling the superintendency role. It often comes down to a chemistry that develops between the candidate and the board; therefore, it is important that you present the real you. If a good chemistry develops under these circumstances and you are offered a job, you are off to a good start. If a false chemistry emanates because you have not presented the real you, relations with the board will probably deteriorate rather rapidly once you accept the job. There is no substitute for frankness and honesty. For a good relationship to exist, the board must not only feel good about you, but you must feel good about the board.

After the interview, a follow-up letter to the board members expressing your appreciation for the interview is appropriate. If additional material has been requested, supply it at this time. Beware of inundating the board with unsolicited materials and press clippings. Having others contact the board members on your behalf is done at times; however, this is risky business.

Usually, boards do not ask more than three candidates back for a second interview. On occasion, only the candidate of their choice is invited back. Whatever the case, the second interview will be much more detailed and will revolve around specific board concerns for the system. The specifics of a contract will probably be discussed, and you, most likely, will be asked at the conclusion of the interview if you will accept the superintendency if offered. If at all possible, be prepared to give a direct response to this query.

Probably before you are offered the position, some or all of the board members will want to visit your current place of employment. Be as helpful as possible in providing a place for them to hold meetings. Arrange meeting schedules if they so request.

If the board visits the home turf of more than one finalist, this practice can possibly pose a problem, because there will be only one winner. Questions of competence and dedication may be raised within the system of the individual who was not selected. This is particularly true for practicing superintendents. The visiting board should extend the courtesy of asking permission from the finalist to visit his/her school and community. However, if board visitation is a problem, it probably should have been addressed during the second interview. It is hoped that, in the future, more boards will visit only the community of their selected candidate.

A word of caution is in order. Don't take rejection personally!! Obtaining a superintendency, particularly the first one, is a very difficult and time-consuming task. Some of the most successful superintendents had to apply a number of times before grabbing the brass ring.

However, while continuing to apply for superintendencies, try to learn from past experiences. Have a knowledgeable person look at your paper credentials and make suggestions for improvement. When possible, obtain feedback on the style and content of your interviews. Above all, throughout what might be a lengthy process, remain enthusiastic, upbeat, and confident.

CROSSING THE FINISH LINE

You have just received a call and been offered a superintendency. At this point, you will talk contract in earnest with the board. You should know what the general salaries and fringe benefits are for similar districts in the area and what you are willing to accept. At this point, most boards will want to bring closure rather quickly to the selection process. This is a delicate time because you and the board are both on a high. Serious negotiating can cool this relationship; however, it is important to get things in writing at this time. In addition to salary and fringe benefits, such things as professional leave, the process to be used in your evaluation, and the conditions under which you may be released from your contract (either at your request or the board's) should be spelled out. It may be necessary to consult an attorney in the process, but it is not recommended, however, that your attorney and the board's attorney do the negotiating on behalf of you and the board. Problems can easily develop under this scenario.

Obtaining one's first superintendency is difficult; therefore, a beginning superintendent is not in a good bargaining position. It is suggested that attempting to get a number of concessions from the board during contract negotiations can be counterproductive. At this point, the board is somewhat at a disadvantage because the word has probably gotten out that you have been offered the position. If they feel that you are taking undue advantage of this situation, they will have the last laugh. On the other hand, if you accept a reasonable offer and do a good job, it is hypothesized that you will be rewarded accordingly in future years.

One last comment is in order as you cross the finish line and proceed to your new job. Leave your present job and district with good feelings. Resist the temptation to get in some parting shots at your former boss, board, or whomever. Leave with dignity and class.

OBTAINING A SUPERINTENDENCY AFTER BEING FIRED

An unfortunate fact of life is that superintendents do get fired. The dismissal does not always show up as a firing in the local newspaper. One may resign under pressure of nonrenewal, the remainder of the contract may be bought out, or another position may be obtained before the hangman performs his dastardly deed. Whatever the case, the local community and the general educational community usually know the real story.

On the positive side, being fired from a superintendency is not the professional kiss of death it was several years ago. In fact, fired superintendents represent a very capable and competent pool of superintendency applicants.

There are professionally viable and acceptable reasons that superintendents get fired. For instance, a superintendent may be hired by a school board having one or more of the following as high priority items: the strengthening of staff evaluation procedures, passing a levy, consolidating or closing schools, etc. These are all tough issues. In accomplishing any one of them, a significant segment of the community can be alienated. If the alienation is great enough, new board members are elected, often with the stated goal of changing superintendents. As another example, some board members, at times, may get inappropriately involved in personnel selection. The superintendent may have to say no, at times, to such unwarranted board member involvement. Even if done tastefully and tactfully, this action can take its toll on board member support. At other times, such as after a strike, the superintendent is the scapegoat as the community and board look for someone to bear the brunt of the unpleasantness. On other occasions, the chemistry between the board and superintendent just isn't good. This generally does not happen overnight but gradually escalates over time. Nevertheless, it is a situation that can lead to dismissal.

As illustrated above, the key becomes *why* one was fired. The examples represent professional superintendency hazards that cannot always be avoided. On the other hand, if the dismissal was for such things as the inappropriate use of public funds or grossly inappropriate personal conduct, it will probably be very difficult, if not impossible, to obtain a superintendency, which is as it should be.

The information contained in the preceding three sections of this chapter also applies to fired superintendents. However, due to the special circumstances, there are some additional considerations that former superintendents in this category need to take into account.

Being dismissed from a prestigious, high-visibility position is a humbling experience. This is particularly true if this is the first major setback in an otherwise successful personal and professional life. It can give even the most confident individual feelings of self-doubt and personal inadequacy. It will raise feelings of bitterness, vindictiveness, anger, and spite. In short, it places one in a very tense and unnatural mental state. Thus, the first thing to do is nothing. Don't say or do things that will be regretted later. Don't overreact. Things generally are not as bad as they seem. You are not the first, nor will you be the last superintendent to be in this predicament. Take time to allow things to settle into their proper perspective. Talk with trusted friends. Attempt to view the situation as an unpleasant professional interlude that can and will be positively overcome.

In applying for another job, be honest. Don't pretend the dismissal or, in the case of a forced resignation, a pending dismissal didn't exist, or, worse yet, don't be misleading about the situation. Probably nothing turns off superintendency screeners or boards quicker than the thought that they are being misled.

Talk with screeners, professional friends, and personnel in the state superintendent and school board associations about your situation. This does two things. It makes them aware of your situation, and it helps make them a party to resolving it.

From your discussions, form a plan for honestly addressing the situation as you apply for superintendencies. Sometimes, a separate letter for inclusion in the application file is appropriate. This is particularly true if you have officially been relieved of duties or are currently employed in a lesser position than a superintendency. Also, consider how you will respond to probing questions during an interview situation.

Whatever your approach to addressing the situation, do not be negative toward the board that dismissed you. Board members relate to other board members. Recognize that a problem did exist, indicate why you believe it existed, and then go on to point out the many positive things that you and the board accomplished together. Your goal is to show that you can work effectively with your boss, in this case, a board of education.

One last bit of advice is that every situation can be a learning situation. Reflect on your past experiences. What can you learn from them? What can or would you do differently? Doing this reflective thinking does not mean that you are accepting personal blame for the problems that led to your dismissal. Rather, it is an attempt to identify ways in which you can be a more effective educational leader in the future.

CHAPTER 20

After the Superintendency, What?

Superintendents are a part of the nationwide trend to retire at earlier ages. In a number of states, superintendents are qualifying for retirement in their early fifties. With the advent of early retirement incentive plans being adopted by some boards, at times, the option to retire presents itself with very little advance notification. Although being eligible for retirement does not mean one has to retire, more and more superintendents are opting for the retirement option.

Unfortunately, retirement is about the only professionally and economically acceptable alternative to the superintendency. Unlike higher education, where returning to a professorship from an administrative post is a professionally and financially feasible alternative, returning to teaching from the superintendency in the public schools is not a viable option. Thus, retirement, in many instances, serves as an escape from the incessant rigors of the superintendency. Many, if not most, superintendents do not really wish to retire. Instead, they are using retirement as an avenue to career change.

Probably the most common error in making a career change is a lack of proper planning prior to making the change. Superintendents are busy people, and this planning process is something that can be easily postponed. Also, superintendents get used to being the center of attention. To many, it is inconceivable that their expertise would not be in great demand when they retire. Thus, it comes as a big surprise when, upon retirement, the telephone, in fact, does not ring off the hook with people and organizations vying for his/her services. This silence serves as a rude awakening to say the least.

Therefore, how should one plan to exit the superintendency when one really doesn't want to retire? First, one should begin thinking, talking, reading, and asking questions about making a career change from two to five years before one anticipates making such a change. In fact, no time is too early to begin. It can be a fun and exciting process for the entire family if it is done when not under pressure to make a decision.

Such questions as: How much money must one make? If one had one's druthers, what would one really like to do? Does one really want to return to teaching, or would one rather be a travel agent? Has one always wanted to have a business of one's own? etc., need to be addressed. There are books and seminars on these topics. Take advantage of them.

Look upon the planning process as an opportunity to stretch horizons and use imagination; it doesn't cost anything to daydream. Perhaps the financial base provided by retirement income will enable you to do something you have always dreamed about. One individual went to a Caribbean island ten years ago and started a charter boat service to explore coral reefs. Perhaps this example is a more esoteric undertaking than you wish to consider; however, the point is, look at alternatives. Don't approach career change with blinders.

If geographic relocation is a consideration, begin to take vacations in the desired area during different seasons of the year. Is this really a desirable location in which to reside the year around?

Once one has begun to narrow the responses to the questions above, an assessment of personal strengths and skills must be performed. Help may be needed in conducting such a task because most individuals possess much more expertise than they give themselves credit for. (This is particularly true of superintendents.) Via the vast array of experiences one has had over the years as a teacher and administrator, many technical and human skills have been acquired. Once these skills have been identified, there is probably no career change area to which they cannot be creatively and innovatively applied. Thus, with proper planning, the number of career change opportunities is limited only by one's imagination. In reality, the superintendency, in conjunction with the path one has followed to become a superintendent, prepares one exceptionally well for life after the superintendency.

While it is impossible to identify all the possible alternatives for career change, there are four general areas that can be explored. Each of these areas will be discussed briefly in the next sections.

PRIVATE SECTOR–NONEDUCATION RELATED

This is a vast arena with unlimited options; however, it is the area with which superintendents are usually the most unfamiliar because it is the farthest removed from education. Thus, it is the area that probably presents the greatest challenge. New networks will have to be developed, and supply-and-demand thinking must be honed.

The human skills one has developed over the years can be put to good use in the private sector. For instance, most of the larger companies have public, customer, and/or community relations departments. In addition, one may have developed some specialized technical skills, such as in personnel management, which will serve one in good stead.

One may wish to strike out on his/her own. Most small businesses fail due to a lack of management skills on the part of the owners. The superintendency experience should put one a step up in this area and increase the probability of success.

PRIVATE SECTOR–EDUCATION RELATED

The private sector spends more money on education than the federal government. With the increased emphasis on well-trained employees who like what they are doing and where they are doing it, human resource management is going to be an exciting area in the years ahead. Training and development activities, writing training manuals, developing innovative fringe benefit packages, and devising innovative ways in which employees can become involved in decision-making are but a few of the areas that are receiving and will continue to receive attention. Former superintendents are uniquely qualified for many of the activities that take place in this area; however, efforts must be put forth to make the appropriate contacts because there is considerable competition from organizational development specialists.

Perhaps during one's tenure in education, some personnel or organizational needs that are going unfulfilled have been identified. For instance, one individual is doing very well selling supplemental retirement insurance. Perhaps there is a new product on the market that fills a void and would be exciting to sell. Thus, there are ways in which one can take advantage of educational contacts to help market products or services that will benefit either educational personnel directly or school systems in general.

PUBLIC SERVICE AGENCIES

There are a host of public service agencies that are constantly looking for innovative leaders who can provide services on a limited budget. This in itself should make superintendents prime candidates. However, there is more. Most of these agencies have volunteer citizen boards that are somewhat akin to school boards. Fund-raising usually is a primary agency activity. While the agency fund-raising schemes differ from school fund-raising efforts, the basic job of convincing individuals that the organization is worthy of financial support is the same. And in the final analysis, these agencies are service agencies like schools. If one really enjoys providing leadership to a public service organization but would like to do so in a less fishbowl-like atmosphere than is possible in the superintendency, then seeking employment with a public service agency could be a very attractive option.

EDUCATION

Many retired superintendents acquire other positions that are in the mainstream of education. This is good if one does this by choice and not by default. To accept such a position because little thought had been given to the direction a career change would take and because this was the only job available does neither oneself nor education a favor.

In most teacher retirement systems, there are restrictions regarding how much one can work and/or how much can be earned in public education and still maintain retirement status. Be sure to thoroughly check out the regulations in your particular retirement system.

Some superintendents retire to a superintendency in another state. Thus, really only the location of their work changes. This move is usually made for monetary reasons, i.e., retirement income, plus the salary from the new superintendency, is much more than just superintendency income.

There is an increasing opportunity for employment as an interim superintendent. Former superintendents are employed for a period of up to one year to fill the void while a board is searching for a new superintendent. This same concept applies to other administrative positions. In fact, some retired superintendents have formed consulting firms to provide interim administrators to school systems.

A number of retired superintendents remain in education at the K–12 level by accepting employment in private schools. This often is a good situation for both the individual and the school. The school gets a quality individual at a salary that is usually considerably less than the going market rate. The individual can negotiate the terms of his/her contract to suit his/her personal desires, and the pressures and pace are less than those experienced in the superintendency.

Many superintendents desire a career change to the professorship at the university level, but full-time positions of this nature are very competitive. If one desires to make such a move, s/he should begin planning early in one's career. For instance, publications are important in obtaining a professorship. Most practitioners have none, which puts them at a distinct disadvantage. Thus, it is important to write for publication along the way. There are many things going on in a school system that are worthy of publication; however, one must take the time to identify what they are and then must put forth the effort to reduce them to writing. Writing for publication is not an easy task. As such, it is easy to let other things take a higher priority. To guard against undue procrastination, set a goal of perhaps one published article a year.

If possible, teach a university course periodically. Do a good job of teaching the course. Do the necessary homework. A good course is much more than the relating of war stories. Teach as you would want your teachers to teach. Perhaps help conduct workshops. These are more concentrated than courses, often lasting only one week or several weekends. Serve on university committees. This not only gets you in contact with appropriate people, but it also enables you to get a glimpse of how universities operate. And of course, above all, be a good superintendent. Universities don't employ poor superintendents.

Also, universities expect that one's knowledge of administrative theory is current. A degree obtained ten or twenty years ago, without evidence of periodic updating, won't be acceptable.

OTHER OPTIONS

There are limited opportunities for employment with professional associations. In addition to executive directorships, there are positions as field representatives, lobbyists, etc. These jobs are not as plentiful as other types of positions, but they can be personally rewarding, as well as providing a service to the education profession.

Some superintendents opt for the consulting route. This is a very demanding and difficult route. The competition is keen whether employment is taken with an established consulting firm or whether one strikes out on one's own. Usually, one must possess a recognized area of expertise to make it in the consulting field. Unless one is employed by an established firm that trains individuals for their specific needs, it is extremely difficult to be a viable consultant on a learn-as-you-go basis. Consulting is a field that requires much thinking and planning prior to retirement.

In conclusion, the thrust of this chapter has been to stress the importance of planning for a career change. Place yourself in a marketable position. Take control of your future. Be able to say more than, "We're going to travel for several months, and then we'll begin to make plans for the future."

PART FOUR

Health, Happiness, and the Superintendency

This final subdivision of the book addresses the *private* life of the superintendent. The topic was deemed worthy of a separate part because the private life of a superintendent is really not so private. The superintendent and his/her family are exposed to constant scrutiny and pressures that are different from those experienced by anyone else in the school system or community, including the mayor.

The prototype individual aspiring to a superintendency has worked full-time while completing the graduate course-work required to receive administrative certification. The aspirant usually has worked as a school-level administrator and probably as a central office administrator. Thus, the aspirant and the aspirant's family are no strangers to long hours of hard work and sacrifice. The aspirant also has been exposed to some intrusions into his/her private life.

While these experiences are a necessary part of the superintendency preparation process, they do not adequately prepare one for the continuous and intense public scrutiny that accompanies the superintendency. Thus, this part identifies some of the intrusions into the private life of the superintendent and his/her family and suggests some coping strategies.

CHAPTER 21

Life in the Fishbowl

When one accepts a superintendency, s/he moves into the fishbowl. One now becomes a big fish in a small pond. This is particularly true in a smaller district where the first superintendency is usually obtained. Having one's every action closely scrutinized and constantly being the center of attention can be very exciting and exhilarating at times, but it can also be frustrating and stressful for the entire family at other times.

Expectations of a superintendent vary both by region of the country and community; however, some commonalities can be identified that are present in most, if not all, situations and must be addressed. They go with the territory. As such, it is necessary to be aware of these intrusions into one's private life and to do some thinking about how they will be addressed.

The chapter is divided into three sections. The first section addresses the personal demands placed on a superintendent. The second discusses the impact on the family, and the third identifies the unique aspects of being a single superindentent.

PERSONAL DEMANDS

In reality, the superintendent is on duty twenty-four hours a day, seven days a week, as long as s/he is within the system. The

Mr. Roger Stiller provided the basic material for the first two sections of this chapter. His children attended school in the district where he was a superintendent.

Ms. Linda Huntley and Mr. Stanley Heffner provided the basic material on the single superintendent. They are both superintendents.

superintendent is always viewed as representing the school system and, as such, is held to a higher standard of conduct than others within the community. Perhaps this is a carryover from the days when female teachers were not to be married.

The community expectations are such that the superintendent generally is not expected to play tennis at a public court on Saturday morning unshaven and without a shirt and probably should not stop at the local pub for a beer on the way home. Appropriate tennis attire is expected, and perhaps a drink at one of the area's choice restaurants is acceptable. A Saturday evening at a local night club could be suspect, and under no circumstances will driving under the influence (DUI) be tolerated. An innocent stop at the hardware store on Saturday morning or a quiet time at church on Sunday morning can turn into a forum on the shortcomings of the football coach or on financial planning. Examples of intrusions could continue, but suffice it to say, that, while the superintendent is in town, there is no time-out period, and it can even be extended to one's home where the phone can be the conveyer of intrusions. This type of intrusion, however, can be controlled to a greater degree than the face-to-face interactions while out in the community. An unlisted number is not recommended, but it is an alternative.

Selecting a bank, an insurance agent, a real estate agent, buying a car, and shopping are subject to scrutiny and possible criticism if inappropriate choices are made. It is an individual preference as to how political one wants to be and should be in making these selections; however, it would be an unwise superintendent who would not at least take into account the potential personal and professional ramifications that could ensue by going against the tide. Perhaps no one will say a word about the selections, but five months later, one may be scratching one's head on why a couple of the power brokers in town are remaining silent on the upcoming school levy.

In many communities, one should have a good reason for going outside the community to make a major purchase such as a car. Whenever possible, local businesses that support the schools should be given consideration, even at a slight cost to the buyer, the superintendent. An extra dollar spent locally may return dividends in a variety of ways in the future.

Usually, the superintendent is expected to join and participate in service organizations and serve on community boards. These may be things that the superintendent would do anyway, but to be expected to do them as a condition of employment tends to diminish one's personal enthusiasm for them at times. In addition to participating in such organizations, there also may be some additional unwritten expectations as to which organizations should be selected for membership and participation. These expectations change over time, but if the superintendent of the district has always been a member of Rotary, Lions, or Kiwanis, it would be prudent to weigh the pros and cons of changing this pattern before making a decision. Incidentally, many of these avenues used to be closed to females. Recent years have seen a change in this area, and, today, females are eligible for membership in most of the service organizations.

If in doubt as to what is acceptable or what would be appropriate in a community, seek advice from several trusted friends and board members. Combine their advice with past history and make a decision accordingly. Perhaps the community is ready to accept a change. However, if there is some doubt as to the appropriateness of a choice, the adage that discretion is the better part of valor probably offers some good advice.

Finally, the selection of a community in which one feels comfortable is the real key. If an individual feels that the mores of a particular community will be unduly restrictive, then another superintendency should be sought. Personal unhappiness or uncomfortableness within a community is very difficult to conceal for long. Because the schools are really their schools, citizens tend not to want an individual leading their school system and influencing their children who does not share their values, and it is difficult to fault this thinking.

FAMILY IMPACT

A good place to start the family impact section is with a continuation of the preceding section, i.e., moving into a community. With greater frequency, school boards are requiring their superintendents to live within their respective communities. Rightly or wrongly, many boards feel that it is not possible for the superintendent to really be a part of the community and have a feel for it unless s/he resides in it. Also, they believe a credibility gap exists for the superintendent if s/he does not pay property taxes in the district or if one's children do not attend school within the system.

If one is serious about obtaining a superintendency, one can count on being questioned during the interview process relative to one's thoughts on moving into the community. Therefore, moving should be thoroughly discussed, and decisions should be reached with the family prior to seeking a superintendency. Moving becomes a particularly important issue if one's spouse also happens to be a professional with limited mobility. Children can also raise some rather strenuous objections at the thought of leaving their friends; however, unless there are extenuating circumstances, such as having a child who is entering the senior year in high school, children seem to adjust nicely. This is particularly true if the parents are positive and excited about moving to the new community. Nonetheless, while in the midst of the newness and excitement of getting established in a new job and town, one should not forget to take time to stay in touch with his/her children's feelings and experiences.

If one is successful in the superintendency, s/he will likely move three or four times during one's superintendency career. Thus, it is imperative that the moving issue be laid to rest at the onset of one's venture into the superintendency.

Once a decision has been made that the family will move into the school district, other things come into play. Are there acceptable houses available in the new school district in a price range one can afford? In fact, will one even be comfortable living in the district? Often, compromises must be made, particularly if one has become accustomed to residing in a more affluent suburban area.

Most school boards will reimburse for moving expenses and may provide living expenses for a short period of time while a residence within the district is being sought. However, unlike the private sector, most school districts do not help in the purchase of residences by providing low interest loans or by picking up the realtor fees.

A number of superintendents have experienced the joy of owning two homes at the same time. This can be particularly burdensome when the housing market is down. It is not unheard of for a superintendent to be a proud dual homeowner for a year or more. Fortunately, some boards seem to be more seriously addressing this problem area and are identifying innovative ways to alleviate this issue. Hopefully, in the years ahead, this trend will continue. A relatively minor financial barrier of this nature (to the board that is) should not stand in the way of a board's ability to employ the best individual for the job.

The superintendency has an impact on school-age children.

Sometimes the superintendent's children will be treated better than other children, and sometimes they will be treated worse. The only certainty is that they will not be treated the same as other children. In this respect, being a superintendent's child is a little like being a child whose parent(s) is part of the clergy; one is held to different standards than other children.

On the negative side, it is unbelievable how nasty some teachers can treat the superintendent's child. For starters, remarks like, "Why didn't your dad/mother close school today?" "Tell your dad/mother that if s/he would give us more money for supplies we could do a better job," and "Your dad/mother wouldn't want you to act like this," are not that uncommon. It escalates from here. In the aftermath of a strike or if a teacher has just been nonrenewed, remarks and actions can get a little wild.

Children can be very hard on other children. If the superintendent's child receives an award or is a starter on the basketball team, allegations will be made by some that the superintendent was an influencing factor and the recognition was not deserved on its own merits.

At times, the child will hear some very disparaging remarks made about his/her parent. Often, these remarks will be overheard, as opposed to being directed to the child. They hurt nonetheless

It is important that parents keep an eye on their children for telltale signs that being the superintendent's child might be taking an undue toll. However, it also is important not to overreact. Some children handle being the superintendent's child very nicely. Others are more sensitive and are bothered by the remarks and actions of others. The parents need to help the children understand why they are being treated differently and encourage them to take things in stride. They should be encouraged to vent their anger and frustrations in family discussions. Fortunately, most superintendent's children survive this period in their lives rather well and, in fact, in future years, are able to laugh about some of the things that occurred.

Being a superintendent's spouse is not easy either. The spouse is looked upon as an extension of the superintendent. It is difficult for the spouse to be viewed as a thinking individual with the right to have ideas different from the superintendent. As with the children, the spouse will be asked questions about which s/he has no knowledge and over which s/he has no control. What the spouse says and does will reflect on the superintendent. If the spouse makes a remark about the schools or about an individual, by the end of the day, the remark will be attributed directly to the superintendent. Even if s/he has discussed a matter with the superintendent, confidence must be maintained on many issues.

Being the superintendent's spouse also carries certain social expectations. S/he may attend more ball games, concerts, and community functions than one thought existed. S/he will be expected to be a hostess/host on other occasions at functions involving the board and staff.

Perhaps the most difficult part of being the superintendent's spouse is biting one's lip while being a party to verbal and/or written criticism of one's spouse. This usually is more difficult than being personally criticized. One's first reaction is to speak out defensively. To respond in this way usually adds fuel to the fire and does little, if anything, to help the situation. As with the children, it is important to keep things in perspective. Enjoy the positive aspects of being in the fishbowl and minimize the negative.

THE SINGLE SUPERINTENDENT

The single superintendent has some additional pressures that are not normally experienced by his/her married counterparts. This is true even though the expectations individuals and communities have for the personal conduct of their leaders is changing. In most instances, it appears as if community leaders are being held to a lesser standard of personal conduct than they were in the past. Today, constituents seem to be more accepting of human frailties displayed by their leaders.

The superintendency has been affected by these changing values but probably not as much as other public leadership positions. Many citizens still view the superintendent as one who ought to represent the traditional American value system, i.e., married with a family, church attender, active in community affairs, etc. Statistics on the personal characteristics of superintendents bear this out. For instance, the divorce rate of superintendents is considerably below the national average, while church attendance and the percent of superintendents who are married are above the national average. Thus, the single superintendent has unique community pressures because s/he does not fit the norm.

It is possible to be a divorcee and a superintendent; however, even though the national divorce rate is approximately 50 percent, the divorced superintendent is often subject to a special type of scrutiny. Divorce is viewed as personal failure, and personal failure doesn't equate with professional competence in the public's mind. It also implies instability, while marriage implies stability and continuity. It raises the question that, if one cannot get along with a spouse, does s/he also have generally poor interpersonal relations skills. It also raises a concern that the individual is so career-oriented that traditional family values have taken a back seat. The bottom line with these types of concerns is that people wonder if an individual with this personal background is the appropriate individual to provide educational leadership for the community's youth.

If one has never been married, this raises questions such as what's wrong with him/her anyway? Why hasn't s/he gotten married? There is the underlying assumption that the individual is somehow different if s/he hasn't found a spouse. In addition, the same concerns about interpersonal relations skills and professional versus family values with which the divorcee must contend also surface.

There is a concern on the part of some that if an individual doesn't have children of one's own, s/he cannot really understand children. The fact that, over the years, the superintendent aspirant has been in contact with many more children for greater periods of time than most parents does not substitute for the fact that one is not a parent. This outlook has an inherent assumption that certain insights relative to understanding children are reserved only for parents. Of course, no theory or research to date supports this view.

In some quarters, the question is raised whether a single individual can be a good role model for kids. Hollywood's image of singles as swingers and rogues stirs fear in the hearts of the prudent. The fact that singles work as hard, have the same bills to pay, manage households, and live lifestyles comparable to their married counterparts is sometimes not given sufficient consideration.

Most of the social world for professionals is designed for couples. The superintendent without a spouse doesn't fit. For example, an individual does not fit nicely into a bridge club if s/he doesn't have a spouse to keep the numbers even, or one does not fit in with a group of couples on a football weekend at the local university if one is the only individual without a spouse. Attending a social function alone often makes others feel uncomfortable. They believe that the single individual feels lonely and/or embarrassed about the situation. The result is that the single individual does not receive an invitation to the function again in the future. These types of exclusions limit the informal social and political networking important for success in the superintendency.

The social activities of single individuals tend to be more suspect than those of married individuals. For instance, a married superintendent takes a vacation in the Bahamas because s/he needs to spend time with the family, while the single superintendent does so for the purpose of partying in the sun. A married superintendent can entertain at will, while whispers will start if a particular car(s) is seen too often or too late at the residence of a single superintendent. A sort of chicken-before-the-egg mentality seems to exist that says it's okay to marry but not to date.

Unfortunately, it is still a reality that, in many communities, the single female superintendent comes under greater scrutiny than her male counterpart. In general, there is not much a single superintendent of either sex can do about the above concerns, except to be aware that they exist and that one's actions will be scrutinized accordingly.

If one is leading a moral life, there is no need to be unduly concerned about the talk of a few. There always will be some individuals who will delight in spreading rumor and innuendo.

Personal behavior over a period of time, perhaps several years, is the only way that concerns relative to the single superintendent will be allayed. In the process of allaying these concerns, one should enjoy the positive aspects of living in the fishbowl. It does present opportunities to be heard and to be influential. Use these opportunities to advantage and enjoy being *the* educational leader.

CHAPTER 22

Confronting the Stress Factor

THE GNAWING GNATS

You have been in the middle of tough negotiations with the teachers for the past five weeks. At times, it seems as if progress is being made; however, during the last week, the sessions have really bogged down. Salary and fringe benefits are the big issues. Just yesterday, you received notice from the state department of education that your state funds would be somewhat less than anticipated this year and that no increases should be projected for next year. This really leaves you in a quandry as to where to go in negotiations. You are beginning to become extremely tired, both mentally and physically. The evening bargaining sessions on top of a full day at the office are taking their toll.

This morning, as you sit in your office and spend a few minutes trying to plan your day, you let your mind wander from the ever-present negotiations for a few moments to some other concerns. The results of student achievement tests published each year by the state should be coming out any day now. You feel that your system has done well this year but that there is room for improvement. You know the inevitable comparisons by the media with other districts will be forthcoming. The football team is not having a particularly good season, and a number of citizens are becoming increasingly more vocal in their comments relative to the football coach. In your opinion, this individual not only is a good coach but also is a good teacher who works well with students. This situation, too, is beginning to make demands on your time. You have a grievance that is going to arbitration tomorrow. You feel very comfortable with your position on the issue, but you must spend several hours today making final preparations for the hearing. Several hours that don't fit easily into your schedule. Your eyes settle on your schedule of meetings for the day. You have a citizens' advisory committee meeting this morning, a Kiwanis presentation at noon, and a meeting with your curriculum committee in the afternoon. You also have to put together an information letter for delivery to your board members by the end of the day. Your thoughts are interrupted by a ringing phone. A board member who has been concerned about the performance of a particular teacher is on the line. The teacher is tenured, and you are doing everything you can do to address the situation, but the board member wants some immediate action.

After spending twenty minutes on the phone with the board member, you hang up and take a moment to collect your thoughts again. You suddenly realize that your stomach has had a constant knot in it for the past two weeks. You never seem to have a moment, either on the job or at home, when your mind is free of school-related matters. You observe that you have been constantly reacting to a myriad of concerns. You have not been able to slow down enough to do any thinking and planning relative to providing long-range leadership for your district. At this point in time, the job just is not very much fun.

This type of schedule and these types of concerns continue day after day. Notice that no one activity or concern is a particularly overwhelming problem in itself. A K.O. punch is not present, i.e., your contract is not in danger of being nonrenewed—not at this point in time at least. It is the "gnawing gnats" that do the damage, not the isolated big events. More specifically, the persistent and unrelenting pressure that comes with constantly being faced with the unexpected; attempting to provide consistent and proactive leadership for the district while at the same time trying to meet the often conflicting expectations of a half dozen client groups, as well as the expectations of the board; and trying to juggle a budget that is stretched to the breaking point combine over an extended period of time to provide the basis for superintendent stress.

Now let us take a more specific look at this thing called stress, the study of which is a relatively recent phenomenon. Around 1950, Hans Selye was the first person to become interested in performing stress-related research. From this beginning, the study of stress mushroomed until, in the early 1980s, approximately 10,000 articles a year were written on some form of stress. Currently, it is estimated that stress accounts for up to 80 percent of all illnesses. Often, only the symptoms of stress, such as a headache, fever, fatigue, etc., are treated by the medical profession.

The human body's stress mechanisms were acquired during man's early stages of development when immediate reactions were required to combat specific dangers or to fulfill very basic human needs. For this reason, the response patterns of the body's stress mechanisms have become known as the fight or flight syndrome.

In a brief period of time, civilization has developed to the point where most of us no longer have to face the daily physical confrontations that once were required if life was to be sustained. Today, stress is primarily mental. People do things that we wish they wouldn't do and, usually, we have no specific and immediate recourse to remedy the situation. Instead, the situation remains within us and causes that gnawing uneasy feeling. The body is still trying to react with a fight or flight response, but it does not have a ready outlet for this internal reaction. Thus, the stress mechanisms turn their fury on our bodies. Stress, in one way or another, affects most of the systems and organs in our body without selectivity. This type of reaction is called a nonspecific response and can be produced by any agent that causes discord in an individual's mind; thus, stress is a very personal phenomenon. What is one person's meat will be another's poison.

Stress has been defined in the following ways (Lazarus and Launier, 1978):

1. The nonspecific response of the body to any demand
2. The body's physical, mental, and chemical reactions to circumstances that frighten, excite, confuse, or irritate
3. A psychological reaction that causes a physiological action
4. Any event in which environmental (external events) or internal demands (goals, values, commitments, tasks, etc.) tax or exceed the adaptive resources of an individual (psychological), social system, or tissue system (physiological).

Some of the common causes of distress (stressors) are as follows:

1. Frustration at one's work
2. Frustration in one's private life
3. Lack of motivation
4. Personality conflicts
5. Role conflicts
6. Time pressures
7. Career frustration
8. Lack of closure
9. Continued uncertainty and strangeness
10. Fatigue

11. Physical violence or threat of it

12. Physical injury or threat of it

Note that all but the last three stressors are mental and/or emotional in nature. Also, the expectation of a stressful event can be every bit as stressful as the event itself, i.e., a board meeting. Therefore, the perceptions or thoughts one has become very important.

It is of more than passing interest to note that many of the first nine stressors are very much a part of the superintendency for most individuals; therefore, stress comes with the territory. In fact, in future years, as education comes under greater scrutiny, as finances continue to be a problem, as more structural changes are required within the organization, as greater emphasis is placed upon being the educational leader, and, in all likelihood, as fewer administrators will be employed to help with these increasing demands, the stress associated with the superintendency will continue to increase.

THE GNATTING DANCE

The constant stirring and agitating of the ever-present swarming gnats identified earlier can cause the mind and body to react in ways that are detrimental to good health and to a productive and enjoyable life. The gnats have started to dance with joy for they know that your stomach is frequently in knots, that you wake up in the middle of the night for no apparent reason with that queasy feeling, and that your effectiveness has been lowered as a person and as a professional. Your body is being gradually torn asunder.

Let us look at some of the specifics that are fueling the "gnatting dance." You have become impatient. You tend not to listen to the whole story in your meetings and conversations. You are making hasty and ill-advised decisions. In short, you are beginning to prove that impatience is probably the single most important factor leading to bad or marginal decisions. At the same time, you are becoming more irritable, causing communication problems with the board, staff, community, and family.

At work, your power of concentration has decreased. As a result, your incidence of mistakes has increased, and the completion of tasks started has decreased. Your already full schedule has been pushed to the breaking point because now it is taking you longer to complete tasks and to correct your mistakes. You're in a vicious circle. The added pressures of time and the inability to efficiently and effectively cope with the myriad of ever-changing demands lead to still more stress. At the same time that the individual tasks of your job are becoming more troublesome, the big picture is also becoming muddled. Your perceptiveness has decreased. You are reading people and events less well. The art of administration is decreasing. You begin reacting to symptoms instead of searching for the real problems. Your alternative identification capabilities have also decreased. You are now operating with blinders on. Each problem becomes a crisis. The feeling that everyone and, yes, that even includes your spouse and children, is working against you becomes more prevalent.

At the same time that your ability to deal with people and situations is decreasing, your body begins to sputter. Consider briefly some of the things that are occurring physiologically. The hypothalamus, which is a part of the brain immediately above the pituitary gland, senses that something is wrong. Your stomach begins to churn. At this moment, physiological changes over which you have no control begin to occur. The hypothalamus sends word to the pituitary that something is wrong. The pituitary, in turn, sends word on to the adrenal glands located just above the kidneys. The adrenal glands spring into action and secrete anti-inflammatory corticoids (ACs) into the bloodstream. These ACs influence connective tissue to inhibit inflammation. Thus, the immunological system of the body is impaired. When the ACs reach the liver, sometimes called the chemical factory of the body, the ACs are transformed into other types of corticoids that affect the body in various, sometimes detrimental, ways. The ACs arrive at the kidneys, and, through a complicated process, hypertension occurs. The blood vessels are constricted throughout the body. The heart is now pumping against greater resistance, causing your blood pressure to rise, and your blood also thickens, causing the heart to work even harder. In addition, the sugar level in the blood rises, and the fatty deposits in the blood vessels (cholesterol and triglycerides) increase. The ACs have also reached the stomach where the digestive juices are very acidic. Selye (1976) found, quite by accident, that the inflammation on the inside of the stomach wall keeps the acidic digestive juices from eating through the stomach lining. The ACs reduce the inflammation of the stomach lining and, thus, permit the acidic digestive juices to begin to eat their way through the stomach wall. The result can be a peptic or gastric ulcer—the common *stress* ulcers.

The central nervous system is also affected. The spinal cord, brain stem, and thalamus are components of the central nervous system that can be affected. The ability of the body to coordinate the various functions of the nervous system becomes impaired.

The body can resist the above physiological idiosyncrasies for a prolonged period of time; however, it is only as strong as its weakest vital part. Seyle (1976), in performing over 2,000 autopsies, claimed that he never saw an individual who truly died of old age, but that, in every case, a weak part of the body gave out. This knowledge was not as important when the average life span was thirty-five years of age. Few, if any, individuals would argue that our ancestors were not under terrific stress with all the trials and tribulations they had to endure. However, the average life span was such that the weakest part of the body was not given the time to completely break down. With a doubling of the average life span to seventy plus years, the weakest part of the body now has ample opportunity to break down. Thus, stress-caused physical problems are increasing. It is evident that treating a kidney or liver problem is not getting at the likely culprit—stress.

It is interesting to note that the same physiological processes occur in eustress (elation and happiness) as in distress, but they don't have the same negative effects on the body. As yet, researchers are not completely able to explain this peculiar phenomenon.

GNEUTRALIZING THE GNATS

We have learned of the deleterious effects stress can have on one's professional and personal life and on one's body. Now we are going to identify ways to "gneutralize" the gnats—to slow their antics down to the point where they are no longer harmful.

The objective in seeking to gneutralize distress is to identify ways to keep it within tolerable limits, not to eliminate it, because a life free of stress would be a boring and unproductive life. To this end, thirteen (a baker's dozen) specific considerations in seeking on-the-job relief from distress are presented.

1. *Work within reason.* Take breaks. It is possible to relax even when going between meetings. Think of some pleasant thoughts.

Make yourself aware of the many positive things going on in your environment. Over the long haul, work reasonable working hours. Productivity is the proper measuring stick, not the number of hours worked. Take vacations. Even short vacations can have wonderful rejuvenating effects. There will always be a reason to postpone a vacation. A vacation missed is gone forever.

2. *Learn to deal with anger.* At best, prevent anger, and, at worst, don't let it linger with you. A negative and angry person is an unhappy person. You have a job to do. While, at times, anger can make the adrenaline flow and help you to rise to the occasion, more often than not it just makes your job more difficult and may even create more problems through spontaneous ill-advised comments and actions.

3. *Do not always take work home.* A briefcase sitting on the dining room table is a nagging reminder all evening of work you could be doing instead of watching the Monday night football game. The same briefcase left on your desk in the office will enable you some peace of mind while watching the game, because your work is no longer just a few steps away.

4. *Come to work rested and relaxed.* Get enough sleep. The specific amount differs for each individual. Get up early enough in the morning to allow ample time to complete your pre-work routine. Arrive at the office relaxed and in a good mood. To do otherwise means that you are starting the day in a hole, and you may not dig yourself out the rest of the day.

5. *Make a plan for the day.* Do not let the entire day just happen and dominate you. Bringing a situation under control is usually the only thing that needs to be done immediately. Don't be constantly fighting zero-hour deadlines.

6. *Break a big job into a series of small ones.* A systemwide curriculum review is a staggering task when looked at in its entirety. Establish a time line for the various components of the review process.

7. *Make lists.* Don't try to remember everything. Make a note and free your mind to concentrate on other more important things of the moment.

8. *When possible, do not arrange stressful activities for late in the day.* Once the anti-inflammatory corticoids are in your blood, they do not leave immediately. Thus, the reason you are not able

to go to sleep until past midnight after a tough board meeting is stress related.

9. *Anticipate crisis situations.* Certain types of crisis situations can be anticipated during the course of the year, i.e., trouble at athletic events. Do thinking and preplanning on how you will deal with them.

10. *Practice selective thinking.* This is difficult, but it can be done. Don't let a problem that occurred Friday afternoon and which you cannot address until Monday morning ruin your weekend. Tune it out of your mind until perhaps Sunday evening.

11. *Arrange for time to be alone.* A few minutes of solitude can do wonders. Plan some time for yourself.

12. *Pursue an avocation.* Identify something that you enjoy doing that is totally unrelated to your professional life, i.e., jogging, tennis, photography, woodworking, recreational reading, etc. This enables you to relax and get your mind off of your problems, thus giving your body a much needed rest from the gnawing gnats.

13. *Keep your job and importance in perspective.* Do the best you can to make your school system the best that it can be. However, remember that the system was operating before your arrival on the scene and will continue to do so after you have departed in search of other mountains to climb (or retire).

In gneutralizing the gnats, it is also necessary to give some attention to the physical needs of the body. Five such considerations follow:

1. *Maintain a proper diet.* The body, like any complex machine, must be properly maintained. Eat regularly and wisely.

2. *Exercise.* Choose your form of exercise, but choose it and do it. Program it into your daily and weekly calendar. Making plans to exercise with another individual can often provide the needed incentive to follow an exercise plan when other activities look more inviting or appear to be more pressing.

3. *Socialize to the extent that it is enjoyable.* It is impossible to be a super professional, parent, and spouse all at the same time—a truism that is difficult to accept. Which activities of yours, your kids, and your spouse are the most important ones? Set some priorities, which by the way, is very difficult to do, for you will have

more high-priority obligations than you will adequately be able to fulfill.

4. *Avoid crutches*. Moderation or abstinence in such things as alcohol, overeating, smoking, prescribed drugs, etc., will pay dividends. Beware of and be alert for unplanned changes in any of these things.

5. *Have periodic physical examinations*. Every finely tuned machine needs a periodic maintenance check. Your body is no exception. Be sure that a treadmill test is included as part of your examination.

It is evident from these lists that health today is more than the absence of disease. It implies wellness that is holistic and includes not only physical but also psychological and emotional well-being. Ryan and Travis (1981) suggest that wellness is "a choice . . . a way of life . . . a process . . . an efficient channeling of energy . . . an integration of body, mind, and spirit . . . the loving acceptance of yourself" (p. 1).

The private sector was the first to recognize the importance of wellness when it began to initiate employee wellness programs. In recent years, the public sector and school systems have also come to recognize that wellness programs can help increase productivity and job satisfaction, reduce absenteeism and tardiness, and improve employee health (Terborg, 1986; Kizer, 1988; Violette and Violette, 1990). Thus, wellness programs can be beneficial not only to the superintendent but for all employees. Terborg (1986) suggests that such programs can be categorized into screening programs that assist individuals in identifying risks, education programs that help employees in understanding the benefits of a healthy lifestyle, and behavior change programs that encourage participation.

Research studies on wellness and health programs for educators are limited, but in 1987, Bradley and Pulak conducted a study of Wisconsin school districts in an attempt to identify the status of health promotion programs. Among their findings were:

1. Nineteen percent of the school districts had established wellness programs.
2. Of the 81 percent who did not have programs, 50 percent indicated an interest in starting one.
3. Over 90 percent of the programs were sponsored on a district-

wide level with district administrator support and leadership provided.

The number of districts sponsoring such programs has risen considerably across the country since this study was performed. Now, a number of universities have wellness centers, and many are very responsive to service requests from local school systems. Services they will provide run the range from a one-time informative session to becoming actively involved in helping a school system initiate its own program. Superintendents are encouraged to become knowledgeable of the wellness services that are available in their areas.

One final comment is in order. Regardless of the wellness approach taken personally and/or for the employees, have the perserverance and self-discipline to stick with it. A wise selection of and follow through on a stress-reducing wellness program will help keep the gnats at bay.

THE GNAT GNOCKOUT

At this point, the coup de grace in the form of a "gnat gnockout" is applied. In the last section, the gnats were gneutralized; now they are going to be put into hibernation.

To apply the gnat gnockout, an individual must stand back and take stock of the important things in life and then assess daily decisions to see if s/he is really leading a life that reflects his/her personal values. A good starting point is to list the five most important things in one's life in order of priority. Most lists will look something like the following:

1. Health
2. Family
3. Religion
4. Job
5. Avocation

Health is extremely important because it has been said that he who has health has hope, and he who has hope has everything. Most individuals will also list family and religion ahead of job. Even Vince Lombardi who is credited with saying, during his heyday as head coach of the Green Bay Packers that, "Winning is not everything, it is the only thing," also stated emphatically many times that nothing was more important to him than his family and his religion. Thus, one's job is often listed as approximately fourth in order of importance. However, when reality is faced as to what actually takes priority on a daily basis and what takes a backseat, one's job often emerges as the top priority. If this is the case, then there probably is a need for some soul searching.

One of the things that all the major religions espouse is the need to go beyond oneself and to express care and concern for others. In fact, a number of studies have shown that some of the people who have the least distress are those who are helping other people. Thus, while the superintendency is fraught with stressors, it can also be used as a vehicle for relieving stress, for the essence of the superintendency is a dedication to helping others. The gnats must not be allowed to obscure this goal. The superintendent must believe that personal efforts on the job are making a difference in the lives of students.

As a final suggestion, when the day has been particularly troublesome, take a few minutes to read and reflect upon the following poem:

THE VALUE OF A SMILE

It costs nothing, but it creates much good.

It enriches those who receive it without
impoverishing those who give it away.

No one is so rich that [s]he can get along without it,
no one is too poor not to feel rich when receiving it.

It creates happiness in the home,
fosters goodwill in business,
and is the countersign of friends.

It is rest to the weary, daylight to the discouraged,
sunshine to the sad, and is nature's best antidote for trouble.

Yet it cannot be bought, begged, borrowed or stolen
for it is something of no earthly good to anyone
until it is given away willingly.

(Anonymous)

REFERENCES

Bradley, C. and Pulak, M. (1987). *A Statewide Survey of Employee Health Promotion/Wellness Programs in Wisconsin Public Schools.* Madison, WI:

Wisconsin Department of Public Instruction and Wisconsin Foundation of Educational Administration.

Kizer, G. (1988). *Health Promotion at Work in California.* Sacramento, CA: California Department of Health Services.

Lazarus, R. and Launier, R. (1978). Stress-related transactions between person and environment. In *Perspectives in Interactional Psychology.* New York, NY: Plenum Publishing Corp.

Ryan, S. R. and Travis, J. (1981). *Wellness Workbook.* Berkely, CA: Ten Speed Press.

Selye, H. (1976). *The Stress of Life.* New York, NY: McGraw-Hill Book Co.

Terborg, J. R. (1986). Health promotion at the worksite: A research challenge for personnel and human resource management. In K. H. Rowland and Ferris (Eds.), *Research in Personnel and Human Resource Management,* pp. 255–267, Greenwich, CT: JAI Press.

Violette, G. R. and Violette, J. A. (1990). Employee wellness is good business. *CPA Journal, 60*(12), 90–92.

The old Indian adage that one cannot really know what another is experiencing until one has walked a mile in the other's moccasins is very apropos to the superintendency. An individual cannot know what it is to be a superintendent until s/he has been a superintendent. Even though the reading of this book has not enabled the reader to obtain a superintendency experience, it is hoped that the reading has given the reader a "feel" for the superintendency and the things that are important in serving as *the* educational leader of a school system.

Obtaining a feel for the superintendency is important. There are a number of things pertaining to the superintendency that can be studied and learned. Some of these are presented in the leadership subsections on the personal and professional competencies of a superintendent. However, such things as one's personal value system, the impact of one's personality on others, specific organizational history, the interpersonal dynamics at play in a given situation, and the domino effect generated throughout the organization caused by a given decision cannot be taught because there is an infinite number of combinations possible in any given situation.

Over a period of years, one mentally catalogs, sometimes unconsciously, many thousands of personal experiences. Intuition or the "art" of leadership is the result of this extended and continuous mental-cataloging process. When applied to the superintendency, this process constitutes a feel for the superintendency.

Decision-making can serve as a specific example of the importance of a feel for the superintendency. Much time is spent in graduate preparation programs on the decision-making process. However, such important points as who should be involved in and responsible for the decision-making and how and when the decision should be made rely greatly on one's feel for the situation.

How and when a decision should be implemented also rely greatly on one's feel for the situation. The best decision in the world is useless if significant others are not committed to work for its successful implementation.

How does one empower others to make decisions and still maintain organizational focus? As presented in the chapter on transformational leadership, there are steps that can be taken to help maintain the organizational focus. However, as position power is minimized in an empowering situation, the art of influencing and motivating others becomes extremely important.

Additional examples and prose could be put forth on the importance of a feel for the superintendency. However, suffice it to say that leadership in general and the superintendency in particular are both an art and a science. Therefore, one must obtain a superintendency before one can combine the art with the science.

The superintendency is more than a job. It is a position for one who is obsessed with the belief that s/he is embarked upon a very important mission. This individual has a burning vision of what this mission entails and what the outcomes should be. The enthusiasm and commitment displayed while pursuing this vision become contagious throughout the organization. Mistakes and problems along the way are looked upon as temporary inconveniences that must be positively overcome so that one can continue pursuing the vision. The vision may be dimmed somewhat, at times, by the daily trials and tribulations inherent in the superintendency, but it is never lost.

Finally, the superintendency is a tough, time-consuming, and demanding job. However, in the words of one of our country's great leaders, Theodore Roosevelt,

> It is not the critic who counts; not the [person] who points out how the strong [person] stumbles, or where the doer of deeds could have done them better. The credit belongs to the [person] who is actually in the arena, whose face is marred by dust and sweat and blood; who strives valiantly; who errs, and comes short again and again, because there is no effort without error and shortcoming; but who knows the great enthusiasms, the great devotions; who spends himself[/herself] in a worthy cause; who at the best knows in the end the triumph of high achievement, and who at the worst, if he[/she] fails, at least fails while daring greatly, so that his[/her] place shall never be with those cold

and timid souls who know neither victory nor defeat. (Hart and Ferleger, 1989, p. 2)

If an individual is committed to the superintendency, s/he should pursue the position with vigor and with the knowledge and belief that it is one of the most important ways in which humankind and this country can be served. In the words of Thomas Jefferson, "If a nation expects to be ignorant and free, in a state of civilization, it expects what never was and will never be" (Seldes, 1966, p. 367).

Have Fun—and—Good Luck!!!

REFERENCES

Hart, A. B. and Ferleger, H. R. (eds.) (1989). *Theodore Roosevelt Cyclopedia.* Westport, CN: Meckler Corp.

Seldes, G. (1966). *The Great Quotations.* Secaucus, NJ: Castle Books.

INDEX